DATE DUE

DEMCO 38-296

The Technology of Clothing Manufacture

The Technology of Clothing Manufacture

Second Edition

Harold Carr and Barbara Latham

b

**Blackwell
Science**

Blackwell Wissenschafts-Verlag GmbH
Kurfürstendamm 57
10707 Berlin
Germany

Blackwell Science KK
MG Kodenmacho Building
7–10 Kodenmacho Nihombashi
Chuo-ku, Tokyo 104, Japan

First edition published 1988
by BSP Professional Books
Second edition 1994
by Blackwell Science
Reprinted 1996, 1998, 1999

Set by Best-set Typesetter Ltd., Hong Kong
Printed and bound in Great Britain by
MPG Books Ltd, Bodmin, Cornwall

The Blackwell Science logo is a trade mark of
Blackwell Science Ltd, registered at the
United Kingdom Trade Marks Registry

DISTRIBUTORS

Marston Book Services Ltd
PO Box 269
Abingdon
Oxon OX14 4YN
(*Orders:* Tel: 01235 465500
        Fax: 01235 465555)

USA
Blackwell Science, Inc.
Commerce Place
350 Main Street
Malden, MA 02148 5018
(*Orders:* Tel: 800 759 6102
                617 388 8250
        Fax: 617 388 8255)

Canada
Login Brothers Book Company
324 Saulteaux Crescent
Winnipeg, Manitoba R3J 3T2
(*Orders:* Tel: 204 837-2987
        Fax: 204 837-3116)

Australia
Blackwell Science Pty Ltd
54 University Street
Carlton, Victoria 3053
(*Orders:* Tel: 3 9347-0300
        Fax: 3 9347-5001)

A catalogue record for this title
is available from the British Library

ISBN 0–632–03748–2

Library of Congress
Cataloging-in-Publication Data
Carr, Harold.
    The Technology of Clothing
manufacture/Harold Carr and
Barbara Latham.—2nd ed.
        p.   cm.
    Includes bibliographical references
and index.
    ISBN 0–632–03748–2
    1. Clothing Trade.   2. Sewing.
3. Dressmaking.   I. Latham,
Barbara.   II. Title.
TT497.C33 1994
687—dc20   93-25907
                                    CIP

For further information on
Blackwell Science, visit our website:
www.blackwell-science.com

Contents

Preface to the Second Edition

The first edition of this book was published in 1988 and since then it has become recognised as a standard textbook on the subject of clothing technology.

A clear need had been perceived for a book which collected together published information on clothing manufacturing technology, related it to current practice in the clothing industry and presented it in a form which would be of use to students studying various aspects of the design, technology and manufacture of clothing, on degree and HND courses, as well as to a variety of people working in clothing manufacturing and retailing.

In writing the second edition, the opportunity has been taken to show how the increasingly market-driven nature of clothing retailing influences the clothing production process and the opportunities that manufacturers have to make use of the technology that is available to support it. Changes in the technology of clothing manufacture in the last five years have been evolutionary rather than revolutionary, but there has been something of a polarisation, between the highest levels of technology that are currently available which are suited to the manufacture of predominantly staple clothing products, and the technology that can fulfil a need for much increased flexibility in an environment that requires a quick response to fashion demands. A number of sections of the book have been rewritten to reflect these changes. The majority of the drawings have been redrawn to improve clarity and the photographs have been updated in many cases to show new generations of equipment. A small number of errors in the first edition have shown up and have been corrected. In line with current practice, any reference to persons as either male or female is intended to refer to either sex.

The book provides a framework, with as much detailed description and analysis as space allows, of the concepts and choices with which clothing manufacturers daily wrestle to satisfy their customers. It starts with the basics of each topic and progresses to more complex notions, covering the full range of technologies available, and relating them to the opportunities that different types of company in different sectors of the industry have to make use of them. The need to maintain quality standards is stressed at all times. The range of opportunities to make use of computer controls, for productivity and quality, is clearly indicated.

The authors owe an enormous debt to former and present colleagues in the clothing industry and to colleagues at the London College of Fashion and the Scottish College of Textiles, with whom many of the ideas in both editions of the book have been discussed, elaborated and verified.

Acknowledgements

We wish to thank the following for help given and in many cases for permission to publish photographs of equipment or quotations from published work:

Mrs P. Danvers of the British Standards Institution, Milton Keynes; Mrs Dennison of Pfaff Bellow Ltd, Leeds; Mr David Bell of Lectra Systems UK Ltd, Shipley, Yorkshire; Mr Ron Rose of Eastman Machine Co. Ltd (and also Mr Rod Josey of Rod Josey Associates, Esher); Mrs Floutier of Bandwise Reliant Ltd, Chesham; Mr R.F.B. Wivell of Continental Pressing Technic, Normanton, Yorkshire; The Victoria and Albert Museum, Department of Prints and Drawings; Miss Sawbridge of the Shirley Institute, for permission to quote from *Productivity in Sewing Operations*; the American Apparel Manufacturers Association, Arlington, Virginia, for permission to quote from *State of the Art Investigation on Automated Handling of Limp Fabrics*, a Report to the Apparel Research Foundation by Arthur D. Little Inc.; Mr David Sinclair for permission to quote from the *Hollings Apparel Industry Review*; Dr P. Weedall and Mr D. Robson for particular assistance in the areas of colour, fabric objective measurement and robotics; Moira Poulton for the three series of stitch formation drawings (Figs. 3.21, 3.25 and 3.30) and Alistair Wright for all the remaining drawings.

Too numerous to mention are those from the clothing industry whom we wish to thank for information, advice and criticism. Finally, we acknowledge the continuous help and support provided by the libraries of the London College of Fashion and the Scottish College of Textiles.

Harold Carr
Barbara Latham

1
Background to the Clothing Industry

The clothing industry in Britain includes a diversity of company types and sizes, of product types and volumes of production, and of manufacturing environments, that is difficult to find in any other industry. It remains a significant force in Britain, whether manufacturing here or using its considerable design and technical skills to control manufacturing abroad. Numbers employed at the end of 1992 totalled 160,000, with the other sewing industries of footwear and home furnishings adding another 70,000. In many areas of the country significant numbers of jobs, especially for women, are in clothing and there is competition between firms for staff.

Clothing companies vary from the small number who employ several hundred or even several thousand workers to the typical traditional company in the large cities employing less than fifty. Of 7,000 establishments in 1985, only 630 employed more than 100 people, though between them they employed about 55 per cent of the labour force. This wide variation of company size and type within the clothing industry is due to two special features of the fashion industry.

(1) Fashion requires a quick response

The world of clothing includes what is conventionally called fashion, as well as what cannot, by any stretch of the imagination, be called fashionable.

Fashion may be couture garments, setting the trends for a season and made in very small quantities at high cost. The dominance of the fashion houses has declined in recent years and sharply dictated shapes or hemlines, for example, are a thing of the past. A strong feature of the fashion scene in the 1980s which is continuing into the 1990s is street fashion – rapidly changing styles, produced a few hundred at a time for a young market that will want something new after a few weeks. Prices are moderate and the clothes are not designed for long life. A process that began by supplying appealing clothes to young women is increasingly supplying a demand from fashion-conscious young men.

At the other end of a spectrum of clothing types are those normally referred to as staple. These include underwear, shirts, schoolwear and suchlike garments where the influence of fashion is minimal and there is a constant demand for large quantities. In particular, they include the garment types where a consumer makes multiple purchases, often of exactly the same thing.

A recent survey compared the number of items of each type of clothing owned by young and middle-aged people today, with similar people in the 1940s and 1950s. For items such as shirts and men's and ladies' briefs it is common that twenty or more of each are owned now compared with three or four formerly. Factories producing such garments are able to set their production processes to run for months or even years without a style change.

Between these extremes are the garments produced in hundreds or thousands with varying levels of style change between each batch. They may be ladies' or children's dresses, men's suits, leisure and sportswear, and many other types. Consumer demand in this area is increasingly for more fashionable garments, but made to the standards of make-up and performance that are more easily achieved in high volume.

Thus the technology that is applied to clothing must increasingly allow for versatility and quick response, except in the limited number of garment types such as shirts where long runs will probably always be the case. This technology makes the management of clothing manufacture relatively uncertain in respect of output, quality and delivery. It makes economies of scale small, except sometimes in the cutting room. It makes the maximum controllable size of factory fairly modest, currently reckoned to be from 100 to 150 operators, although there are some larger. The technology must also cope with a continuous input from a pipeline of product development whose output varies in colour, fabric, shape, feature and size, changing ever more frequently to meet opportunities in a competitive marketplace. The point which will be made throughout this book is that the levels of technology used in clothing manufacture are closely related to the quantity and length of manufacturing run of a style of garment that is made.

(2) The clothing industry is labour-intensive and does not require much fixed capital

Entry into the clothing industry is relatively easy. A new entrepreneur needs primarily design flair, a niche in the market, some working capital, but only a small amount of fixed capital. The reason for this relates to the simplicity of the central process in clothing manufacture which is sewing. Although fabric must be cut before it can be sewn, and pressed after it has been sewn, it is the process of sewing which dominates the output of a clothing factory, however large or small it is.

The sewing machine is no more than a power-operated needle, with other mechanisms in synchronisation, which produces a series of stitches continually. All the rest is left to the operator. The operator controls the size of the stitch, the tension of the sewing threads and the rate of stitch formation. The operator controls the shape of the sewing line and hence the shape of the finished garment part, as well as the matching and fitting of one ply against another. In addition, the operator must interpret instructions on a work ticket about different styles, have the knowledge to thread up the machine correctly, often a highly complex process, and be able to judge acceptable quality during and after the operation. Thus, apart from a small number of operations where some form of automatic machine can be used, the operations in clothing manufacture are largely operator-controlled. This does not apply to quite the same extent in cutting and pressing.

A sewing factory produces low added value, because it is generally limited to a one operator-one machine organisation. In addition, the machine's output is limited by practical mechanical constraints on the speed of stitch formation, as well as the machine speed the operator can effectively use, especially on short bursts of sewing. This is not, however, as significant as the fact that however sophisticated the engineering of stitch formation, its technology occupies only about one-fifth of the time of the average sewing operation. The other four-fifths of the time are occupied in activities such as preparing the fabric to be sewn, trimming, folding, creasing, marking, disposal after sewing and bundling. These activities are often referred to as ancillary handling. In fact, they are the core of the typical clothing operation, and they have not yet been mechanised to a significant extent.

The reasons for the continuing dominance of the human hand stem largely from the nature of the raw materials used in clothing. First, fabrics are limp; in particular, they bend in all directions. It is therefore much more difficult and expensive to invent jigs and automatic equipment for performing sewing operations than it is for operations on the rigid materials used in other industries. Second, fabrics vary in extensibility. A certain minimum extensibility of yarn is necessary in order that the needle may penetrate the fabric satisfactorily, but exentsibility which is less than that minimum and very high extensibility both give trouble in making up. This extensibility then varies, not only from fabric to fabric, but also according to the angle of the line of sewing to the lengthwise grain of the fabric. One of the difficulties inherent, for example, in the operation of sewing a sleeve into an armhole – following a complete circle round the armhole – is that the line of sewing includes all degrees of bias in the fabric and therefore all degrees of extensibility in it. Third, fabrics vary in thickness. There are problems associated with sewing very thin or very thick fabrics, and within one garment the overall thickness the operator is required to handle will vary as different numbers of plies are sewn.

Fourth, because the joining must achieve compatibility with the flexibility, drape and handle of fabrics, no satisfactory general alternative to sewing has yet been generally applied. In mechanical terms, a stitch is a flexible universal joint, and it is still the only type of joint whose properties approach those of fabrics.

A contrast with the sewing room situation described above is provided by the activity of cutting which must precede it. The cutting room must produce as many accurately cut garments as are required by the sewing room but, instead of working to join together single sections of garment in a three-dimensional form, the cutting process operates on flat fabric. This is significantly easier to handle and, if many plies of fabric can be piled up and some kind of vertically operating knife used, it is possible to cut out garment parts in large quantities at a time. This has led to a great deal of technical development in the various processes relating to cutting, the spreading of fabric, as well as the actual cutting itself. This in turn has led to extensive investment in cutting room equipment by the larger manufacturers who are able to cut large amounts of garments using only a small staff. This is in sharp contrast to the labour-intensive nature of sewing. Visually, a cutting room is a vast area of large tables and few people while a sewing room always seems relatively crowded with people.

The labour-intensive nature of the sewing room in a company means that there is a limit to how large it can conveniently be. Although they vary in size, and a small number have as many as 500 people, sewing units of not more than 150 people are much more common. Above this size the management of so many people becomes difficult, in a situation where close personal contact is normally needed to maintain motivation and quality of work. There is also the problem that a local area will rapidly become exhausted of people wishing to work in clothing and, in an industry where pay levels are not particularly high and where the majority of the workforce is women, there is a reluctance to travel very far. It is thus common for the larger clothing companies to separate their assembly of garments into small factory units rather than to concentrate it in one large one.

The economies of scale that are now available to companies requiring to cut large quantities of garments are such that it makes sense to concentrate the cutting for several sewing units into one large cutting factory which, as was explained above, will not need to employ a very large number of people. Cut garments are transported to sewing factories by road, with completed garments frequently being brought back to a central warehousing facility.

What has been described here does not, of course, apply to the whole of the clothing industry, but it is applying increasingly to companies outside the traditional clothing cities such as London and Leeds which manufacture moderate to large quantities of garments to be sold through the large mail order and direct retail companies. The smaller companies, especially those producing rapidly changing styles of fashion garments, still work in small units which generally cut and sew within the same premises.

Another typical feature of the clothing industry in terms of company structure is the number of situations where the manufacturing is separated from the design and development which precedes it. In the large, bulk production companies this situation may arise because the design department is in London, close to retail customers, while manufacturing takes place in a less expensive part of the country where labour is more readily available. In some fashion companies, small or large, it is often the case that they do not own or run any manufacturing capacity, choosing instead to place contracts with other companies whose business is to make garments on an outworker or CMT (cut, make and trim) basis. In many cases the subcontractor supplements his production by using homeworkers. These smaller sewing units, and the homeworkers, tend to have basic sewing machines only but the machinists are very skilled. It will be seen later that this combination is necessary to achieve the flexibility of style inherent in the short run situation of fashion.

A further significant factor in the differences between the cutting and sewing activities in clothing manufacture relates to costs. The cutting room may employ a small number of people for the amount of work it produces but, because about half of the wholesale cost of a garment is in the materials, the cutting process consumes about half the company's turnover when it cuts cloth. The result of this is a strong emphasis on economy of materials in everything the cutting room does, though it will be seen that this must sometimes be compromised to fulfil the overriding need to keep the sewing room supplied with cut work. By contrast, the typical major cost in the sewing room is that of labour, which generally contributes 20–25 per cent of the total cost of a garment. Of that labour cost, 95 per cent is likely to be incurred in the sewing room and only 5 per cent in the cutting room. This leads to pressure on the productivity of sewing room labour and on labour cost. The work of the managers in many companies involves improving the efficiency of training methods so that operators may become productive as soon as possible, control of individual operator or group performance, the use of individual or, increasingly, group monetary incentives where possible, and great attention to quality control at the workplace because a high level of defects is detrimental to output.

2
Cutting

With the exception of one-piece knitted garments, clothing is generally assembled from several parts. This is necessary to introduce shape, to overcome the limitations of fabric width and because a piece of fabric wrapped around the body must be joined somewhere. The first stage in the manufacture of garments is the cutting of the materials into the necessary pattern shapes. These are then joined together by means of seams to create three-dimensional garments. When a single garment is cut out, the garment pattern is attached to one or two plies of the fabric in a way which allows for any special requirements such as matching of the design on the fabric. The garment parts are then cut out with hand shears, electric cutters or dies. Where large quantities of a garment style must be cut, a lay is created which consists of many plies of fabric spread one above the other. From this must then be cut all the garment pieces for all the sizes which it has been planned to cut from that lay. The pattern shapes for these garments may be drawn on a paper marker placed on top of the lay, or information as to their shape and position may be held within a computer, to be plotted similarly on a paper marker or used to drive an automatic cutter. Depending on the method of cutting that is used, there is not always a need for the pattern shapes and positions to be physically drawn on a paper marker, but whether the marker is drawn out or not, a marker plan must be made in which the pattern pieces are closely interlocked to achieve minimum fabric usage. In spreading the fabric to form a lay, the plies of fabric in the lay will be nominally the same length as the marker plan. A diagram of a lay, showing a paper marker, is given in Figure 2.1.

The sizes that will be cut and the number of plies of fabric in the lay are determined by the requirements of the order for the garments, the availability of materials and the constraints of physical equipment, and will not be discussed in detail here. The purpose of this chapter is to study the technology of the cutting room which has as its objective the cutting of garment parts accurately and economically and in sufficient volume to

Fig. 2.1.   A lay with paper marker on top.

keep the sewing room supplied with work. The three processes involved are:

(1) the planning, and if appropriate, the drawing and reproduction of the marker;
(2) the spreading of the fabric to form a lay;
(3) the cutting of the fabric.

(A) THE PLANNING, DRAWING AND REPRODUCTION OF THE MARKER

It is useful to break marker making down into:

(a) marker planning, or the placement of pattern pieces to meet technical requirements and the needs of material economy, and
(b) marker utilisation, which may include drawing the marker plan directly onto fabric, drawing it onto a paper marker by pen or automatic plotter, or, where the cutting method allows it, recording pattern piece information on the paper marker or on the fabric without actually drawing pattern lines on it. Provision may have to be made for the same marker plan to be used many times.

Although the original diagram of a lay and a marker implied a large sheet of paper on which were drawn the edges of all the pattern pieces, this is only appropriate when cutting is by manually controlled knife and a line must be provided for the cutting operator to follow. Even then, it is sometimes more appropriate to mark the pattern lines directly onto the fabric rather than onto paper. Increasingly though, cutting is by computer-controlled knife and drawn pattern shapes are unnecessary.

Where a paper marker is used, it is normally stabilised on the top ply of the lay by stapling or by ironing so that an adhesive backing on the paper may lightly stick to the surface of the fabric. The paper marker is cut along with the fabric plies, and thus destroyed. Since a marker may be required for use more than once, this method needs an economical way of duplicating to provide copies. Where marking is done directly onto the fabric, it must, of course, be repeated for each spread of fabric.

The requirements of marker planning

The industry has always paid great attention to marker planning, because when the cutting room cuts cloth it spends around half the company's turnover. Any reduction in the amount of cloth used per garment leads to increased profit.

Marker planning is a conceptualising, intuitive, open and creative process, in contrast to making up a jigsaw puzzle, which is an analytical, step-by-step and closed process. There is no final solution to a marker planning problem, only a more tightly packed and therefore shorter marker the more time is spent on it. In order to plan efficiently it is necessary to visualise the marker as a whole, to see it at a glance. The planner proceeds by first positioning the larger pattern pieces in a relationship which looks promising and then fitting the smaller pieces into the gaps. Since most of the pieces are irregular and often tend to be carrot-shaped, one skill lies in discovering those edges which fit together most neatly, and placing side by side across the marker those pieces which fill the width most nearly. The planner will then try a number of pattern placements, selecting the one which gives the shortest marker. The work of the marker planner is subject to a number of constraints. These relate to:

(1) the nature of the fabric and the desired result in the finished garment;
(2) the requirements of quality in cutting;
(3) the requirements of production planning.

(1) The nature of the fabric and the desired result in the finished garment

(a) Pattern alignment in relation to the grain of the fabric

Pattern pieces normally carry a grain line. When pattern pieces are laid down the piece of cloth, as is commonest with large pattern pieces, the grain line should lie parallel to the line of the warp in a woven fabric or the wales in a knitted fabric. Where pattern pieces are laid across the piece, the grain line should lie parallel to the weft or course direction. In bias cutting, which is often used in large pattern pieces as part of the garment style in ladies' dresses and lingerie, as well as in small pattern pieces such as pocket facings and undercollars in menswear as a requirement of satisfactory garment assembly, the grain lines will (normally) be at 45° to the warp. The designer or pattern cutter may define a tolerance which allows the marker planner to swing the grain line a small amount from parallel. If the marker planner lays down a pattern outside the stated rules for grain lines, then the finished garment will not hang and drape correctly when worn. This requirement to follow grain lines restricts the freedom the marker planner has in choosing how to lay the patterns in the marker.

(b)   Symmetry and asymmetry

Many fabrics can be turned round (through 180°) and retain the same appearance and these are designated *'either way'* or *'symmetrical'*. They require no special action on the part of the marker planner. More restricting are fabrics known as *'one way–either way'* or *'asymmetrical'*. In this case, if a fabric ply is turned round it does not retain the same appearance, especially when the two opposite ways are sewn together. However, as long as the pattern pieces of an individual garment all lie in the same direction, the direction they lie in does not matter. Examples of such fabrics are those with a nap or pile which is brushed in one direction and thus presents surfaces which show different reflection of light, knitted fabrics where the loops of the wales always point in the same direction, and fabrics with a surface design which does not run the same way when turned round but where either direction is acceptable. Because of the frequently tapered shape of pattern pieces, an economical marker is usually still possible provided an even number of sets of patterns are fitted together. Even more restricting are fabrics which are *one way only*. This applies to fabrics with a heavy surface pile or nap or a print design which includes a recognisable object which can only be used one way up. Typical of the former would be velvet which should be cut with the pile pointing upwards. The marker planner must ensure that the top ends of the pattern pieces, as they will be worn in the garment, all face the same way. This is likely to be less economical than other markers. It will be seen later that care must be taken to spread the fabric in the lay in such a way that effects built into the marker are retained.

(c)   The design characteristic of the finished garment

For example, if a vertical stripe does not show a complete mirror image repeat, the right and left sides of a garment may be designed to be mirror images of each other. In this case, a marker is planned which uses a half set of patterns, and the required effect is created in the spreading of the fabric which places pairs of plies face to face.

(2)   The requirements of quality in cutting

(a)   For the majority of cutting situations where a knife blade is used, the placements of the pattern pieces in the marker must give *freedom of knife movement* and not restrict the path of the knife so that it leads to inaccurate cutting. A blade, which has width, cannot turn a perfect right angle in the middle of a pattern piece and space must always be allowed for a knife to turn such corners. Also, in practice, a curved part of a pattern such as a sleevehead, when placed abutting a straight edge, leads to either a shallow gouge in the straight edge or the crown of the curve being straightened. The amount of space which must be left will depend on the actual cutting method employed.

(b) A *pattern count* must always be made at the completion of the planning of a marker to check that the complete menu of patterns has been included. This is not just a formality when, for instance, a 12 garment trouser marker, where each garment may have 16 pattern pieces, signifies a complete marker of 192 pattern pieces.

(c) *Correct labelling of cut garment parts* is essential if, in sorting and bundling a multi-size lay after cutting, operators are to identify correctly the parts which make up whole garment sizes. It is the responsibility of the marker planner to code every pattern piece with its size as the marker is planned.

(3) The requirements of production planning

When an order is placed for a quantity of garments, it normally specifies a quantity of each size and colour, the former often given as a ratio. For example, in the still common situation of orders being placed in dozens, 500 dozen of a blouse may include 200 dozen red, 200 dozen blue and 100 dozen green, across sizes 12, 14, 16, and 18 in the ratio 2:4:4:2. The requirements of production planning and control will be to supply the sewing room with an adequate amount of cut garments at sufficiently frequent intervals, consistent with availability of fabric and the best utilisation of cutting room resources. Among the latter considerations are that, for a given quantity of garments, a high lay rather than a low lay gives a lower cutting labour cost per garment. The higher lay will, of course, also be shorter, giving a lower overall cutting time which is important if the sewing room requires the cut work urgently. The shorter lay will also require a shorter marker and in the above example the marker planner may make two markers, each containing six garments, one with two size 12s, two size 14s and two size 16s and the other with two size 14s, two size 16s and two size 18s. The planning of two shorter markers may not take more time than the planning of one long one, and since shorter markers are easier for the planner to work on, a more tightly packed and efficient marker could result, though for complex garments long markers generally offer more opportunities for savings than do short ones.

The mixing of sizes in a marker, as opposed to cutting single sizes at a time, is termed *scrambling* and, up to a point, the more sizes that are included in a marker, the greater is the scope for fabric savings. In simple terms, there are smaller spaces between the patterns and a bigger percentage of fabric actually cut out in garment parts. If, in the above example, the marker planner could create a marker which contained the pattern pieces for a dozen garments, it would include the pieces for two size 12s, four size 14s, four size 16s and two size 18s. Unfortunately, there are a number of reasons, in addition to the production planning restrictions given above, why this may not be possible. The marker will be very long and may even be too long for the cutting tables. A piece of cloth when spread to this length will not give many plies before it runs out, and it may not be possible to mix garments cut from it with garments cut from another piece because the shade may not be exactly the same. In many sewing rooms, the operators work on bundles of garments, a bundle consisting of garments which are all the same style, size and colour. Small numbers of plies of one colour spread in a lay lead to small bundles and increased costs of handling those bundles.

An alternative to the scrambled marker described above, when feeding the sewing room is an overriding priority, is the use of single size markers on a stepped lay. If it is required to cut 100 singles of a size 14 dress and 50 singles of a size 12 dress, all in the same colour, two markers would be made with one containing the size 12 pattern pieces and one containing the size 14 pattern pieces. Fifty plies of the fabric would be spread to a length to include both markers, followed on top and at one end by a further 50 plies of a length to fit the size 14 marker. The marker containing the size 12 patterns would then be placed on top of the 50 plies and the marker containing the size 14 patterns on top of the 100 plies. This is illustrated in Figure 2.2. Greater fabric savings, and often lower total cost, although with more time taken, would normally result from cutting this stepped lay as some combination of lays with scrambled markers.

Fig. 2.2. A stepped lay with paper markers on top.

Efficiency of the marker plan

The marker planner measures his success by the efficiency of the marker plan created. A formula describes this:

$$\frac{\text{Area of patterns in the marker plan}}{\text{Total area of the marker plan}} \times 100\%$$

Since the reduction in fabric cost is so important, the company expects the planner to discover opportunities for improvements in marker efficiency by suggesting alterations to patterns and cloth, the two elements brought together in marker planning. The first sort of opportunities are commonly designated pattern engineering. Chief among these is an examination of seam location to ensure the best possible placement of patterns in the marker. In one case the shift of a seam might allow the placement of small parts in areas otherwise wasted, for instance in the armhole of a jacket or shirt lying next to the edge of a marker. In another case the seam is moved to enable the better placement of large panels across the whole width of the fabric. It goes without saying that the seam shift should not affect the appearance or balance in such a way that the designer's intentions are significantly diverted. If no change is made, however, at least the effect of not changing can be analysed, and the costs of the two alternatives presented will be known at the time the decision is made.

Again the planner may spot opportunities arising from needlessly generous seams, turnups, hems and alteration allowances. Sometimes there is an opportunity to 'piece' a pattern. This means dividing a large, awkwardly shaped pattern into two pieces, the better to accommodate it in the marker. One example is the fork on the underside of trousers, which projects from the main contour very prominently. It is common practice to cut off from the point of the fork, a nearly triangular pattern piece, adding the seam widths to both new edges. This allows both the closer placement of the larger piece and the 'hiding' of the smaller piece in a waste area of the marker. The cost saving in this instance is greater than the cost of seaming the parts together.

The second sort of opportunity arises in the influence the marker planner has on the selection of fabric widths where a choice is available. The 'best' width depends among other factors on the costs of various fabric widths per square metre, the typical number of sizes in a marker, the potential pattern engineering changes at various widths and the marker efficiency of a series of test markers.

An important consideration is the value of the material. Low cost linings promise much smaller savings than worsted suitings at many pounds per metre. The possibility of bigger material savings should stimulate more effort to achieve higher marker efficiency through longer lays. On the other hand, if the more expensive fabric is commonly only cut in lays a few plies high, whereas the cheaper fabric is cut several hundred plies high, then the situation reverses, because what is significant is the total value of the fabric in the lay.

The range of markers used varies from perhaps shirt markers containing up to 20 garments in many sizes, through 6–12 garment trouser markers and 2–6 garment dress markers to single suit markers, but there is a considerable variation in practice even within one sector of the industry.

Methods of marker planning and marker use

(1) Manual marker planning with full size patterns in a full size marker

Prior to the development of computerised marker planning systems, all markers were planned by working with full size patterns. For many companies in the industry this method is still used, because the more modern alternatives are expensive, and because these companies make only short or single size markers and the planner can see the whole of the plan relatively easily. The planner works by moving around the full size patterns until a satisfactory plan is obtained.

In a few clothing companies this planning is done directly on the fabric to be cut and the pattern shapes marked in immediately. This can only be done when the length of the marker is predictable and in marking directly onto fabric, the necessary accurate reproduction of the pattern and good definition of line can be difficult to achieve. Patterns are usually made from card and it is important that the edges do not become worn and that the pattern is held firmly while drawing takes place. Various chalk or wax materials can be used to draw with but whatever is used needs to be easily held and readily sharpened. The quality of the line also depends on the surface nature of the fabric.

This method takes considerable skill to achieve accuracy and it takes considerable time, but it is economical for single garments and also for check fabric since it allows the patterns to be manipulated during the marking process. In many companies, more than one lay is cut using the same marker plan. If the plan is drawn directly onto the fabric, this process of drawing round the patterns has to be repeated for each lay.

It is much more common for a paper marker to be used for cutting and in this case the pattern lines and style and size information are usually drawn on spot and cross paper to ensure adherence to grain lines. It is still essential that patterns do not become worn but a satisfactorily fine line is easier to achieve than when marking directly onto fabric as a pencil or a ballpoint pen can be used. Again, multiple copies of the paper marker are normally needed. These copies can either be made when the marker plan is first drawn, or the master marker can be reproduced as needed by a variety of methods.

(a) Carbon duplicating

For copies to be made as the original is drawn, and where small numbers of copies only are needed, use can be made of carbon paper, usually double-sided, or the same effect can be achieved with special NCR-type (no carbon required) paper. In either case, 6–8 copies can be made without too great a deterioration in the fineness of the line. Where double-sided carbon is used with asymmetrical pattern pieces, the sequence of markers created would be used alternately with a lay spread all right side up and a lay spread all right side down. This method of duplicating has the advantage of low capital and material costs.

(b) Spirit duplicating or hectograph carbon system

In this process, the master marker is drawn on paper with a layer of special hectograph paper underneath it. This paper transfers a blue line onto the back of the master as it is drawn. The master is then used to make one copy at a time in a duplicating machine. The machine uses alcohol to wet a plain white paper which is then passed with the master between two rollers, transferring the lines onto the copy. It is a messy process but many copies can be produced. Its use is decreasing in favour of the following method.

(c) Diazo photographic method

This process makes as many copies of the marker as are needed, one at a time, following the drawing of a master marker. The master marker and a light-sensitive paper are passed under high intensity ultraviolet light and the light-sensitive paper is developed using ammonia vapour. The lines and other markings on the master marker prevent exposure of the light-sensitive paper which forms the copy and when developed the lines remain visible. It is a clean process which can make unlimited numbers of copies with good line definition but it must be used with ample ventilation to remove ammonia fumes. The paper is expensive but the equipment is comparatively cheap.

An alternative to making multiples of paper markers, is the creation of a perforated marker from the initial hand-drawn version by means of a punch perforator. This has been used in the clothing industry but is more commonly used for cutting upholstery fabrics. The perforator punches about four suitably sized holes per inch through the paper along the pattern lines. The perforated marker is placed on the lay and by means of special lay powder the pattern lines are transferred to the top ply as a series of dots. Care must be taken that corners and notch positions are adequately defined. The powder is available with various degrees of adhesion to suit various fabrics.

(2) Computerised marker planning

This method is normally part of an integrated system which includes digitising or scanning of full-size patterns into the computer, facilities for pattern adaptation, and, by inputting appropriate grade rules, the means to generate all the sizes required. The planner uses a visual display unit with keyboard, tablet and data pen, puck or mouse.

Methods and equipment vary slightly between manufacturers but a typical example is as follows. The planner specifies the exact make-up of the marker plan: the width of the fabric, the pattern pieces to be used, the sizes to be included and all constraints to be applied, including any matching of checks. The system produces a marker plan automatically or interactively. Automatic marker planning involves calling up data defining the placement of pieces in markers previously planned, and selecting, from a series, that marker conformation which gives the highest marker efficiency. There is no guarantee that the best marker plan will be achieved, but this is a rapid method of achieving a relatively efficient plan and it has the advantage of not needing an operator.

Interactive marker planning is more common and is the process by which the operator plans markers by interacting directly with the system through a VDU screen. All the pattern pieces are displayed in miniature at the top of the screen. In the middle of the screen are two horizontal lines defining the marker width and a vertical line at the left representing the beginning of the marker. The right end is for the moment open. At the bottom of the screen is a written marker identification, with marker length and efficiency constantly updated during the planning process. A view of a computer system for marker planning, and also for pattern development and grading, is shown in Figure 2.3.

A data pen (or puck or mouse), tablet and the computer keyboard are used to manipulate the pattern pieces. The tablet, which rests on the desk in front of the operator, represents the display screen and consists of a grid of fine wires immediately below the surface. When using a data pen, the pen is touched on the surface of the tablet and it registers a position on the grid which shows as a position on the screen. A combination of movements of the pen and commands via the keyboard enable pattern

Fig. 2.3. Computer system for pattern development, grading, marker planning and marker plotting. (Reproduced by permission of Lectra Systems Ltd.)

pieces to be moved about the screen and positioned in the marker. The system finally positions the pattern pieces precisely according to the marking rules specified. This process enables the planner to produce a trial marker very rapidly and accurately, thus enabling the planner to run through the feasible placements of pattern pieces more quickly than with non-computerised systems. After selecting the most economical marker plan devised in the time available, the computer will provide an accurate piece count, calculate a marker plan efficiency percentage and total the length of the pattern peripheries. When the marker plan is complete it will be stored in a marker plan file for future retrieval. The system is not limited to large marker plans but can be used, when combined with a pattern adaptation facility, to provide single size marker plans for made-to-measure cutting of men's suits.

An alternative to the data pen in some systems is the puck or mouse. In this case keys are pressed to achieve the same effect as pressing the data pen on the tablet.

The quality of marker planning is more consistent than with manual methods, because instructions regarding grain lines are always followed, because the butting of pattern pieces is precise with no overlapping, and the pattern count is automatic, a boon in complex markers.

It is difficult to compare the capital cost of the computer system used in marker planning with the other methods described previously because in all cases the computer system provides a pattern development and grading facility as well. It also enables the reproduction of as many copies of a marker as are required without resorting to additional methods of reproduction such as the manual methods require. However, the fact that the cost of such a package of computer equipment is many times that of a manual marker planning and reproducing system indicates a difference in scale which makes it unsurprising that the computer systems are used by the larger companies making substantial quantities of many garment styles, where small percentage savings in fabric can mean saving large amounts of money.

After planning the marker on the computer, the marker planner instructs the computer to plot the marker automatically onto paper. Granted a well-maintained mechanical plotter, this provides the most accurate marker. The plotter operates on a dual axis system, the x direction determined by a beam travelling along the table, the y direction by the pen's travel along the beam. The process requires minimum attention since the plotter uses a continuous roll of paper, and a series of markers can be plotted continuously. In practice, plotters are commonly left to run overnight. If required, markers may also be plotted to a slightly larger scale, such as a one per cent increase lengthwise, to allow for shrinkage on certain fabrics. Reference copies in miniature can also be plotted. It is, of course, the cleanest system of marker making. As was stated before, the planning and plotting systems involve a high capital cost, which is justified by its potential to achieve the most economical use of fabric, its savings in expensive marker planning and plotting time and its storage of large amounts of information.

When methods of cutting are discussed later, it will be seen that it is possible, for a further considerable capital cost, to feed the marker plan to a computer-controlled cutting knife. This knife does not require that the pattern shapes are drawn on paper, indeed does not require a marker at all, but for the cut work to be sectioned off correctly into garment parts and sizes there is a need for a means of showing the size code of each garment section the knife cuts. In this case, the plotter will not actually draw the pattern outlines, it will only write the size codes in the correct positions on the marker and mark a corner reference point which gives an initial position to the knife. The plotting of markers by computer is shown, along with the rest of the system, in Figure 2.3.

As an alternative to plotting even this amount of information on a marker, it is possible, when cutting will be by computer-controlled knife, not to plot any of the marker but to attach adhesive labels to the top ply of fabric to give the information necessary to section garment parts into bundles. This saves both the time of plotting and the cost of plotter and paper. Instead, a system is mounted over the lay of fabric, similar in principle to the plotter described above. A beam travels along the table and a label dispenser travels along the beam, the x and y coordinates again giving the position. In some systems the label dispenser also prints the labels, in others they are printed separately and loaded into the dispenser. Positioning is faster when printing is done separately. The labels carry bar coded or alphanumeric information.

An example of equipment for top-ply labelling is shown in Figure 2.4.

Fig. 2.4. Top-ply labelling system. (Reproduced by permission of Lectra Systems Ltd.)

(B) THE SPREADING OF THE FABRIC TO FORM A LAY

The objective of spreading is to place the number of plies of fabric that the production planning process has dictated, to the length of the marker plan, in the colours required, correctly aligned as to length and width, and without tension. Although in certain sections of the clothing industry, notably bespoke menswear, it remains necessary to cut single garments, most of the industry is able to cut garments in bulk and by doing so achieves the savings in fabric that are available through the use of multi-garment marker plans and the savings in cutting time per garment that result from cutting many plies at the same time. However, there are a number of prices to be paid for this saving in the time and cost of cutting and the cost of materials.

First, the spreading of multi-size lays of many plies demands strongly constructed tables, usually with steel legs and braced frames, a heavy laminated, smooth wood top, and sometimes centre legs. A 10 metre lay of shirting fabric with 200 plies can weigh up to 600 kg and with 150 cm wide fabric can exert a downward pressure of up to approximately 40 kg per square metre on the table surface. The table may also bear the weight of a spreading machine, travelling on steel rails at the edge of the table. The type of table surface is critical for the spreading and cutting operations. It is usually covered with a plastic laminate or tempered hardboard, which provide a low level of friction, but in more sophisticated examples the table incorporates a source of compressed air, giving the facility of air flotation through perforations in the table surface. This enables heavy sections of lay to be moved easily along the surface of the table to the cutting operation. It is also possible to fit tables with a vacuum facility so that a high lay may be sucked down, compressed and stabilised before cutting.

Second, spreading is itself a time-consuming operation. With the highest lays it can consume more time in total than cutting, especially if the cutting is by computer-controlled knife. Just as with the marking and cutting operations, the efforts of engineers have produced sophisticated equipment designed to reduce spreading time and make the operation more automatic. Before the advent of computerised marker making and computer-controlled knives, the largest capital expenditure in the cutting room was usually the purchase of spreading equipment. With a few exceptions, spreading machines can spread only one ply at a time and most developments have had the objective of simply spreading individual plies more quickly and accurately. It has to be remembered that spreading is no more than a sophisticated method of material handling, adding nothing to the manufacture of garments, yet in conventional cutting rooms it is the technological bottleneck.

A study of spreading must include the following considerations:

(a)   the requirements of the spreading process;

(b)   methods of spreading;
(c)   the nature of fabric packages.

The requirements of the spreading process

Spreading must achieve a number of specific objectives:

(1)   Shade sorting of cloth pieces

Lays commonly require more than one roll of cloth and lays which include several colours normally require more than one roll of each colour to achieve enough plies in total. It is likely that cloth pieces that are nominally the same colour will have been dyed separately and are not an exact shade match. A garment made from parts cut from these different pieces would be likely to show a shaded effect between its different panels. Thus when deliveries of a number of rolls of cloth of the same colour are received, they should be sorted into batches such that shade differences between them are undetectable. This is normally done by a trained colourist but can more easily be done by a computer after measurement of the colour has been carried out using a spectro-photometer or a colorimeter.

It was stated earlier that the size of bundles of garments supplied to the sewing room is related to the number of plies of fabric of the same shade in the spread lay. Batching together of rolls of the same shade gives a greater number of plies that in turn give larger bundles. Where rolls of cloth of the same colour but different shades do have to be spread adjacent to each other in the lay, they are separated by a layer of interleaving paper, a roughened tissue in a bright colour which can be seen easily at the edge of each cut stack, and which assists in easy separation of the plies for bundling. (Lays containing more than one colour are spread with the colours changing from one roll to the next to make bundling very easy.) Occasionally the relationship between roll length and marker length gives bundles which are too large for convenient handling in the sewing room. In this case the plies would be separated at suitable intervals of perhaps 10 or 12 plies with interleaving paper. The paper can also assist in holding the spread firm where fabric surfaces may slip against each other.

(2)   Correct ply direction and adequate lay stability

These two factors must be considered together as the opportunities for achieving them are related. They depend on fabric type, pattern shape and the spreading equipment that is available.

The various types of fabric, in terms of surface direction, that are available, designated either way, one way–either way or one way only, were described in the section on marker planning. For one way–either way and one way only fabrics, where the pattern pieces have been positioned in a particular direction in the marker plan, it is essential that the fabric is spread in a way that maintains that direction.

In addition to the visual effects of a surface design or fabric construction, problems of instability and creep can arise with fabrics with special frictional characteristics such as those with a nap or a pile surface. This can require that some fabrics are spread with all the plies face up, some with all the plies face down and some face to face.

As far as pattern shape is concerned, many garments are constructed from symmetrical pattern pieces in which case the fabric may be spread all the same way up or face to face. If the pattern pieces are asymmetrical, however, the fabric can only be spread with all the plies face up or face down as a face to face spread will result in half the garments being asymmetrical the wrong way and produce, for instance, a double-breasted garment fastening the wrong way.

If fabric is being spread by hand or if a spreading machine with a turntable is available, there are four possible types of spread which can be achieved, combining the two directional possibilities with the face up, face down, and face to face possibilities. Some are faster than others but, aside from the question of speed, which ones are possible depend on the various constraints described above. Fortunately a great many garments have symmetrical pattern pieces and fabrics which are completely plain; the fabrics are also stable spread in any configuration. The fabrics for these garments can be spread in any of the four ways provided the necessary machinery is available.

Figure 2.5 shows the spreading possibilities diagrammatically, with the unrolling of the fabric piece giving a ply laid with a lengthwise direction, and an up or down direction, as indicated by the arrows.

Methods of spreading which lay alternate plies in different directions can only be used for either way fabrics. In this case the pattern pieces can face in either direction in the marker and the following opportunities are available:

(a) For symmetrical pattern pieces, and fabric which is stable spread face to face, the fabric can be spread along face up and immediately back again face down.

(b) For asymmetrical as well as symmetrical pattern pieces, and fabric which is stable spread all the same way up, the fabric can be spread along and immediately back again but the roll must be turned on a turntable before returning.

Methods of spreading which lay each ply in the same lengthwise direction can be used for any surface direction of fabric but, if the fabric was one way–either way or one way only, the pattern pieces would be positioned appropriately. These represent the other two spreading opportunities:

(c) For asymmetrical as well as symmetrical pattern pieces, and fabric which is stable all the same way up, the spreader spreads in one

Fig. 2.5. Types of spread. (a) Alternate plies in different directions; symmetrical pattern pieces; fabric stable face to face. (b) Alternate plies in different directions; fabric stable face up; turntable spreader. (c) All plies in the same direction; fabric stable face up. (d) All plies in the same direction; symmetrical pattern pieces; fabric stable face to face; turntable spreader.

direction only and 'dead heads' back to spread the next ply in the same direction.

(d) For symmetrical pattern pieces, and fabric which is stable face to face, the spreader spreads in one direction only but after 'dead heading' back, a turntable is required to rotate the roll before the next ply is spread in the same direction.

(3) Alignment of plies

Every ply should comprise at least the length and width of the marker plan, but should have the minimum possible extra outside those measurements. The nature of textile materials means that pieces of fabric, as delivered from suppliers, vary in width, both from piece to piece and to a lesser extent within single pieces. The marker plan is made to fit the narrowest width. The surplus width is usually distributed outside the edge of the marker plan farthest from the spreading operator by aligning the straight edges of the plies nearest the operator. Alternatively, plies are centred and the surplus distributed equally to both edges. Inaccuracy in this alignment could mean that plies do not cover the whole area of the marker plan and parts of some pattern pieces would be missing when cut. In addition the ends of the plies must be cut off squarely, allowing the smallest possible loss at both ends, and having regard to the weft grain.

(4) Correct ply tension

If the plies are spread with too slack a tension they will lie in ridges with irregular fullness. If plies are spread in a stretched state they will maintain their tension while held in the lay, but will contract after cutting or during sewing, thus shrinking the garment parts to a smaller size than the pattern pieces. In a non-stretch fabric practically all elongation of the fabric occurs in such a manner that rapid relaxation and recovery ensues. Thus the use of spreading machines with positive feed to give tension-free spreading normally obviates stretched plies being bound into the lay. On the other hand stretch fabrics containing elastic or texturised yarns or knitted fabrics designed to have 10 to 50 per cent stretch present special problems.

In addition to the tension which may be produced by a conventional spreading machine, there are likely to be tensions inherent in the fabric roll arising from the twist, texturising or elasticity of the yarn and the relationships of loops in the knitted structure. These elements of stretch do not allow rapid relaxation and recovery. Hence, stretch fabric plies are commonly positioned by hand, and, although the fabric may be dispensed from a travelling spreader, it may in some cases be required to be unrolled and allowed to relax overnight before spreading. The width of most fabrics means that two operators are normally required for spreading. A further difficulty lies in building an accurate edge to the spread, since knitted fabric plies, once spread on top of each other, cannot easily be shifted without localised distortion. To make use of the speed of spreading in a modern spreading machine and the accuracy of placement that comes from an alignment shifter actuated by photo-electric guides, it is necessary not only to avoid adding to the tension in the fabric but also to reduce or eliminate the inherent tensions in a stretch fabric. This can be done by agitating, flexing and vibrating the fabric in a regular manner between its dispensing from the rolled piece and its placement on the spread, just as the operators do by hand in a somewhat irregular manner.

(5) Elimination of fabric faults

Fabric faults (flaws, holes, stains, etc.) may be identified by the fabric supplier, and additional faults may be detected during examination of the fabric by the garment manufacturer prior to spreading. In either situation a 'string' or plastic tag is attached to the fabric edge level with the fault. It is possible that the spreading operator may also discover faults missed in previous examinations. Unless it has been decided, as it sometimes is with small and inexpensive garments, that faults will be left in garments and 'inspected out' at the end of manufacture, the spreading operator is responsible for ensuring that faults do not occur in cut garment parts.

The simplest way to achieve this is by creating a splice. The spreader cuts across the ply at the position of the fault and pulls back the cut end to overlap as far back as the next splice mark. Splice marks are marked on the edge of the spreading table prior to spreading, by reference to the marker, and ensure that whenever a splice is created the overlap of fabric is sufficient to allow complete garment parts rather than sections only to be cut. How much fabric is wasted when a splice is made thus depends not just on the size of the fault but on the size of the garment panels in that part of the marker. The waste can be considerably greater than that allowed for in the price by the cloth supplier.

If more time is available it may be possible to consider the position of a small fault in relation to the marker and move the ply so that the fault occurs in a waste area. This may waste less fabric than making a splice. Computerised methods of achieving this are now available which provide a display of the marker plan on a computer screen on the spreading machine. A reference light is mounted on the crossbar of the machine which can be moved to a position directly over the fault each time the spreading operator stops the machine at a string on the selvedge. Various options are available to the operator to deal with the fault, once it can be seen where it will come in relation to the marker plan. If the fault will lie in an area of waste then no action is needed. Alternatively, a conventional splice may be seen as the best option or the third course of action available is to add a fabric patch of sufficient size over the flaw so that a separate recutting operation is avoided later.

A frequent fabric fault which can apply to a complete piece of a woven fabric is tight selvedges which cause fullness in each ply in the central area of the spread. It must be corrected by cutting into the selvedge to release the tightness.

(6)   Elimination of static electricity

In spreading plies of fabric containing man-made fibres, friction may increase the charge of static electricity in the fabric. The spreading operator will experience difficulty in laying a ply neatly on top of the others owing to either the attraction or repulsion of those plies according to how they are charged. He cannot align the plies accurately nor create a compact spread. Friction may be reduced by changing the method of threading the fabric through the guide bars of the spreading machine. Humidity in the atmosphere of the cutting room may also be increased, thus allowing the static electricity to discharge continuously through the atmosphere. In some cases it may be necessary to earth the lay.

(7)   Avoidance of distortion in the spread

A layer of glazed paper, laid glazed side down, is normally placed at the bottom of the spread. This helps to avoid disturbing the lowest plies of material in the spread when the base plate of a straight knife passes underneath, and also gives stability to the lay if it is to be moved on a flotation table. In addition, it prevents snagging of the fabric on the table surface which often becomes roughened with use.

(8)   Avoidance of fusion of plies during cutting

Cut edges of thermoplastic fibre fabrics may fuse together during cutting if the cutting knife becomes hot as a result of friction with the fabric. In this case, anti-fusion paper may be used in the same way as interleaving paper. It contains a lubricant which lubricates the knife blade as it passes through the spread, thus reducing the increase in temperature of the blade arising from friction.

Methods of spreading

Before describing the methods of spreading which can be used, the two different forms of spread which can be created must be described.

The commonest form of spread in bulk production is one where all the plies of fabric are the same length, underlying the complete marker plan. Though this plan can contain the parts for only one garment style, it is normally scrambled, that is it contains the pattern pieces for a number of garments, usually in different sizes, interlocked together in the most economical manner.

An alternative type of spread is the stepped spread in which a series of separate, usually single-size markers are positioned on top of varying numbers of plies. This was shown in Figure 2.2. Spreading a stepped lay may take less time than the alternative of several scrambled lays, and this shorter time may be crucial if the sewing room is to be fed with cut parts on time.

The methods of spreading which the industry uses can be divided into:

(1)   spreading by hand;
(2)   spreading using a travelling machine.

(1)   *Spreading by hand*

Despite the advent of spreading machinery which will cope with a wide variety of fabrics, there is still a frequent need to spread fabrics by hand. It is a time-consuming method, requiring an operator at each side of the table.

The fabric is drawn from its package which, if it is a roll, may be supported on a frame, and carried along the table where the end is secured by weights or a clamp. The operators work back from the end, aligning the edges and ensuring that there is no tension and that there are no wrinkles. The ply is normally cut with hand shears or with a powered circular knife mounted on a frame, though a few fabrics are ripped at the end of the ply to discover the exact weft grain and enable some straightening of a slightly crooked fabric to take place. Typical fabrics which must be spread by hand are checks, crosswise stripes and other regularly repeating patterns, as well as those with a repeating design at intervals of a garment length. If accurate 'stacking up' of the design vertically through the spread is necessary, the fabric may be 'spiked' on to a series of sharp spikes set vertically on the spreading table. These are available with an adjusting mechanism which controls the amount of spike showing above the table and which also enables the complete spikes to be lowered after spreading to allow for cutting or for moving of the lay along the table to a different cutting site.

The cost of hand spreading is partly offset by the ability to cut a fabric in bulk which might otherwise have to be cut in single garments.

(2)   *Spreading using a travelling machine*

Spreading machines carry the piece of fabric from end to end of the spread, dispensing one ply at a time onto the spread. Their basic elements consist of a frame or carriage, wheels travelling in guide rails at the edge of the table, a fabric support, and guide collars to aid the correct unrolling of the fabric. In the simpler versions, the operator clamps the free end of fabric in line with the end of the spread, pushes the spreader to the other end, cuts off the ply in line with that end, clamps the beginning of the next ply, pushes the spreader to the other end and so on.

More advanced spreading machines may include a motor to drive the carriage, a platform on which the operator rides, a ply-cutting device with

Fig. 2.6. Spreading machine with robotic loading equipment. (Reproduced by permission of Pfaff Bellow Ltd.)

automatic catcher to hold the ends of the ply in place, a ply counter, an alignment shifter actuated by photo-electric edge guides, a turntable, and a direct drive on the fabric support, synchronised with the speed of travel, to reduce or eliminate tension in the fabric being spread.

The maximum fabric width which can be handled is normally 2 m although extra wide machines capable of handling up to 3 m are available. The maximum weight of cloth roll that can be carried by the larger spreading machines is 120 kg, the maximum spreading speed around 100 m/min and the maximum height of spread cloth 28 cm. When a spreading machine dispenses fabric when travelling in one direction but returns to the first end without spreading to begin the next ply, the return pass is known as 'dead heading'. Many spreaders will travel at a considerably higher speed when 'dead heading'. Heavy piece machines are usually automatic, incorporating specialised braking facilities. A modern spreading machine is shown in Figure 2.6.

The advent of microprocessor control has enabled the development of more automatic functions on spreading machines. Thus a spreader can be pre-set to a selected number of plies, emitting an audible signal when it has reached the selected number or has come to the end of a piece of fabric. Automatic turntabling gives automatic spreading even for corduroys which are normally spread face to face. With robotic spreading, when the piece is finished, the spreader returns to an auto-lifter at the end of the table, transfers the empty centre bar to the lifter which then advances the next piece to the spreader. It repeats the process until it achieves the required number of plies. This method requires automatic sensing of previously marked flaws and damages. As the flaw moves past the sensor the spreader will halt, the ply cutter will cut across the ply, the spreader will reverse direction and move back to the nearest splice mark on the marker plan, and then it will continue its run to the end of the ply.

Rolls of cloth have increased in length and hence in weight over the years and even without the level of automation described above there is a need for mechanical assistance with lifting rolls of cloth from warehouse to cutting room and with loading them onto the spreading machines.

The nature of fabric packages

Fabric packages vary in length, width, and make-up. The choice of package to be delivered to a cutting room relates to the characteristics of the fabric and the method of spreading employed. The forms of fabric piece which can be used are as follows:

(1) Open fabric – rolled

Most fabrics are supplied rolled as a single ply directly on to a disposable, tubular cardboard core about 7 to 8 cm in diameter. The packages are suitable for spreading by machine. When spread by hand they often require two spreading operators, one each side of the table. Open fabric may vary from less than 75 cm wide to over 3 m, especially with knitted fabrics. In recent years the width of fabric has tended to increase, since its manufacturing costs per square metre tend to decrease with increasing width. This process is limited by the size of knitting machines and by what the garment manufacturer is prepared to handle.

(2) Tubular knitted fabric – rolled

This is usually used for the manufacture of garments such as sports shirts or tee-shirts and in specialised cases the fabric width is that required for the shirt body. The fabric fits the designed girth rather than vice versa. Tubular knits can usually be spread by machine.

(3) Folded fabric – rolled

This form is traditional with the woollen and woollen mixture fabrics used in tailored garments. The fabric is rolled onto a disposable, flat board approximately a centimetre thick. It is not suitable for spreading by machine, but its lesser width allows it to be spread manually by one spreader on narrower tables. Its width commonly varies from about 70 to

80 cm folded. With folded fabric the marker contains only a half set of patterns, since the fabric by its attitude is spread face to face.

(4) Folded fabric – cuttled

This form occurs usually with check fabrics and some tubular knits and aims to avoid the distortions which may ensue from tight rolling. The doubled fabric is folded accurately backwards and forwards in lengths of approximately 80 to 90 cm, the end of the piece being wrapped around the pile of folds or cuttle.

(5) Velvet – hanging

More rarely, some velvets may be delivered wound on specially constructed frames to prevent the pile becoming crushed.

An important trend is towards heavy pieces of 500 or even 1,000 metres. The longer the piece of fabric, in general, the lower the cost of manufacture and packaging per square metre. This benefits the fabric supplier, but in a competitive market part of the benefits will be passed on to the garment manufacturer as lower priced fabric. In addition garment manufacturers can reduce handling costs although specialised handling equipment is required. In spreading, the heavy piece reduces total loading and threading times on the travelling spreader, and increases the number of plies available from each piece. With effective control of shading over a larger area, it will reduce also the garment maker's costs in demarcating different shades from piece to piece. Finally, the longer the piece the smaller is the percentage of wastage through remnants.

(C) THE CUTTING OF THE FABRIC

The use of the term cutting can present a difficulty. It is used in the sense of 'cutting room', an area which normally includes the activities of marker planning, spreading and preparation for sewing, as well as being used to refer to the actual cutting out of garment parts from the lay.

The objective of cutting

The objective of cutting is to separate fabric parts as replicas of the pattern pieces in the marker plan. In achieving this objective, certain requirements must be fulfilled:

(1) Precision of cut

Garments cannot be assembled satisfactorily, and they may not fit the body correctly, if they have not been cut accurately to the pattern shape.

The ease with which accuracy is achieved depends on the method of cutting employed and in some cases on the marker planning and marker making, as described earlier. In manual cutting using a knife, accuracy of cut, given good line definition, depends on appropriate, well maintained cutting knives and on the skill and motivation of the cutter. In both die cutting and computer-controlled cutting, the achievement of accuracy comes from the equipment.

(2) Clean edges

The raw edge of the fabric should not show fraying or snagging. Such defects come from an imperfectly sharpened knife.

(3) Unscorched, unfused edges

The build-up of heat in the knife blade comes from the friction of the blade passing through the fabric. This, in extreme cases, leads to scorching of the fabric, and, more frequently, to the fusing of the raw edges of thermoplastic fibre fabrics, such as those containing polyamide or polyester. The cutter cannot separate individual plies from the pile of cut parts. Forced separation causes snagged edges, and, in any case, the hard edge is uncomfortable in wear. Solutions to this problem lie in a well-sharpened blade, a blade with a wavy edge, the use of anti-fusion paper during spreading, spraying the blade with air coolant/lubricant, slowing down the speed of the blade and reducing the height of the lay.

(4) Support of the lay

The cutting system must provide the means not only to support the fabric but also to allow the blade to penetrate the lowest ply of a spread and sever all the fibres.

(5) Consistent cutting

The cutting system should not be limited in the height of plies it will cut, because of progressive deterioration in cutting quality, though there may be mechanical or human reasons, such as toppling or leaning, for the height of lay being limited.

Methods of cutting

Numerous attempts have been made over the years to develop methods of cutting cloth other than by means of some kind of metal blade. Work continues in this direction and some of the possibilities will be described later, but in the majority of cutting rooms today, the cutting process makes use of hand shears, a mechanised knife blade in one of several possible types, or a die press which stamps out the garment shapes.

In all of these methods, a sharp blade is pressed against the fibres of the fabric. The blade must present a very thin edge to the fibres, to produce a bearing pressure high enough to shear the fibres without exerting a force against the fabric which will stretch or deform it. All fibres must be severed to allow the blade to pass through the fabric and produce free-standing cut parts. The act of cutting dulls the blade, which must be regularly sharpened to renew the thin sharp edge. This wears the blade and leads to its eventual replacement. Where an upright, mechanised knife blade is used, the blade must point in the direction of travel through the fabric when cutting straight or at a tangent to the line of cut on a curve. These methods of cutting remove no material between the cut parts (in contrast to the act of sawing wood which creates sawdust). The blade opens the cut after the fibres are severed, and the rest of the blade passes through the cut by compressing the material on either side (especially when cutting a curve). Normally fabrics return to their original shape after cutting. The following cutting systems are currently in use, separately or in combination.

(1) Hand shears

Hand shears are normally used when cutting only single or double plies. The lower blade of the shears passes under the plies, but the subsequent distortion of the fabric is only temporary and accurate cutting to the line can be achieved with practice. Left-handed shears are available since the cutting line will not easily be seen if right-handed shears are used by a left-handed person. This method is flexible enough to accommodate any fabric construction and pattern shape. The obvious disadvantage of the method lies in the time it consumes and the consequent high labour cost per garment, but it is appropriate for made-to-measure garments.

(2) Straight knife

Most cutting rooms which cut garments in bulk, but not in sufficient bulk to justify the purchase of computer-controlled cutters, make use of straight knives. The elements of a straight knife consist of a base plate, usually on rollers for ease of movement, an upright or standard carrying a straight, vertical blade with varying edge characteristics and an electric motor above it, a handle for the cutter to direct the blade, and a sharpening device. The base plate on its rollers slides under the glazed paper which is spread below the bottom ply of fabric in the lay. A typical straight knife is illustrated in Figure 2.7. Both this and the round knife mentioned later are hand-held power tools requiring an overhead cable feed and statutory safety precautions.

Two kinds of power are required to operate a straight knife. Motor power drives the reciprocating blade and operator power drives the knife through the lay. The motor power needed is determined by the height of the lay, the construction of the fabric, the curvature of the line being cut

Fig. 2.7. Straight knife. (Photo by Susie Lang, reproduced by permission of Eastman Machine Co. Ltd.)

(which causes the rear of the blade to press against the cut fabric plies) and the stroke of the blade. The greater the power of the motor the heavier the machine. The taller the standard the thicker its cross-section and the greater its width, adding resistance to the forward movement on a curve. Normally available blade heights vary from 10 cm to 33 cm. Normally available strokes vary from 2.5 cm to 4.5 cm. The greater the blade movement the faster the blade cuts the fabric and the more rapidly and easily the operator can push the machine, although proportionately greater motor power is required. The most important consideration in selecting a straight knife is the power required from the operator to move the knife through the lay. Operator effort is affected by the weight of the motor, the shape of the standard, handle height (awkward if too far above the lay), stroke, sharpness of blade, and the effect of the baseplate rollers on the table surface. The first four are involved in the choice of machine and the remainder in effective maintenance at the workplace. In particular, the sharpness of the blade and its constant bevel is most consistently achieved by the use of a continuous abrasive belt, available in a series of grits from coarse to fine. The normal blade has a straight edge, varying from coarsely ground for use with densely woven and coated fabrics, through various grades of roughness to a fine edge for cutting synthetic fabrics, knits and loose wovens. As stated previously, knife blades are also available with wavy edges to reduce heat generation and the possibility of fusing synthetic materials. Variable speed machines are available, allowing the same machine to be used to cut natural and thermoplastic fibres as well as allowing for a change of speed between long straight cuts and tight curves. The option of selecting a machine with a different blade stroke provides another way of solving the problem of the fusing of synthetics, as an alternative to varying the machine speed.

The straight knife is a common means of cutting lays in conventional cutting rooms because it is versatile, portable, cheaper than a band knife, more accurate on curves than a round knife and relatively reliable and easy to maintain. Even if a bandknife is used for the main cutting operation, a straight knife will be used to separate the lay into sections for easier handling.

The straight knife as described here has been in use for many years. More recently, a travelling suspension system has been available for use with a straight knife. This system supports the knife from above and means the heavy baseplate and rollers are replaced by a small, flat base, which reduces the possibility of distortion during cutting which can arise from the thickness of the conventional base plate. Suspension from above also reduces the need for a heavy gauge standard behind the knife, and the width of the blade is also reduced, allowing easier cutting of sharper curves. The drive trolley of the support arm moves automatically along rails on the side of the table supports as the straight knife is moved during the cutting process, allowing the best support to the knife at any part of the lay. These systems enable a much higher degree of cutting accuracy than unsupported straight knives, with less operator skill required. In many cases they allow a standard of cutting to be achieved with a straight knife that is normally only achievable by transporting roughly cut work to a band knife. The system is shown diagrammatically in Figure 2.8.

(3) Round knife

The elements of a round knife, pictured in Figure 2.9, are a baseplate, above which is mounted an electric motor, a handle for the cutter to direct the blade, and a circular blade rotating so that the leading edge cuts downwards into the fabric. Blade diameters vary from 6 cm to 20 cm. Round knives are not suitable for cutting curved lines in high lays because the blade does not strike all the plies simultaneously at the same point as

Fig. 2.8. Straight knife with automated arm support. (Reproduced by permission of Eastman Machine Co. Ltd.)

a vertical blade does. Therefore a round knife is used only for straight lines or lower lays of relatively few plies. It is naturally much more difficult for a circular blade to negotiate a tight curve, such as an armhole.

(4) Band knife

A band knife comprises a series of three or more pulleys, powered by an electric motor, with a continuously rotating steel blade mounted on them. One edge of the blade is sharpened. The principle of operation is different from a straight or a round knife in that the band knife passes through a slot in the cutting table in a fixed position and the section of lay to be cut is moved past it. The blade is usually narrower than on a straight knife and there is no standard behind it, both factors which assist the cutting of tight curves. A band knife workplace may be so arranged that the operator either pushes or pulls the section of lay towards the knife. The latter is most common in Britain. A band knife is shown in Figure 2.10.

Band knives are used when a higher standard of cutting accuracy is required than can be obtained with a straight knife. Space must be left around garment parts when planning the marker so that they can be sectioned out using a straight knife and then cut exactly using the band knife. When small parts such as collars, cuffs and pockets are cut, a template of metal or fibre board in the shape of the pattern piece may be clamped to the section of lay on top of the marker which is then drawn past the band knife blade, cutting exactly along the hard edge. Band

Fig. 2.9. Round knife. (Reproduced by permission of Eastman Machine Co. Ltd.)

knives are used more in menswear than in womenswear and are often used to cut large garment parts such as the large panels of jackets and overcoats.

(5) Notchers

Many garment parts require that notches are cut into the edges of them to enable alignment during sewing with other garments parts. The previous four methods of cutting can be used to cut notches, but accuracy depends on the operator. Specialised notching equipment provides greater accuracy because a guide lines up the notcher with the cut edge to give consistent depth of notch at a consistent right angle to the edge. Both

Fig. 2.10. Band knife. (Reproduced by permission of Pfaff Bellow Ltd.)

Fig. 2.11. Hot notcher. (Reproduced by permission of Eastman Machine Co. Ltd.)

straight notches and vee notches are available. A further machine, the hot notcher, incorporates a heating element in order that the blade may slightly scorch the fibres adjacent to the notch in order to prevent it fraying and disappearing. This cannot be used with thermoplastic fibres or certain unlined garments. One fabric requiring it may be a loosely woven tweed. The notcher is illustrated in Figure 2.11.

(6) Drills and thread markers

Where reference marks are needed away from the edge of a garment part, such as for the position of pockets, darts and similar features, a hole is often drilled through all the plies of fabric in the lay. The drill mounting includes a motor, a base plate with a hole to allow the drill to pass through, and a spirit level to ensure that the base is horizontal and hence the drill vertical. Figure 2.12 shows the essential features. On many fabrics the drill is used cold and the hole remains visible until the sewing operator comes to use it. On looser weave fabrics, where the hole may

Fig. 2.12. Hot drill. (Reproduced by permission of Eastman Machine Co. Ltd.)

close up, a hot drill is used, which will slightly scorch or fuse the edges of the hole. A hypodermic drill may also be used which leaves a small deposit of paint on each ply of fabric. If it is important that no mark remains on the fabric, a long thread may be passed through the lay which is then cut with scissors between each ply, leaving a few centimetres visible on each garment panel. All drill holes must eventually be concealed by the construction of the garment.

(7) Computer controlled cutting knives

In describing the use of computer systems for marker planning and marker making, the possibility of using the information stored in the computer to drive a cutting knife was mentioned. This method provides the most accurate possible cutting, at high speed, and to keep the larger systems fully occupied they are frequently used in a central cutting facility that supplies a number of separate sewing factories. Increasingly, though, smaller, cheaper systems are being developed which are suitable for companies wanting to cut lower lays of smaller quantities of garments and these are appropriate for a single-factory operation. The main elements of a computer-controlled cutting system are shown in Figure 2.13.

A typical computer cutting system has a table with a cutting surface consisting of nylon bristles which support the fabric lays but are flexible enough to permit penetration and movement of the knife blade which is supported only at the top. The bristles also allow the passage of air through the table to create a vacuum, reducing the height of the lay and holding it in place. The carriage supporting the cutting head has two synchronised servo-motors which drive it on tracks on the edges of the table. A third servo-motor positions the cutting head on a beam across

Fig. 2.13. Computer-controlled cutting head and table. (Reproduced by permission of Lectra Systems Ltd.)

the width of this carriage. These two movements are co-ordinated to give a knife position at any point on the table. The cutting head contains a knife, automatic sharpener and a further servo-motor which rotates the knife to position it at a tangent to the line of cut on curves. A further facility controls the deflection of the knife which inevitably occurs on curves by adjusting the angle to equalise the pressure on each side of the blade. This ensures accurate cutting through all layers. A sheet of airtight polyethylene covers the top of the lay which assists the creation of a vacuum and allows significant compression of the lay. A control cabinet houses the computer and the electrical components required to drive the cutter, its carriage and the vacuum motor.

The spreader spreads the lay on a conventional cutting table equipped with air flotation. Paper is spread below the bottom ply so that the lay can be moved onto the cutting table without distortion and so that the bottom plies are supported during the cutting operation. This paper is perforated to enable the vacuum on the cutting table to operate to compress the lay.

After loading the disc into the computer, the operator positions the cutting head's origin light over the corner of the spread. This provides the computer with a reference point. A lift and plunge feature enables the knife to negotiate sharp corners and straight or vee-shaped notches can also be cut. A motorised drill behind the cutting head can provide drill holes as required. Different systems are available which are designed to cut different heights of compressed plies. The maximum height is usually 7.5 cm when compressed, with the height before compression, and hence the number of plies, being dependent on the nature of the fabric. The type of powerful cutting head designed to cut this high is more costly than one designed for lower ply heights and it cannot cut as fast. A manufacturer who cuts only low lays, e.g. 2 cm compressed, would invest in the less expensive, faster system. Quoted figures for actual knife speeds can be as high as 80 m/min but the overall speed of cutting garment parts is generally between 5 and 12 m/min, with the higher overall speeds being obtained when cutting large garment parts rather than small.

Different arrangements of cutting room tables are possible, but they must allow for the fact that in this situation the cutting process takes very much less time than spreading and somewhat less time than bundling. A typical arrangement would consist of four spreading tables supplying each cutting table. The cutting table and its carriage and cutting head is able to move between the spreading tables by means of tracks on the floor and has, beyond it, four bundling tables onto which the cut garments are moved. When the cutting table is lined up with a table on which a lay has been prepared, the lay is floated onto it in sections which are then cut and moved on to the bundling table. The cutting table does not need to be as long as the lay and its bristle surface can consist of a conveyor which assists in the transfer of the lay, in sections, from the spreading table and of the cut work onto the bundling table. The rotation of the conveyor with its bristle surface also assists in cleaning waste material from the surface. An alternative arrangement is for a flotation cutting table to be used as a transfer table to a fixed cutting table carrying the cutting head. The transfer table has to be as long as the lay and a table for bundling would be required beyond the cutting table.

Since the computer-controlled knife cuts according to instructions from the computer rather than by following a pattern line drawn on a marker, it is possible, as indicated previously, to dispense with the use of fully plotted paper markers and either just plot the information necessary for bundling on the marker, or elimininate the marker completely and just label the garment parts that are being cut. Care must be taken that the correct disc is loaded into the computer so that the correct garments are cut. An error here would be costly in wasted fabric and, without a plotted marker on top of the lay, it may not be immediately obvious that the computer-controlled knife is cutting a different style from that intended.

(8) Die cutting

In contrast to the fast-moving blades used in the methods of cutting previously described, die cutting involves pressing a rigid blade through the lay of fabric. The die (called a clicker in the shoe industry) is a knife in the shape of a pattern periphery, including notches. One or more tie bars secure its stability. Free standing dies generally fall into two categories. They can be of strip steel, manufactured by bending the strip to the shape required and welding the joint. These cannot be sharpened and must be replaced when worn. Alternatively, they can be heavier gauge, forged dies which can be resharpened but which are about five times the price of strip steel. The position of the tie bars determines the depth of cut, which is generally greater with forged dies.

Free standing dies cut the small parts of larger garments such as collars and trouser pocketing or the parts of smaller garments such as bras. They can also be used for part of a larger garment part, such as the neck area of a coat front. They provide a high standard of accuracy of cutting but, because of the cost of the dies, they are only appropriate to situations where large quantities of the same pattern shape will be cut. Die cutting also offers much faster cutting than knife cutting for the same depth of cut. It is proportionally more economic for small parts which have a greater periphery in relation to their area than do large parts. In addition, the level of accuracy demanded of small parts is not only greater but correspondingly more difficult to achieve with conventional knives.

The die press generally has a cutting arm supported by a single pillar at the back of the machine. It swings to the side to allow the placing of dies on top of the fabric. The downward cutting stroke of the press should be so controlled that the edge of the die just penetrates the cutting pad or surface in order that the fibres of the lowest ply are completely separated. Die presses are of two types: impact, which makes a single press on the die, and, more commonly, hytronic (hydraulic and electronic) which exerts continuous pressure on the die until it has cut the fabric and made contact with the soft metal or nylon pad. Once the pad, after repeated cutting, reaches an unsatisfactory state of wear, its surface is recut and re-levelled.

For die cutting, the spreader spreads a lay to the required number of plies and may place a marker on top to guide the placement of dies. The spread is cut into sections to allow transport to the cutting pad. In some cases, no marker is used, the operator placing the dies by eye to the correct grain line and as close together as this method allows.

One important disadvantage of die cutting is its greater use of fabric. When the die press forces the dies through the fabric it also forces a narrow wedge of fabric between the dies. The narrow wedge exists because the sharpened cutting edge of the die is necessarily of narrower gauge than the top of the die. Thus if dies are butted together, they touch at the top but show a small gap at the level of the cutting edges. The action of the press will compress this narrow wedge of fabric to the point where it will rupture the dies. Hence it is necessary to leave a significant gap between two dies, say 2 to 3 mm. Similarly a single die will not cut satisfactorily if placed closer than 3 to 4 mm to a previously cut edge.

Large area die cutting presents a number of technical problems. A complete lay of free dies several metres long on top of the fabric could be cut by a twin pillar or four pillar press extending across the lay. For economic and engineering reasons the depth of the press is limited. Hence the lay is cut in sections, the downward stroke of the press alternating with the forward movement of a conveyorised bed. This gives partial coverage of larger dies at certain strokes of the press, causing the dies to break. One solution is the die forme, for instance, a plywood backing with strip steel dies set in it blade upwards. The fabric plies are spread on top of the die forme and the strokes of the die press successively press the fabric down onto the blades. Foam inserts within the dies assist the operation of stripping out after cutting. Some fabric stretch may result when the press head does not completely cover a die, because while part of the fabric is pressed onto the die, the area just outside the head remains on the surface. The capital cost of large area die presses is high but more important, the cost of tooling up with die formes, to cover all markers in all styles and fabric widths, is prohibitive in a frequently changing market. Hence, the circumstances where large area die cutting is profitable are rare. An exception is the cut-and-sew knitwear industry.

All the cutting methods described so far have made use of a metal blade in some form, powered by hand or machine. This is not the only way to separate materials but it is reliable in that a cut is assured whichever of the methods is used. Several high energy sources which can be concentrated into a moving point have been tried for the cutting of fabric. It will be seen that some of them can be effectively used but all carry the possibility of insufficient energy and hence poor quality cutting or even complete lack of cutting. All are controlled in a similar way to the computer-controlled knife already described.

(9) Laser cutting

A laser produces a beam of light which can be focused into a very small spot (0.25 mm), producing a very high energy density. The energy transfers to the material on which it is focused, producing a rapid increase in temperature. Cutting takes place by vaporisation. Charring is prevented by the use of a jet of inert gas which also removes debris and smoke from the cutting area. A laser beam does not become blunt and need renewing but it does suffer from limited depth of focus. This limits the depth of fabric it can cut and the best results are achieved when cutting single plies. If several plies are cut, the accuracy is not perfect as it is a V cut rather than a straight line. There is also a risk that the edges may fuse together.

The system includes a stationary gas laser, a cutting head carrying a system of mirrors which reflect the laser beam to the cutting line, a computer which operates the entire system and a means of removing cut parts from the conveyor carrying the single ply of fabric. In installations currently in use in the USA, cutting speeds of around 13 metres per minute are quoted. A practical limitation on the speed of cutting is the speed of movement of the carriage bearing the mirrors.

Automatic, single ply, laser cutting is fast compared with automatic multiple ply knife cutters, with speeds of 30–40 m/min being achieved compared with 5–12 m/min quoted already for knife cutting. However, when the cutting of a number of plies is taken into consideration, knife cutters are faster per garment cut, especially with the recent developments towards faster and cheaper equipment for cutting at low and medium ply heights. Such equipment is cheaper to purchase than a laser cutter, and that, combined with its higher cutting speed per garment, has ensured that, for the present, laser cutting seems unlikely to become widespread in the cutting of garments. There are advantages to single ply cutting which relate to the use of information stored in the computer that is controlling it. This can enable local adjustments to be made to allow for fabric width variation, check matching, avoidance of flaws, and immediate recutting of parts that are flawed. However, most manufacturing units require garments to be transported and presented in some quantity greater than singles which further discourages the use of single ply cutters.

Laser cutters are rare in the UK clothing industry but are being used successfully in the cutting of sails where single ply cutting is the norm and a slight fusing of the edge of the synthetic, woven materials that are used is actually desirable. They are also used for cutting in some areas of home furnishings.

(10) Plasma cutting

Plasma cutting was originally developed to satisfy a demand for high quality cutting on stainless steels and aluminium but it can also be used to cut textile materials. Cutting is achieved by means of a high velocity jet of high temperature ionised gas (argon). If engineering problems could be overcome, this method has the potential to become the faster cutter of single plies, but as explained above, there is not currently a high demand for single ply cutting.

(11) Water jet cutting

A very high velocity, small diameter stream of water is created by applying high pressure water to a nozzle. The high pressure jet acts as a solid tool when it encounters the material to be cut, tearing the fibres on impact. As the jet penetrates successive plies in a spread, the momentum decreases and cutting ability is reduced. The jet spreads out and the cut is wider and rougher at the bottom of the spread. Here the jet of water is normally caught and drained away. There is a danger of wet edges and water spotting. The water used must be filtered and de-ionised.

Water jet cutting is most effective with harder sheet materials, including leather and plastic. A complete computer system has been developed for leather in which hides are inspected and blemishes marked, and the hides are then scanned into the computer. A marker plan is made in which the pattern pieces are planned onto the hide, allowing for blemishes and for the varying thicknesses that occur in leather, and the hide is then automatically cut, in a single layer, by water jet. Capital costs are high and it is difficult to see such systems being taken up by the many small companies in the leather side of the industry. Currently, much leather is cut by hand-held knife blade on a glass surface, with the visual appearance and thickness of the hide being taken into account as every pattern piece is placed. There is no grain direction to be considered.

(12) Ultrasonic cutting

Most recently developed is a cutting system using an ultrasonically driven knife blade. Vibration frequencies in the 20 kHz range produce ½0 mm movement in the blade, small enough to remove the need for a bristle base to the cutting table. Disposable knife blades save sharpening time and last for 10–14 days. In the systems developed so far, two cutting heads are used, moving in different but synchronised paths. Up to 10 plies can be cut and low vacuum only is needed.

3
Sewing

The dominant process in garment assembly is sewing, still the best way of achieving both strength and flexibility in the seam itself as well as flexibility of manufacturing method. Much of the application of technology to clothing manufacture is concerned with the achievement of satisfactorily sewn seams.

It is necessary to define the term seam at an early stage in any discussion because its application is broader than is generally realised. In common parlance, a seam is a joint between two pieces of fabric. Indeed, this was the essence of the British Standard definition of seams as contained in the 1965 version of BS 3870: Schedule of Stitches, Seams and Stitchings. The noun 'stitching' then applied to situations where there is only one piece of fabric, such as when fabric edges are neatened or hems created, and where decorative sewing is involved.

The current BS 3870: Part 2: 1991: Classification and Terminology of Seam Types, and the earlier 1983 edition, define a seam as 'the application of a series of stitches or stitch types to one or several thicknesses of material'. Thus the term includes virtually all sewing that goes into garments. Perhaps in the future, the further development of non-sewing methods of seaming will cause this definition to be altered, but the current definition is appropriate to present purposes.

The properties that seams have to achieve can be stated quite simply at an introductory level, but the factors involved in achieving those properties are complex and interrelated. It is proposed that the general properties of sewn seams in garments should be discussed in the present chapter in order to relate the many relevant factors together as rapidly as possible. The following chapter will then explore the technical considerations in greater depth by studying the machinery used.

The properties of seams

The objectives of sewing are the construction of seams which combine the required standards of appearance and performance with an appropriate level of economy in production.

Good appearance in a seam normally means smooth fabric joins with no missed or uneven stitches and no damage to the material being sewn. Alternatively it may mean regular gathering to create a style feature or a varying but controlled amount of ease to ensure a good fit to the body. In yet other cases fabric may be deliberately stretched to achieve an effect but the amount should still be predetermined and controlled. With the wide variety of fibre types and fabric constructions available, good seam appearance during manufacturing demands varying techniques. Once it has been achieved, it must be maintained throughout the designed lifetime of the garment, despite the additional problems that arise during wearing and during washing and dry cleaning processes.

Performance of seams means the achievement of strength, elasticity, durability, security and comfort, and the maintenance of any specialised fabric properties such as waterproofing or flameproofing. Seams must be as strong as the fabric, in directions both parallel to and at right angles to the seam. They must also stretch and recover with the fabric. Stretch fabrics are increasingly being used in garments, both low level 'comfort' stretch as used in stretch corduroy or denim where the amount of stretch may be up to about 30 per cent, and high level 'action' stretch for swimwear and dancewear where 100 per cent or more is normal. Such levels of stretch place very heavy demands on seaming. Seams must also be durable to the kind of abrasion experienced in wearing and washing as well as secure against fraying apart or the unravelling of stitches. A seam in a close-fitting or underwear garment must not present an uncomfortable ridge or roughness to the skin. If a fabric is coated in PVC, neoprene or polyurethane to make it totally waterproof, a simple form of sewn seam joining two sections will leave gaps between those sections, as well as needle holes along the join, and the seam will not be waterproof. According to the nature of the coating, the seam must be welded, taped or 'doped' to seal over the join and block up the needle holes. A fabric used for a child's nightdress which must by law conform to specified flammability requirements, must be constructed with sewing threads which will not propagate a flame along the seam. Finally, seam performance as well as seam appearance can be spoilt by the fact that damage may occur to the fabric along the stitch line.

The question of economy of seaming in production arises because many seams can be constructed in a variety of ways. Many of the newer machines and stitch types enable shortcuts to be taken in the joining and neatening of seams but the appearance and performance of the seams vary with the different methods. A balance must be achieved when planning garment production between the demands of the end use of the garment, its price and the machinery available for its construction.

Assuming that the fabric is sewable and suitable for garments, the achievement, at an economical level, of the various requirements of appearance and performance of sewn seams, both initially and during use, is the result of the selection of the correct combination of five factors during manufacturing:

(a)   the *seam type* which is a particular configuration of fabric(s);
(b)   the *stitch type* which is a particular configuration of thread in the fabric;
(c)   the *sewing machine feeding mechanism* which moves the fabric past the needle and enables a succession of stitches to be formed;
(d)   the *needle* which inserts the thread into the fabric;
(e)   the *thread* which forms the stitch which either holds the fabric together, neatens it or decorates it.

These factors are closely interrelated and discussing any one of them without reference to at least one of the others is not possible. When dealing with seam types it will be seen that seams drawn as sections of flat or folded fabric(s) with no indication of the position of the stitches holding them together are meaningless. Thus an indication of the position of the needle(s) in the seam is normally given. Similarly, a stitch type and the particular configuration of fabric to which it is applied cannot easily be separated and diagrams of stitch types inevitably show a variety of seam types. In order to depict fully the construction of sections of a garment, both the type of seam and the type of stitch must be given. The use of a sewing thread is also assumed. It is proposed to begin by describing the basic seam types and their method of representation with only the minimum reference to the types of stitch which would be used on them. Stitch types will then be described in detail, with applications to a wider variety of seam types.

(A) SEAM TYPES

The choice of seam type is determined by aesthetic standards, strength, durability, comfort in wear, convenience in assembly in relation to the machinery available, and cost. BS 3870: Part 2: 1991, referred to above, allows for eight different classes of seam, including some where only one piece of fabric is involved. Examples are the hem of a garment folded up on itself and a raw edge which has been neatened by means of stitches. This alters the traditional concept of a seam as a joint between fabrics.

The British Standard divides stitched seams into eight classes according to the minimum number of parts that make up the seam. These parts can be the main fabrics of the garment or some additional item such as a lace, braid or elastic.

To indicate how the various seam types are formed, several styles of diagram can be used. The one which most clearly relates to garment parts as sewn shows a perspective view of a section of the seam, and, when the various stitch types are being discussed, it is useful to show a section of the reverse side of the stitch. This is shown in Figure 3.1.

The diagram shows two pieces of fabric laid one on top of the other and sewn close to one edge. The straight lines to the right are the edges which are relevant to the seam being described, the wavy lines to the left

Fig. 3.1. Seam diagrams.

(i)   (ii)

Fig. 3.2. Simplified seam diagrams.

represent the rest of the garment parts, of no importance to the seam under consideration. When seam types are being discussed purely as a configuration of fabric, these diagrams are unnecessarily elaborate, especially on complicated seams. Once familiarity with seam types has been established, it is often sufficient to draw the diagrams in a shorthand version which shows a cross-section through the fabric represented by lines, with short lines at right angles showing the point of needle penetration of the stitch. This is shown in Figure 3.2. Once familiarity with stitch types has also been established, the British Standard stitch number, as given in BS 3870: Part 1: Classification and Terminology of Stitch Types, can be used.

Certain conventions are observed in depicting the penetration or passage of the needle(s). Thus Figure 3.2(i) shows the representation when the needle passes through the material, whereas (ii) shows the situation when a stitch type or needle shape is used such that the needle does not pass through the material.

A common seam used on the sides of garments is shown represented in three different ways in Figure 3.3. This shows a seam consisting of two pieces of fabric with neatened edges, joined with a further row of stitches. This type of seam can be pressed open. If the third, shorthand diagram is initially difficult to understand, a cast off garment can be examined and, if some of the seams are cut into at right angles with scissors, the layout of the diagram will be more clearly seen.

The British Standard gives an identifying number for each of the hundreds of different seam types which it depicts. Seams are relatively simple to draw and remember and a great many of them will be encountered. More important than remembering the numerical

Fig. 3.3. Methods of representing seams.

designation is the ability to relate diagrams to existing or possible garments, as a way of considering the suitability of the seam for its purpose, and the machinery that would be used in its construction. Accordingly, it is not proposed to use the seam type numbers but, if needed, they can be obtained from the British Standard. By contrast, the number of British Standard stitch types in common use is quite small but they are much more complicated to draw and to remember and it will be seen later that it is essential in this case that their identifying numbers are used.

Six seam classes were included in the 1965 British Standard and at that stage they were given names which usefully describe their constructions. Two more classes were added with the publication of the 1983 edition, but without the descriptive names, and the total of eight continues in the 1991 edition. In the following sections these names have been included in brackets. This breakdown of seams into classes is included here as it provides a framework within which seam constructions can initially be explained and an indication given of the variety that exists.

Class 1 (superimposed seam)

This is the commonest construction seam on garments and the one used in Figure 3.3, above, to illustrate the various methods of depicting seam constructions. The simplest seam type within the class is formed by superimposing the edge of one piece of material on another. A variety of stitch types can be used on this type of seam, both for joining the fabrics and for neatening the edges or for achieving both simultaneously.

The seams shown in Figure 3.4(i) and (ii) can be pressed open, that shown in (iii) cannot. Not all the seams shown in these diagrams can be sewn in one operation. The diagrams normally show the final version and it should be clear from the positions of the needles and the folding of the fabric if it was constructed in one step or several. An example of this is

Fig. 3.4. Superimposed seams.

Fig. 3.5. French seams.

Fig. 3.6. Piped seams.

the type of superimposed seam known as a French seam which is done in two stages. This is shown as (i) in Figure 3.5. A similar, and in many cases an equally acceptable seam, could be constructed using a folding device and a multi-needle machine, though only on a straight, rather than a curved, fabric edge. This is shown in (ii).

Fig. 3.7. Lapped seam.

Fig. 3.8. Lap felled seam.

Fig. 3.9. Welted seam.

An example of a superimposed seam with an additional component would be one that contained an inserted piping, and even here more than one construction is possible, as is shown in Figure 3.6.

Class 2 (lapped seam)

The simplest seam type in this class is formed by lapping two pieces of material as shown in Figure 3.7.

In practice, this simple seam is not common in clothing because it causes problems with raw edges and at least one of the edges must be neatened in a decorative manner. Where it is commonly used is in the joining of panels in sails where a strong seam is achieved by using two or three rows of zig-zag stitching. Sail fabrics are very finely woven and fray very little.

Much more common on long seams on garments such as jeans and shirts is the so-called lap-felled seam, sewn with two rows of stitches on a twin needle machine equipped with a folding device. This provides a very strong seam in garments that will take a lot of wear though there is a possibility that the thread on the surface may suffer abrasion in areas such as inside leg seams. The lap felled seam is illustrated in Figure 3.8.

(i)   (ii)

Fig. 3.10. Bound seams.

The type of raised, topstitched seam often used down skirt panels is also technically a lapped seam although at the beginning of its construction it appears to be a superimposed seam. It is often referred to as a welted or a raised and welted seam and is shown in Figure 3.9.

Class 3 (bound seam)

In this class, the seam consists of an edge of material which is bound by another, with the possibility of other components inserted into the binding.

The simplest version of this class is again unusual as it cannot be constructed with self-fabric binding because of the problem of raw edges. It can, however, be made with a binding which has been constructed to a specific width. Figure 3.10(i) shows the simplest bound seam while (ii) shows a common version where the garment fabric, or even a contrasting colour of the garment fabric, has been cut into narrow strips. A folding device turns the edges under and wraps the strip over the edge of the main fabric. Bias cut strip would normally be used, unless the fabric had an element of stretch. A bound seam is often used as a decorative edge and the binding may continue off the edge of the garment to provide tie ends.

The types of folding device which can be added to sewing machines to create these bound seams will be discussed further in the next chapter. Their development has given designers the scope to use a wide variety of complicated seam constructions, both functional and decorative. Examples in common use on underwear and leisurewear and on skirts, jeans and ladies' trousers are shown in Figure 3.11. In (i) is shown a common finish used on the neck edge of tee shirts and also on the edges of men's vests and briefs. In (ii) it has an insert of another cut strip. This would normally be in a contrasting colour to the garment and both could contrast with the outer binding. In (iii) an elastic has been included in a sufficiently stretched state to draw the edge of the garment in to a snug fit.

(i)   (ii)

(iii)   (iv)

Fig. 3.11.   Common bound seams.

On all these seams, a stitch type would be used which has two needles and incorporates a thread passing between the needle threads on the underside and covering the raw edge of the fabric. Self-fabric in the same or another colour is usually cut into strips for the bindings and the fabrics are normally knitted. In (iv), a waistband, usually with an interlining fused to it, is bound on to the top of a skirt, jean or trouser using a folder and twin needle machine. The ends of the waistband require stitching separately.

Class 4 (flat seams)

In this class, seams are referred to as flat seams because the fabric edges do not overlap. They may be butted together without a gap and joined across by a stitch which has two needles sewing into each fabric and covering threads passing back and forth between these needles on both sides of the fabric. Knitted fabrics are most commonly used because the advantage of this seam is that it provides a join that is free from bulk in garments worn close to the skin such as knitted underwear. The machine

Fig. 3.12. Flat seams.

trims both fabric edges so that they form a neat join. Alternatively, various zig-zag stitches could sew back and forth between the fabrics which might then have a decorative gap between them. Examples of flat seams are shown in Figure 3.12.

Fig. 3.13. Decorative seams. (i) 2 × 301, (ii) 4 × 401, (iii) pin tucks, (iv) channel seam.

Class 5 (decorative stitching)

This is the first of the two classes of seam which, in the old British Standard, were not regarded as seams at all and were given the name 'stitching'. The main use of the seam is for decorative sewing on garments where single or multiple rows of stitches are sewn through one or more layers of fabric. These several layers can be folds of the same fabric. The simplest seam in the class has decorative stitching across a garment panel. One row would have little effect but multi-needle stitching is common.

Figure 3.13(i) shows twin-needle stitching with a ribbon laid under the stitches while (ii) shows four rows of stitches. This type of multi-needle stitching has further decorative possibilities if an attachment is added to the machine which lays embroidery threads back and forth under the stitches on the surface of the fabric.

Other possibilities, given the right folding devices, are pin tucks, often sewn in multiples, and channel seams. These are shown in Figure 3.13(iii) and (iv). This type of pin tuck is different from the traditional version which consists of a fold in the fabric sewn close to the edge. When multiple, parallel tucks are required, the original method is slow and potentially inaccurate. In the version shown here, the folder ensures the tucks are parallel as all the tucks are sewn simultaneously. The tucks must, however, be set to face one way or the other and a decision as to which must be made in relation to the design of the garment.

Class 6 (edge neatening)

This is the other seam class that was called a stitching. Seam types in this class include those where fabric edges are neatened by means of stitches (as opposed to binding with another or the same fabric) as well as folded hems and edges. The simplest is the fabric edge inside a garment which has been neatened with an overedge stitch, as shown in Figure 3.14.

In considering hems on the sleeves and lower edges of garments, there are many possibilities when the variety of stitch types that can be used is taken into account. A selection only is given in Figure 3.15 and at this stage it is assumed that the reader can interpret the construction through

Fig. 3.14. Edge neatening.

Fig. 3.15. Hemmed edges. (i) 504/103, (ii) 301, (iii) 2 × 301, (iv) 2 × 401.

the use of the shorthand type of diagram only. The need to know the stitch type used, in order to appreciate fully the construction of the seam, should now become clear. Numbers for stitch types which might be used have been included so that the diagrams can be referred to again later when the reader is familiar with these numbers. In Figure 3.15, (i) is typical of the hem on a dress or a pair of trousers in a woven fabric which has been neatened and then sewn up invisibly (blind stitched). In a knitted fabric the neatening might be omitted. In (ii), a folding device is used in the construction of the hem of a shirt or a skirt lining; (iii) and (iv) show a method of folding an edge that is sometimes used on the buttonhole front of a shirt. Two different constructions are possible, the first one requiring the sewing to be done in two stages, the second one requiring a twin-needle machine.

The remaining two seam classes in the 1991 British Standard are an addition to the original standard, added in the 1983 edition, to include seam types commonly seen in modern garment construction. No general descriptive title has been given to either of them.

Class 7

Seams in this class relate to the addition of separate items to the edge of a garment part. They are similar to the lapped seam except that the added component has a definite edge on both sides. Examples would be a band of lace attached to the lower edge of a slip as in Figure 3.16(i), elastic braid on the edge of a bra as in (ii) and inserted elastic on the leg of a swimsuit as in (iii).

Fig. 3.16. Addition of separate items. (i) 304 lace, (ii) 321, (iii) 406/504.

Fig. 3.17. Shirt buttonhole band – 2 × 401.

An example where the additional item is self-fabric plus interlining is another version of the buttonhole band on a shirt, shown in Figure 3.17. This is another instance where, by using two folders and a twin-needle machine, a complicated construction can be completed in one step. Without such machinery, achieving a similar, let alone identical, result would be very difficult.

Class 8

The final seam class in the British Standard is another where only one piece of material need be involved in constructing the seam. The commonest seam type in this class is the belt loop as used on jeans, raincoats, etc. This is shown in Figure 3.18(i). Also included in this class are belts themselves and two possible constructions for these are shown in (ii) and (iii).

The use on the belt loop of the stitch type mentioned before which has two needles and a bottom covering thread ensures that the raw edges are covered over on the underside while showing two rows of plain stitching on the top. The belt shown in (iii) is quicker and cheaper to construct than the one shown in (ii) but, as always, a special machine attachment is required to fold the fabric.

In this study of seam types, a selection only has been given to demonstrate some of the commoner constructions used in garments. More will be studied when considering stitch types. It will be seen that many of the seams require complicated folding prior to sewing while even the simple ones require to be accurately controlled if the sewing is to be

Fig. 3.18. Belt loop and belts. (i) 406, (ii) 301, (iii) 301.

neat and the garment the correct size. Sewing machine attachments which fold fabric have already been mentioned and others are available which control or guide fabric and enable a relatively unskilled operator to sew quickly and with a high level of accuracy. However, their use is only justified where considerable quantities of the same sewing operation are to be performed. Small volume production is heavily dependent on skilled operators if the manufacturing quality standards are to be high. These high standards will only be achieved at high cost. Thus, cheaply produced fashion garments tend to be inaccurately sewn. The use of sewing machine attachments will be considered in more detail, along with other aspects of machinery, in the next chapter.

(B) STITCH TYPES

In discussing seam types it has been necessary to make some mention of stitch types and it should already be evident that a wide variety is required for even the limited number of seam types already demonstrated. There is a need for stitches which join and stitches which neaten, for machines with more than one needle and for stitches which form a covering layer over the fabric. Certain stitch types can also aid economical garment production by performing several functions at once such as joining and neatening or by adding decoration at the same time as either of those.

British Standard 3870: Part 1: 1991: Classification and Terminology of Stitch Types, is the standard reference to the wide range of stitch types now available for use in garment construction. It defines a stitch as: 'one unit of conformation resulting from one or more strands or loops of thread intralooping, interlooping or passing into or through material'.

Intralooping is the passing of a loop of thread through another loop formed by the same thread, interlooping is the passing of a loop of thread through another loop formed by a different thread, and interlacing, a term also used in relation to certain stitches, is the passing of a thread over or around another thread or loop of another thread. These apparently obscure distinctions are illustrated in Figure 3.19. Their importance in relation to stitch security will become clear as the various stitches are described.

A series of recurring stitches of one configuration is defined as a stitch type. BS 3870 divides the many types which are available into six classes which variously cover the demands of joining fabrics together, neatening raw edges, or providing decoration, or offer the economy of doing more than one of these at a time.

Of the seventy or so stitch types covered by BS 3870, the number in regular use is a selection which includes at present around eighteen to twenty types. Even that number is only in use at the high volume, bulk production end of the industry where the demands of speed, economy, and high standards of seam performance prevail over flexibility of

(i)   (ii)   (iii)

Fig. 3.19. Stitch formation. (i) Intralooping, (ii) interlooping, (iii) interlacing.
The diagrams of stitches used here and the codings are extracts from BS 3870:
1991: *Schedule of Stitches and Seams* Part 1: Classification and terminology of
stitch types. They are reproduced with the permission of BSI. Complete copies of
the standard can be obtained by post from BSI Publications, Linford Wood,
Milton Keynes, MK14 6LE.
British Standard 3870 is identical with ISO 4915: 1991: *Textiles—Stitch types:
Classification and Terminology* published by the International Organisation for
Standardisation (ISO).

manufacturing method. In small volume or more traditional production,
garments are constructed with two or three stitch types only, and many
garments on sale show evidence of having been made by homeworkers
with access only to the domestic lockstitch machine or its industrial
equivalent.

The diagrams which accompany the following descriptions of stitch
types show the stitches as a configuration of thread in the manner used in
the British Standard. Stitch diagrams alone can be difficult to relate to the
real thing as seen on garments and for this reason they are shown in use
in at least one seam type as well.

The six classes of stitch included in the British Standard are as follows:

- Class 100 chainstitches
- Class 200 stitches originating as hand stitches
- Class 300 lockstitches
- Class 400 multi-thread chainstitches
- Class 500 overedge chainstitches
- Class 600 covering chainstitches

At the same time as describing the appearance, characteristics and uses
of the most important stitch types contained within these classes, it is
appropriate to consider how a sewing machine works and in particular
how the stitch forming mechanism works. Whilst the subject of
machinery will be dealt with in more detail later, the various parts of the
simpler sewing machines and their function will be mentioned many times
in the course of the present chapter and are best introduced here. Thus, a
selection of stitch types will be described additionally in terms of the
machines which produce them.

The commonest stitch type in use in industry is the lockstitch. It is also
the one with which people are initially most familiar since it is almost

universally used in domestic machines. For this reason it is the most appropriate to describe first, although it is not the first in the BS classification.

Class 300: lockstitches

The stitch types in this class are formed with two or more groups of threads, and have for a general characteristic the interlacing of the two or more groups. Loops of one group are passed through the material and are secured by the thread or threads of a second group. One group is normally referred to as the needle threads and the other group as bobbin threads. The interlacing of thread in stitches of this class makes them very secure and difficult to unravel.

Straight lockstitch, 301, with a single needle thread and a single bobbin thread, is still the commonest stitch used in the clothing industry, especially in small volume manufacturing of a variety of garment types. The appearance of the stitch is shown in Figure 3.20 and the mechanism of stitch formation in Figure 3.21.

Lockstitch has enough strength for most purposes, provided that suitable thread is used, and enough stretch, when correctly balanced, for conventional and comfort stretch fabrics stretching up to 30 per cent or even more. It has the same appearance on both sides, an advantage denied to virtually all other stitch types, and of significance in the assembly process of garments, especially where topstitching is required. It is also, in its straight stitch version, the only stitch type which reliably forms the stitch when it is necessary to sew round a corner by pausing and pivoting on the needle. This is also important in topstitching as well as in seam joining of facings, collars, pockets and many similar garment parts. The stitch is secure because the breaking of one stitch in wear will not cause the whole row to unravel and additionally the end of a line of stitching can be secured by reversing or 'backtacking'. Alternatively, if the backtack lever is deliberately restricted, a group of small or condensed stitches is formed which secures the end of the stitching without the machine actually sewing in reverse. The thread in a lockstitch generally beds well into the fabric which improves abrasion resistance.

In its single throw, zig-zag version, type 304, it is commonly used for

Fig. 3.20.   Stitch type 301.

Fig. 3.21. Formation of two thread lockstitch, type 301.

attaching trimmings such as lace and elastic where a broad row of stitching but no neatening is needed. In its three step zig-zag version it is commonly used to provide a secure but stretchy stitch for the edges of stretch bras and other corsetry. The single and the three step zig-zag are also used, in two or three parallel rows, in the type of simple lapped seam used for joining the fabric panels in sails. These zig-zag stitches perform a

Fig. 3.22.   Stitch type 304.

Fig. 3.23.   Stitch type 321.

very useful function on seams of the type given here but would not give a good appearance on a superimposed seam. They are shown in Figures 3.22 and 3.23.

Stitch type 306 provides a lockstitch blind stitch. This is more secure than the traditional 103 which will be discussed shortly, but close study of the stitch construction in Figure 3.24 will show a straight bobbin thread which if caught and broken can allow sections of the stitching to come undone. It also tends to show pucker on fine fabrics.

The main disadvantage of the lockstitch is that it uses a bobbin to provide the lower thread and this bobbin can only contain a limited length of that thread. Changing bobbins is time-consuming in production, as is the unpicking of topstitching when a thread runs out at a point where a join is visually unacceptable. Where garments are sewn with twin or multi-needle machines, especially where complicated fabric folding is involved, the loss of stitching on one row because of one bobbin running out would be a major problem. Multi-needle stitching with many closely spaced needles is not actually possible because of the space that the

Fig. 3.24.   Stitch type 306.

bobbins would require. Two is the maximum number of needles commonly in use on lockstitch machines.

Optical bobbin run-out detectors, which pick up a reflection from a flat side on the centre of an otherwise round bobbin as the last of the thread begins to run out are being used now on some machines, as are automatic counters which stop the machine after a pre-determined number of cycles which will leave the bobbin or bobbins almost empty. Even a manual count of the number of garments sewn will tell the operator when another complete seam will not be achieved. On buttonholing, where restitching is possible provided that the hole has not been cut, the machines normally stop without cutting the hole if the bobbin runs out or the needle thread breaks.

The other disadvantages of lockstitch are its limited stretch for today's high stretch fabrics and its unsuitability for edge neatening, other than by a simple rolling of the fabric edge or the use of a zig-zag, both of which are untidy.

Thus, a wide range of additional stitch types replaces the traditional lockstitch in manufacturing situations which allow it. These are primarily situations where large quantities, perhaps thousands, are made of the same style of garment. Small sections only are sewn by each operator who can then use a sewing machine which is specially suited to the purpose. To a greater or lesser extent, virtually all the stitch types other than 301 are in this category.

Having studied the lockstitch class of stitch as the most common and the one most likely already to be familiar, the other stitch classes will be studied in numerical order, each having its own special contribution to make to garment construction.

Class 100: chainstitches

The stitch types in this class are formed from one or more needle threads, and are characterised by intralooping. One or more loops of thread are

Fig. 3.25. Stitch type 101 (bottom looper not shown).

passed through the material and secured by intralooping with a succeeding loop or loops after they are passed through the material. Since each loop is in this way dependent on the succeeding one, stitches in this class are insecure and if the finishing end of thread is not passed through the last loop or separately through the fabric, or if a stitch is broken, it unravels very easily.

One of the simplest of all stitch types is 101, which is formed from a single thread. The appearance of this stitch and the mechanism of stitch formation is shown in Figure 3.25.

Precisely because of its insecurity, it can be easily removed, and it is used for 'baisting' operations in tailored menswear and womenswear garments, using a white, soft cotton thread. It can only be used where the marks of needle penetration close up afterwards in pressing. A baisting operation, in positions such as edges, flaps, collars and so on, is a temporary stitch, allowing accurate placement of permanent stitching.

It is too insecure to be used for seams involving the joining of fabrics but it is widely used in multi-needle machines. A range of decorative effects can be achieved using some or all of a bank of closely spaced needles which may number as many as sixty-five. An additional device can be used to lay embroidery threads back and forward on the surface of the fabric under the needle threads in a variety of patterns to create further decoration. If elastic thread is used in the needles, and sewn into the fabric in a stretched state, it then relaxes and draws the fabric in, enabling garment features such as elasticated waists and cuffs to be created. This stitch type is particularly useful in this case as any other stitch which could cope with elastic thread would not use as much and would not enable as much stretch to be included. Multi-needle elastication is illustrated in Figure 3.26.

This stitch type cannot be chained-off, that is, sewn without fabric, nor can the stitching be brought to a halt and the needles removed from the fabric in the middle of a garment part. In the construction of a garment it is necessary to start and finish at a fabric edge, and that edge may need to be a small piece of temporary fabric held to the garment edge by the stitches. The fabric edges must then be joined securely through the ends of the chain stitching in order to prevent the stitches running back. Where

Fig. 3.26. Multi-needle elastication.

Fig. 3.27. Stitch type 103.

multi-needle stitching is functional rather than solely decorative, stitch type 401, to be described shortly, is increasingly used because of its higher security.

Another common use of class 100 stitches is in the special sewing processes of buttonsewing, buttonholing and blind hemming or felling. The first two hardly merit the description 'seams' but they deserve a mention when considering this particular class of stitch. They utilise the zig-zag version and the machines are fast and require no bobbin but their use generates a high level of consumer dissatisfaction as the stitching, especially on buttons, often does not last the lifetime of the garment. Careful machine adjustment, along with a small thread tail left at the end is necessary for maximum security.

The blind stitching version, 103, utilises a curved needle in order to, successively penetrate partially into the fabric, and then into the hem edge, while showing minimally or not at all on the right side of the garment. If required, the machine can be set to skip stitch, that is to pick up the fabric on alternate stitches only. This renders it even less visible. The stitch structure is shown in Figure 3.27.

Again, the level of insecurity is often high but can be improved by the use of slightly hairy rather than smooth sewing threads. Machines are available which condense a few stitches at the beginning and end of the seam, though since run-back only occurs from the finishing end it is not really necessary at the beginning. Careful machine adjustment is necessary with all these single thread chainstitches if the garments carrying them are to survive normal wear and tear.

Class 200: stitches originating as hand stitches

The stitch types in this class originated as hand stitches and are characterised by a single thread which is passed through the material as a single line of thread, and the stitch is secured by the single line of thread passing in and out of the material.

Handstitching is used at the expensive end of garment production because the consumer expects it at that price, the skills are available and it may be the only way to a perfect finish. Occasionally it is the only way to achieve a particular sewn effect though it should be said that if a large

Fig. 3.28. Stitch type 209.

enough quantity of a garment style is being made it is frequently possible to engineer the garment so that everything is done by machine.

In some cases, machines have been developed to simulate hand stitching, the best example being stitch type 209 which is used around the outer edges of tailored jackets. This is referred to as pick stitching and is shown in Figure 3.28.

A double-pointed, centre-eyed, needle sews short lengths of thread in a near-perfect simulation of the hand-sewn version. The machine can be set to show a longer stitch on the top than the bottom or *vice versa*, with instant change-over at the break point of a lapel. Thread ends are trimmed close if the stitch is small or sewn in invisibly by hand. A button sewing version is also available which both sews the button and wraps the shank.

The machines are not fast by lockstitch standards, achieving a maximum of a few hundred stitches per minute, but this is considerably higher than the rate achieved in hand sewing and a consistently high quality standard is guaranteed.

Class 400: multi-thread chainstitches

The stitch types in this class are formed with two or more groups of threads, and have for a general characteristic the interlooping of the two groups. Loops of one group of threads are passed through the material and are secured by interlacing and interlooping with loops of another group. One group is normally referred to as the needle threads and the other group as the looper threads.

The simplest version of this class of stitch, 401, is shown in Figure 3.29. It has the appearance of lockstitch on the top but has a double chain effect formed by a looper thread on the underside. The chain generally lies on the under surface of the material, the needle thread being drawn through to balance the stitch. The mechanism of stitch formation is given in Figure 3.30.

Fig. 3.29. Stitch type 401.

Stitches in this class are sometimes referred to as 'double-locked' stitches (not to be confused with class 300 lockstitch) because the needle thread is interconnected with two loops of the underthread. Because of the geometry of the stitch, a two-thread chainstitch is stronger than a similar lockstitch and, with no threads interlocking within the fabric it is less likely to cause the type of pucker that arises when closely woven fabrics are distorted by the sewing thread. Its great advantage is that both the threads forming the stitch are run from large packages on top of the machine so there are no problems with bobbins running out. It is frequently used on long seams in garments such as trousers. On twin-needle folded seams such as are used on jeans it is by far the most suitable stitch to use. A bobbin run-out in that situation would be disastrous. It will unravel from the finishing end if broken, but less easily than 101 and, provided the machine is correctly adjusted, there should be no problems. If not sewn across at the end in the course of the garment's construction, 1 cm of thread chain should be left. It does not backtack well but the stitches can be condensed.

When normally adjusted, the stretch with this stitch is about the same as with lockstitch but, if a small amount of seam grin is acceptable, the thread tensions can be loosened and a small increase in stretch obtained.

Lower thread tensions are normally used with these machines, compared with lockstitch, and this enables higher machine speeds to be used with less chance of thread breakage. Typical maximum speeds for lockstitch would be 6,000 spm whereas with two-thread chainstitch 8,000 spm can be achieved. It should be remembered, though, that these are theoretical maxima and although the machines will run at these speeds, practical garment-making situations rarely allow it. Limitations of seam length and the requirements of operator handling often cause machines to be set to run at lower speeds. Acceleration and braking are often more important than top speed.

Stitch type 401 is also often used in combination with an overedge stitch for economy of seam joining and neatening in bulk production. This will be illustrated later.

Fig. 3.30. Formation of two-thread chainstitch, type 401.

Another increasingly used stitch in this class is 406 which uses two needles and has a looper thread covering the fabric between them on the underside. It is used for attaching lace and braid trimmings to garments where the edge of the fabric must be neatened and also for turning up

Fig. 3.31. Stitch type 406.

(i)   (ii)

Fig. 3.32. Stitch types 407 and 411. (i) 407, (ii) 411.

hems where stitching showing on the right side is acceptable. In each case, the raw edge of the fabric can be contained under the cover stitching. It is shown in Figure 3.31.

Both 406 and the three needle version, 407, are used for attaching elastic edging to briefs where, in order to achieve a comfortable edge to the garment, a broad band of stitching is needed. Alternatively, a decorative effect can be achieved by folding an edge of garment and attaching a plain elastic braid by means of the three step zig-zag 411, sewn with the chain showing on the right side of the garment and a contrast thread in the looper. Examples of these uses are shown in Figures 3.32(i) and (ii). In situations where elastic is attached to garments, the elastic is stretched by a pre-set amount whilst being sewn to the fabric and on relaxing draws the garment part in to the correct measurement. The methods of achieving this will be described in the next chapter.

The straight or zig-zag version of 401 can be chained off the edge of the fabric and further decorative effects can be created by this means. If 411 is sewn along a garment edge which has previously been neatened or hemmed in some way, and it is sewn with the chain effect to the right side

Fig. 3.33. Stitch type 411.

of the garment, an effect similar to a crocheted picot edge can be achieved. With a twin-needle version of the same stitch, sewn with the needles moving in opposition, an openwork join between two folded edges of fabric can be achieved. These effects are shown in Figure 3.33.

Class 500: overedge chainstitches

The stitch types in this class are formed with one or more groups of threads, and have as a general characteristic that loops from at least one group of threads pass around the edge of the material. The most frequently used of these stitch types have one or two needle threads and one or two looper threads and they form a narrow band of stitching along the edge of the fabric with threads intersecting at the edge and preventing the fabric from fraying. All have high elasticity, they do not unravel easily, and a trimming knife on the machine ensures a neat edge prior to sewing. This knife can also allow excessive amounts to be trimmed off, thus altering the dimensions of the garment. These stitches are commonly referred to as 'overlocking' although the term derives from a trade mark and is only really correct when used in relation to a particular machine. The correct term is 'overedging'.

Stitch type 504, shown in Figure 3.34, is formed from one needle thread and two looper threads and is used for neatening edges and, in knitted fabrics, for joining seams. It has excellent stretch and recovery properties when sewn with suitable threads though its narrow bight (distance from needle to fabric edge), typically 3–5 mm, does not provide enough strength on fabrics which fray or slip. The bight can be adjusted within these limits to provide satisfactory appearance and an acceptable amount of bulk, according to the nature of the knitted fabric being joined. When joining fabrics with this stitch, a thread chain end must be left and the seam then secured by some means. This may be a cross seam or if the seam ends on the edge of the garment it may be necessary to secure the thread chain and the seam end by means of a short lockstitch

Fig. 3.34.   Stitch type 504.

Fig. 3.35.   Stitch type 503.

tack or a bar-tack, or a short zig-zag of stitching of fixed length. A special machine attachment is available which can 'latchback' the chain end at the starting end of the seam and recently finishing-end attachments have also been developed. The operation of such attachments will be described later.

This stitch type can also be used to provide a decorative neatened edge if sewn with a high stitch density and a narrow bight over an edge which, after the usual trimming, has been rolled under to the width of the stitch, usually 2 mm. A contrast coloured thread is often used, of a type that spreads out and forms a good cover over the edge. On suitable fabrics, the edge can be stretched while sewing to give a soft frill.

Stitch type 503, formed with one needle thread and only one looper thread, is less versatile and is used mainly for edge neatening, often referred to as serging, especially in menswear. It is particularly suitable for trousers because the two-thread construction is less likely to show an impression of the edge after pressing the legs. The construction is shown in Figure 3.35. It is not normally used for conventional joining of two pieces of fabric as the stitch opens up when stressed transversely but there

Fig. 3.36. 'Overlock welting' with stitch type 503.

(i)   (ii)

Fig. 3.37. Stitch types 512 and 514. (i) 512, (ii) 514.

are some situations where this feature can be used to advantage. One such is on tee shirt hems where careful fabric folding ensures a neatened edge as well as a sewn hem with the minimum of stitching showing on the right side. This process is often called 'overlock welting' and is illustrated in Figure 3.36.

Also in this class, and illustrated in Figure 3.37, are stitch types 512 and 514 which use two needles and a total of four threads. They provide a wider bight than 504 and this, combined with the second needle, gives a securer seam when fabrics are joined. They are used on light and medium weight woven fabrics, especially lingerie and shirts. They also provide good stretch and recovery when used on knitted fabrics.

As mentioned under type 401, a combination of 401 and 503 or 504, sewn simultaneously on one machine, is very common where a joined and neatened seam is required that does not need to be pressed open. It is referred to as safety stitch and provides an economical seam on both woven and low-stretch knitted fabrics. It can be used on the same kind of lightweight fabrics as 512 and 514 as well as on heavier fabrics such as denim and cord for jeans. It is written as (401.503) or (401.504), the dot indicating a combination stitch and the brackets denoting simultaneity of sewing. It has the level of stretch of 401 since that is the stitch that actually holds the seam. For brevity, the US Federal Stitch Type Numbers

Fig. 3.38. Stitch type (401.504) (US Federal type 516, excerpted from BS 3870: 1965, now withdrawn).

are often used in the case of these combination stitches and they then become 515 and 516 respectively. (401.504) is shown in Figure 3.38. Because of its similar appearance on one side to safety stitch, stitch type 512 is often referred to as mock safety stitch.

Seam joining with any of the overedge stitches, whether 504, 512 or 514, or a combination stitch, gives a closed seam where the seam allowance must be pressed to one side rather than opened out. The appearance that this gives will not always be acceptable; for example, it is common on youths' trousers but not normally on men's.

Class 600: covering chainstitches

With the exception of the very first type, stitch types in this class are formed with three groups of threads, and have for a general characteristic that two of the groups cover both surfaces of the material. Loops of the first group of threads (the needle threads) are passed through loops of the third group already cast on the surface of the material, and then through the material where they are interlooped with loops of the second group of threads on the underside of the material. The second and third groups are usually referred to as the top cover threads and the bottom cover or looper threads. Stitches in this class are the most complex of all and may have up to nine threads in total including four needle threads. They are used in similar situations to 406 and 407, making a broad, flat, comfortable joining of elastic, braid or binding to the edges of garments such as briefs with the scope for a decorative top cover stitch as well as the functional bottom cover over the raw edge of the garment fabric.

Fig. 3.39. Stitch type 602.

Careful study of 602 in Figure 3.39 will show that it is actually the same as 406 with the addition of the top cover thread.

Most types of stitch join fabrics where the two plies are placed one on top of the other, and when the faces of the fabric are opened out the seam is wholly inside the garment. Alternatively, they join fabric to fabric or fabric to a trim of some kind in a lapped manner as already described. The most complicated stitch type in this class, 606, which is known as flatlock, can be used to join fabrics which are butted together in what used to be called, in the old British Standard, a flat seam. Two trimming knives ensure that neat fabric edges butt together and four needles and nine threads provide a smooth join with good extensibility. It is used on knitted fabrics, especially underwear fabrics, to give a seam with low bulk that can be worn comfortably against the skin. With the top cover thread in a contrast colour, it can be used decoratively on other knitted leisurewear. It is shown in Figure 3.40. With this class of stitch a chain end is left at the end of the seam which must be secured if not crossed by another seam.

In this study of stitch types, those currently in common use have been described. New stitches may be developed and the existing ones will come and go in popularity as machines are developed and garment styles and fabrics change. For as long as stitching remains the normal method of joining, neatening and decorating garments this level of variety of stitch types is likely to be needed.

(C) SEWING MACHINE FEED MECHANISMS

In achieving the objectives of good appearance and performance in seams, correct and even stitch length is essential, along with fabric joins which are either smooth and unobtrusive or evenly eased or gathered, according to the requirements of fit and style. In the construction of seams and the

Fig. 3.40. Stitch type 606.

formation of the stitches that hold them together, these requirements are achieved by means of the mechanism that feeds the fabric(s) past the needle. This can either be a mechanism at the needle point, conventionally referred to as a sewing machine feed system, or some external system of materials control such as is found in certain specialised machines which are part of mechanised workplaces. These latter types will be described in more detail in the next chapter.

The simplest sewing machine feed system, and still the commonest, is known as the *drop feed* and the subject is best introduced by describing the constituent parts of this system and their function. The limitations of this system will then become clear and the alternatives which aim to overcome these limitations can be considered.

The three sewing machine parts which together constitute the drop feed mechanism are the presser foot, the throat plate or needle plate, and the feed dog. These are illustrated in Figure 3.41.

The throat plate is the most passive of the three parts and its function is to provide a smooth, flat surface over which the fabric passes as successive stitches are formed. It has one or more slots in it which match the sections of the feed dog and it has a hole through which the needle passes as it goes up and down. The needle hole should be only about 30 per cent larger than the size of the needle since, if this hole is too large, fabric can be pushed into the hole with each penetration of the needle, a problem known as 'flagging'. Most throat plates are made of steel with a polished surface to enable the material to pass freely over it.

Fig. 3.41. Drop feed system.

The purpose of the feed dog is to move the fabric along by a predetermined amount between successive stitches. The amount of fabric movement, and thus the stitch length, is controlled by means of a stitch length regulator. The feed dog consists of a toothed surface which rises through the openings in the throat plate, engages the under surface of the fabric, moves that fabric along towards the back of the machine, and drops away again below the throat plate before commencing the whole cycle again. As the feed dog drops below the throat plate, this plate supports the fabric so that it loses contact with the feed dog and is not carried back with it. The motion of the needle in an up and down direction must be accurately synchronised with the elliptical motion of the feed dog so that movement of the fabric only takes place when the needle is out of the fabric. Although the movement of the fabric during sewing appears to be one of continuous motion, it actually happens as a series of discrete steps. If this was not the case, distortion of the fabric and the needle would occur and the stitch might not be formed properly. The movement of the fabric after the completion of each stitch aids in setting the stitch and drawing the correct amount of thread into it, as well as positioning it ready for the next stitch.

Even in the simple drop feed, the feed dog can vary in the number and position of the sections comprising it and in the nature of its toothed surface. A single row feed dog has only a small area gripping the fabric and there is a tendency for the fabric to slip to the right or left instead of passing straight through the machine. It is normal in a lockstitch machine to have feed dogs situated both to the right and to the left of the needle hole to ensure that the fabric is fed in a straight line. In an overedge machine, the feed dog is usually mainly to the left of the needle drop point, because it trims and sews the fabric to the right of the needle and because there is a chaining-off finger on the throat plate over which the stitch is formed. Here again the fabric tends to be guided to the left. The problem can be overcome if a machine has a three row feed dog with one row in front of the needle. This is adequate to prevent sideways feeding. A typical feed dog for an overedge machine is illustrated in Figure 3.42.

Fig. 3.42.   Feed dog on an overedger.

The teeth on the surface of the feed dog can be of different types and sizes but they are generally slightly slanted towards the direction of feeding. For sewing of light to mediumweight fabrics, a tooth pitch (distance from peak to peak) of 1.3 to 1.6 mm is normal, with the peaks slightly rounded off if damage occurs on fine fabrics. On very lightweight fabrics, sagging can occur between the teeth and pucker can appear after sewing as a result. Fine-toothed feed dogs with a pitch of only 1.0 to 1.25 mm can be used to prevent this. By contrast, on heavyweight fabrics, a certain amount of sagging is required for satisfactory feeding in order to keep both plies together. In this case, coarser feed dogs of 2.5 mm tooth pitch may be needed.

On very delicate fabrics, damage or marking of the fabric may arise against the feed dog, despite rounding off the tops of the teeth. In this case a rubber-coated feed dog with no sharp teeth at all may be used, though it tends to wear out quickly. Of more importance in preventing damage during feeding is a deliberate mismatch between stitch size and feed dog size. If, for example, a seam is sewn at 6 stitches per cm using a feed dog with 6 teeth per cm, then a tooth will repeatedly hit the same section of fabric as it moves past and marking of the fabric or even damage could occur.

The presser foot is required to hold the fabric down firmly against the throat plate, thus preventing the fabric rising and falling with the needle. At the same time, it holds the fabric against the teeth of the feed dog as it rises up to transport the fabric. It is normally held down by spring pressure in order to 'give' slightly whilst the fabric plies are being fed. Minimum pressure should be used consistent with correct feeding of the particular fabric in use. Unfortunately, in high speed sewing there is a tendency for the presser foot to bounce as the feed dog makes contact with it and this reduces the effective contact between the presser foot and the fabric and thus the control of the fabric.

In the drop feed system, the presser foot remains stationary with the fabric sliding over its sole and this surface must have low friction characteristics. The use of PTFE-coated feet helps reduce friction though care must be taken not to run the machine without fabric between the PTFE surface and the feed dog or the surface will be damaged.

Presser feet are available in a great many types, both to match the varieties of feed dog which exist and to perform additional functions. The simplest type of general purpose presser foot is spring-hinged to ride over slight variations in fabric thickness and it has two toes so that pressure is maintained on the fabric against the feed dog on both sides of the needle. This type was shown in Figure 3.41.

Even the simplest of presser feet, feed dogs and throat plates all have to be shaped around whether a particular machine has a single or twin needles and whether it sews a straight stitch or a zig-zag. They may also have to be shaped so that a folding device can be situated close in front of the needle to control the folding of fabric right up to the point where it is stitched. An example is shown in Figure 3.43.

Additional functions which a presser foot can perform, if suitably designed, are such things as guiding stitching a specific distance from a fabric edge or raised seam, positioning a cord and folding a narrow hem. These will be discussed in the next chapter.

Although this simple drop feed system is still very common in clothing manufacturing, it suffers from a serious limitation in its ability to produce seams of perfect appearance on all types of material. Most seams on garments require to be joined smoothly without any pucker showing in

Fig. 3.43.   Feed system for use with a folder.

Fig. 3.44. Problems of differential feeding.

any of the materials. Assuming that two or more thicknesses of fabric are being sewn, regardless of whether they are separate fabrics or folded sections of the same fabric, the problem arises that the friction between the bottom ply and the feed dog is normally greater than that between intervening plies. The tendency is for the lower ply to be taken satisfactorily through the machine by the feed dog and the top ply to be retarded by the presser foot. The problem is variously known as inter-ply shift, differential feeding pucker or just feeding pucker. On a seam which joins two pieces of material together, it causes pucker on the lower ply and spare material left over at the end of the seam on the top ply: spare material which it is tempting to trim away. The seam when pressed may show a curve because of the excess of fabric along one side. In sewing a hem, twisting may occur between the layers of material and the problem known as 'roping' will arise. These problems are illustrated in Figure 3.44.

A well-trained and skilled machinist may be able to minimise the problem by careful handling of all the plies of material both in front of and behind the needle, but is likely to have to work more slowly in order to do so. With the variety of materials which are used in garments, the seam being joined could consist of two layers of slippery, woven polyester, or heavy elastic net and polyester satin, or two layers of a pile fabric such as velvet or corduroy, or a heavy woollen cloth and a viscose lining, or two layers of smooth shirting. All of these can cause difficulty. In addition, the machine may be fitted with a folding device which achieves a particular construction of seam but prevents the operator controlling the exact feeding of the several plies of fabric that are involved. For the sake of both quality and speed in production, machine feed systems are needed which can be adjusted to enable smooth sewing of any fabric regardless of operator skill or seam type. A variety of these now exists and, in addition to being adjustable to prevent undesirable pucker or easing, some of them can be adjusted so that deliberate, controlled amounts of easing or gathering can be sewn into a seam.

In the drop feed system which has already been described, the constituent parts of the system are the feed dog, throat plate and presser foot but only the feed dog plays an active part in fabric movement. Thus, successful feeding of more than one ply is dependent on friction holding the plies together. In the more advanced feeding systems, positive fabric control and feeding is achieved either by a divided feed dog which can be adjusted to alter the rate of feeding of the lower ply, by the action of a moving presser foot on the top ply, by a moving needle which assists in holding the fabric plies together, by a roller puller feed behind another feed mechanism controlling both plies, or by a computer-controlled top and bottom belt drive in place of the conventional presser foot and feed dog. All are devices which must be built into the machine during its construction rather than added afterwards and in some machines two or more are used in combination.

Differential bottom feed is the name given to a feed dog which consists of two sections, one behind the other. The movement of each section is similar to the movement of the whole feed dog in the drop feed system but the stroke or movement of each part can be adjusted separately or differentially. In the situation where differential feeding pucker, as described above, is a problem, correct adjustment of this feed system to create slight stretch on the bottom ply will overcome the tendency of the feed dog to take in that ply while the presser foot retards the top ply. The adjustment in this case consists of setting the stroke of the rear section of the feed dog so that it is longer than the stroke of the front section. It is also possible to deliberately gather the lower ply into the top ply by setting the front section of the feed dog to a longer stroke than the rear section. The correct setting in each case must be achieved by trial and error with a particular fabric. These possibilities are illustrated in Figure 3.45.

Differential feed is available on chainstitch, overedge and safety stitch machines as well as on lockstitch machines. When overedge joining soft, knitted underwear fabrics where there is a high level of friction between

(i)   (ii)

Fig. 3.45. Differential feed systems. (i) Bottom feed set to stretch lower ply. (ii) Bottom feed working fullness into lower ply.

the plies, there is a tendency for the presser foot to stretch both plies and thus to sew in some stretch along the seam. A differential feed system can be set to prevent this as in this case the friction between the plies is sufficient for the motion of the split feed dog to be transmitted to both of them.

Adjustable top feed systems can take more than one form but all provide positive control of the top fabric ply in a way which allows for adjustment so that the fabric plies will either be fed through exactly together or, if required, the top ply will be gathered onto the bottom ply. The general arrangement of such top feed systems is that the presser foot is in two sections, one holding the fabric in position while the needle forms the stitch and the other having teeth on the lower side and moving or 'walking' in such a way that the top ply is taken along positively while the needle is out of the material. A total feed system would normally be formed from a combination of an adjustable top feed system and either a non-adjustable, drop feed or a differential bottom feed. Machines are available where the vibrating presser acts in front of the needle, behind it or all round it and companies would normally purchase machines appropriate to their typical sewing situations. These situations may include sewing of lightweight fabrics without inter-ply shift, marginal stitching to a right or a left fabric edge, the addition of binding to an edge and many other possibilities.

When a variable top feed is combined with a drop feed, there is the opportunity to speed up the movement of the top ply to achieve shift-free sewing, or, by further adjustment of the top feed mechanism, to introduce a deliberate amount of ease or gather to the top ply. This is shown in Figure 3.46.

When a variable top feed is combined with a differential bottom feed, all possibilities are available for achieving ease or gather in either the top

Fig. 3.46. Variable top feed combined with drop feed. (i) To finish even. (ii) To work fullness into top ply.

Fig. 3.47. Variable top feed combined with differential feed. (i) To work fullness into top ply. (ii) To work fullness into bottom ply.

or the bottom ply, and for achieving shift-free sewing. Such a combination of feeding systems, with both the top feed and the bottom feed being independently variable, is the most logical to apply to most seaming situations since it can be adjusted to feed each ply exactly as required in relation to the other. Machines are available on which the required amounts of fullness can be pre-programmed and altered by the action of a finger, knee or foot switch as needed along the length of the seam. Diagrammatic representations of the variable top and bottom feed systems are shown in Figure 3.47.

Overedge machines are also available with differential bottom feed and variable top feed with the top feed able to act in front of or behind the needle in order to give the best effect on a particular fabric. Thus narrow, closed seams can also be obtained that are free of ply shift or have the correct amount of gathering or stretching incorporated into one ply.

Needle feed is the name given to the feed system in which the needle itself moves forwards and backwards. Used on its own it tends to produce elongated needle holes in the fabric and to avoid this it is normally combined with a drop feed and given the name *compound feed*. The needle enters the fabric, moves back with it as it is moved along by the feed dog to form one stitch and then rises up and foward again to begin the next stitch. Thus the needle is in the fabric while feeding is taking place and the plies of fabric are held together. It is particularly useful in bulky sewing situations such as when quilting through fabric and wadding. Exact synchronisation of the movement of the needle and the drop feed is needed. The needle hole is generally within the feed dog. Stitch length adjustment is normal with the needle stroke changing with the stroke of the feed dog. Compound feed is illustrated in Figure 3.48.

Unison feed is a further combination of feeding mechanisms which provides needle feed in addition to positive top and bottom feeding. Of the two part presser foot, shown in Figure 3.49, the centre part moves

Fig. 3.48.   Compound feed system.

Fig. 3.49.   Unison feed system.

with the needle. Its applications are limited since, once needle feed is included in a system which also has variable top and bottom feeding, it removes any opportunities for adjusting the amount of feeding in the top and bottom plies by means of the separate upper and under feeds. However, it is valuable in the sewing of certain problem materials, especially those with tacky surfaces, and it can achieve seam joining and edge binding without ply shift.

A *puller feed* is a way of providing positive control of all the plies of fabric as they leave another feeding mechanism such as a drop feed. Two rollers exert a pulling motion on the fabric immediately behind the presser foot or a short distance behind it. Both rollers may be driven or the top roller only may be driven while the lower one idles. This is shown in Figure 3.50. Puller feed is particularly useful in multi-needle stitching of parts such as waistbands and it may be set slightly faster than the main machine drop feed to overcome any tendency for the seam to twist. It will be seen later that it can also form the second stage of an elastication system.

Fig. 3.50. Puller feed system.

Fig. 3.51. Top and bottom belt feed.

In a move away from traditional presser feet and feed dogs, machines are being developed with computer-controlled top and bottom belt drive systems. One that has been developed for the insertion of sleeves on tailored jackets can be programmed to insert different amounts of ease in the different sections of the sleeve head by adjusting the speed of the top belt compared with the bottom belt. A secondary top belt to the right of the main one can move faster on curves and assist in taking in the excess material in the seam allowance compared with that along the stitch line. The belts have a lifespan of several years provided they are not allowed to run against each other with no fabric between them. This feed system is illustrated in Figure 3.51.

In the construction of garments it is frequently necessary to ruffle (gather, gauge, ruck – the terms are interchangeable) one fabric onto another fabric intermittently rather than continuously. If the type of machine with programmable adjustment of fullness described above is not available, other methods are possible. In common use on safety stitch machines is a differential feed accompanied by a blade ruffler. For flat joining of two plies, the presser foot holds the material against the rear section of the differential feed only. When a section of the seam is reached where the lower ply is required to be gathered into the top ply, a metal blade is swung into place between the two plies of fabric. This has the effect of extending the presser foot forward and allowing the front section of the differential feed, which has been set to gather, to join in the feeding motion. The lower ply is gathered into the top ply for as long as the blade is left in place. This mechanism is often used in sleeve attachment on dresses and blouses where a section of ruffling is needed over the sleeve head. Notches are cut into the fabric edges during cutting to indicate to the operator where to begin and end the ruffled section. Another option on a safety stitch machine with differential feed is to cancel the operation of the differential feed by means of a lever mechanism. This could be hand operated or controlled by an air cylinder activated by a switch on the treadle. Both these methods of achieving gathers give the pre-set amount of ruffling or nothing, rather than the programmable different amounts of easing or ruffling described earlier.

The very simplest ruffling mechanism and one often used if gathers must be set continuously into a single ply of fabric before attaching it to another in a garment, is a ruffling or gauging foot for use on a lockstitch machine. A small step on the underside of the foot allows fabric to be taken in by the drop feed and it is then drawn back into a small pleat as the stitch is set. The amount of ruffling is controlled by adjusting the stitch size and thread tension or by using a foot with a different height of step. A diagram of the foot is shown in Figure 3.52(i).

Another special presser foot which can be used in conjunction with a differential feed to ruffle one fabric onto another without any tendency for the top ply to ruffle as well is a split ruffling foot. The top ply misses the front section of the differential feed by passing above a section of the foot; the lower ply passing under it is ruffled by the feed just prior to being joined to the top ply. This is used for continuous rather than intermittent ruffling and is shown in Figure 3.52(ii).

(i)   (ii)

Fig. 3.52.   (i) Gauging foot. (ii) Split ruffling foot.

In all situations where easing or ruffling must be sewn into a seam, the machine must be set to incorporate the exact amount that has been allowed for on the patterns. In order to take maximum advantage of the types of mechanism that have been described here, pattern cutters must be familiar with their scope and limitations, particularly the need for the same ratio of ruffling across all graded sizes.

It should now be appreciated that a wide variety of feed mechanisms is available in order that materials can be sewn flat or appropriately eased or ruffled, as well as unstretched where there is a tendency for stretch to occur in normal sewing. Such mechanisms are much in evidence in factories which make up a wide variety of fabrics in moderate to large volume and in which high standards of seaming have to be achieved at high speed, often with relatively unskilled labour. Such factories are accustomed to investing in the most suitable machinery for a particular purpose. The shorter run, fashion side of clothing manufacturing has tended to achieve its output on less expensive machines but with a higher dependence on skilled labour and a higher risk of a low quality finish, but even here, such machines are becoming more common.

(D) SEWING MACHINE NEEDLES

The way in which fabric is penetrated by the needle during sewing has a direct effect on seam strength and on garment appearance and wearable life.

The functions of the sewing machine needle in general are:

(a) to produce a hole in the material for the thread to pass through and to do so without causing any damage to the material;

(b) to carry the needle thread through the material and there form a loop which can be picked up by the hook on the bobbin case in a lockstitch machine or by the looper or other mechanism in other machines;

(c) to pass the needle thread through the loop formed by the looper mechanism on machines other than lockstitch.

The function of the sewing machine needle in relation to the hook or looper of the machine was described earlier but it is now appropriate to study the details of the separate parts of the needle and their role in satisfactory seam construction and performance. The commonest needle shape, with its various sections labelled, is shown in Figure 3.53.

The *shank* is the upper part of the needle which locates within the needle bar. It may be cylindrical or have a flat side, according to how it is secured into the machine. It is the support of the needle as a whole and is usually larger in diameter than the rest of the needle for reasons of strength.

The *shoulder* is the section intermediate between the shank and the *blade*, the latter forming the longest part of the needle down to the eye.

Fig. 3.53. Parts of a sewing machine needle.

The blade is subject to the greatest amount of friction from the material through which the needle passes. In needles designed for use in high speed sewing machines the shoulder is often extended into the upper part of the blade to give a thicker cross-section which just enters the material when the needle is at its lowest point on each stitch. This supplementary shank or reinforced blade strengthens the needle and also enlarges the hole in the material when the needle is at its lowest point, thus reducing friction between it and the material during withdrawal after each stitch. Alternatively, the blade can be gradually tapered along its length from shank to tip, as another way of reducing friction. It will be seen later that this friction can create enough heat to cause serious problems when sewing synthetic fibres.

The *long groove* in the blade provides a protective channel in which the thread is drawn down through the material during stitch formation. Sewing thread can suffer considerably from abrasion during sewing as a result of friction against the fabric and a correctly shaped long groove, of a depth matched to the thread diameter, offers considerable protection to the thread.

The *short groove* is on the side of the needle which is towards the hook or looper and is a groove which extends a little above and below the eye. It assists in the formation of the loop in the needle thread.

The *eye* of the needle is the hole extending through the blade from the long groove on one side to the short groove on the other. The shape of the inside of the eye at the top is critical both in reducing thread damage as the needle penetrates the material and in producing a good loop formation. On some needles, known as bulged eye needles, the eye area has a larger cross-section than the rest of the blade. This serves a similar purpose to the reinforced shoulder mentioned above in that, as the needle enters the material, it creates a larger hole than is needed by the main part of the blade, thus reducing needle to fabric friction. The penalty to be paid for this cooler running needle, however, is a tendency to distortion in fine fabrics, and other methods of reducing needle heating are generally preferred.

The *scarf* or *clearance cut* is a recess across the whole face of the needle just above the eye. Its purpose is to enable a closer setting of the hook or looper to the needle. This ensures that the loop of needle thread will be more readily entered by the point of the hook or looper.

The *point* of the needle is shaped to provide the best penetration of each type of material according to its nature and the appearance that has to be produced. It is also the part of the needle which must be correctly selected in order to prevent damage to the material of the seam being sewn.

The *tip* is the extreme end of the point which combines with the point in defining the penetration performance.

The features described above are those found on the majority of sewing machine needles but other fundamentally different types do exist. Some overedge and safety stitch machines use needles which are curved rather than straight. The needles themselves are costly and do not last as long as straight needles but the machine mechanism that makes use of curved needles can achieve higher speeds than that using straight needles. Blind stitching machines, used particularly for felling of hems, use needles which are also curved but in this case it is to avoid penetration right through the fabric. In the case of single thread chainstitch felling, the needle penetrates partially through the fabric of the garment and the fabric of the hem edge but re-emerges and forms the stitch with a looper on the same side. Machines which form the simulated hand stitch, type 209, use a double-pointed needle which has an eye in the middle through which is threaded the short length of thread with which this machine sews. In the course of forming the stitches, the needle is passed between a gripper above the throat plate and another gripper below the throat plate. A rotating device catches the loop of thread each time and pulls it right through the fabric. Two of these special needles are shown in Figure 3.54.

For use in a particular machine, needles must conform to the machine manufacturer's specification as regards shank diameter, length from butt to eye and total length. In addition, the different needle manufacturers add their own design features as a result of development work to overcome the problems caused by higher machine speeds and the demand for finer needle sizes to reduce pucker, fabric damage and needle heating effects. Needle strength must remain adequate despite smaller size. Needle thread loop formation is critical if slip stitching is to be avoided, especially on zig-zag machines where the hook cannot be set as close as on straight-stitch machines.

Fig. 3.54. Special needle shapes. (i) Blind stitch needle. (ii) Pick stitch needle.

Needles are available in a wide range of sizes and the choice of size is determined by the fabric and thread combination which is to be sewn. As has already been suggested, correct size is essential to good sewing performance but as fabrics tend to become finer and, in many cases, more densely constructed, the demand is for needles and threads which can be used satisfactorily in smaller sizes.

If the needle is too small for the thread, the thread will neither pass freely through the eye nor fit properly into the long groove and will suffer from excessive abrasion as a result. This can lead to costly thread breakages in production because the machinist must stop to rethread the needle and possibly also to unpick some of the stitching so that a join does not show in an important part of the garment. Even worse, a break in a situation of multi-needle sewing with fabric running through folders could be impossible to repair. The use of too fine a needle when sewing heavy plies of material can lead to the needle being deflected which can affect the stitch loop pick up and cause slip stitches or it can even lead to needle breakage.

If the needle is too large for the thread there will be poor control of the loop formation which may cause slipped stitches. There will also be holes in the fabric which are too big for the stitches and give an unattractive seam appearance. An unnecessarily large needle also tends to give rise to damaged fabric along the stitch line and, in closely woven fabrics, pucker along the seam line due to fabric distortion.

Different needle manufacturers use their own nomenclature to describe *needle sizes* but the simplest sizing system is the metric one. The metric

Examples of diameter

in mm	Nm
0.65 × 100 =	65
0.90 × 100 =	90
1.10 × 100 =	110
1.30 × 100 =	130
2.50 × 100 =	250

Fig. 3.55. Metric needle sizing.

Thread sizes in synthetic ticket numbers	Needle sizes in metric system	Needle sizes in Singer system
8	180	24
16	140	22
30	120	19
50	110	18
75	90	14
120	80	12
180	70	10
320	60	8

Fig. 3.56. Needle and thread sizes.

size or Nm of a needle is related to the diameter at a point at the middle of the blade above the scarf or short groove but below any reinforced part, as shown in Figure 3.55. This measurement, in millimetres, multiplied by 100, gives the metric number. Thus a diameter of 0.9 mm is an Nm 90, a diameter of 1.1 mm is an Nm 110. Typical metric needle sizes are shown in the table in Figure 3.56, along with the equivalent sizes in the Singer system and typical thread sizes, given in the ticket number system for synthetic threads which will be described later.

Selection of needle and thread sizes for a particular seaming situation is a question of achieving a balance between minimum damage and pucker, which is usually a matter of small needle size and fine thread, and seam strength which may require a more substantial needle and thread. As will be seen, the answer normally lies in the greater strength for size provided by synthetic rather than cotton sewing threads, especially in the newer versions which, like the needles, provide greater strength for their size than did earlier versions.

So far in this section, needles have been discussed with regard to their various parts, with a brief description of the purpose of each. This must be expanded, particularly in relation to needle points, but first the question of needle quality and condition must be considered. A sewing machine needle is a precision item and if it becomes misshapen in any way it will either fail to form the stitch properly or it will damage the material, or both.

A needle which is bent may cause slip stitching if the hook or looper fails to pick up the loop in the needle thread. In a lockstitch this leads to poor appearance and possibly poor strength in the seam. In a chainstitch it can lead to an insecure seam which unravels. The reason why the needle became bent could be related to faulty operator handling as well as to incorrect needle size for the fabric being sewn.

A needle where the point has become burred or damaged in some way will almost certainly cause damage along the stitch line. On a woven material this will cause fibres or whole yarns to become broken but because of the nature of a woven fabric there is unlikely to be a complete breakdown of the seam unless the damage is very severe. All that will show is a slightly fluffy appearance along the stitch line. On a knitted fabric the problem is more serious because a damaged yarn is likely to lead to laddering in the fabric which is very unsightly and could weaken the seam. A yarn in a knitted or a woven fabric can become damaged because it has been broken by the impact of the damaged needle but in a knitted fabric there is also the possibility that the needle is too large for the size of the knitted loop in the fabric construction and, unless yarn can be quickly drawn into the loop from adjacent loops, it will burst.

Needles can become damaged after striking some part of the machine, usually the throat plate. Occasionally this is caused by the operator in the way the fabric is handled but more commonly it arises when the needle becomes deflected during sewing by fabric which is too thick for the size of the needle. Evidence of the cause of the damage may be present in the form of pock marks on the throat plate where the needle has missed the hole. Bevelling out the edge of the hole may help but if the deflection is too severe, a larger size needle may be necessary. Needles can also become damaged as a result of striking a harsh material over a period of time. Material such as the type of denim used for jeans which is made up in a stiff state and then washed in garment form can require that the needles sewing it are changed every two hours before they become so damaged that they in turn damage the material.

The problem of materials suffering damage during sewing as a result of using damaged needles must be mentioned before the nature of perfect needle points is discussed because perfect needles can also cause damage in certain circumstances. The question of damaged needles causing damage to fabrics is, in some ways, a straightforward one. It is not surprising that damaged needles cause damage to fabrics and the remedy is simple in that the needle must be changed for an undamaged one, along with an investigation into the cause of the damage to the needle so that it does not continue to happen. The more surprising problem is that a needle with a perfect, undamaged point can cause damage to materials because the point is of an unsuitable shape for the particular material or because the material itself has some inherent problems of sewability. Thus a variety of needle point shapes is needed to sew the variety of materials that are used and, in addition, steps may sometimes have to be taken to alter the construction or finish of a material in order that it can be sewn without damage.

The basic division of *needle points* is into *cutting* points and *cloth* points. This division is necessary because of the fundamentally different constructions of the two types of material which must be sewn, namely leathers and plastics which are essentially sheet materials with no gaps within the structure, and textile fabrics which, whether woven, knitted or made from bonded textile fibres in a non-woven form, have spaces within the structure through which a needle can penetrate. In a sheet material, the needle point must cut a sufficient hole that the needle blade and thread can pass through it without excessive friction, but there must be sufficient strength of material left between the holes that they do not run together, especially when under stress, and cause the garment to split. In a textile material cutting of the fibres is precisely what must be avoided since, depending on the fabric construction, yarns may run back from the hole that is created, causing poor appearance and a weak seam.

Cutting point needles all have sharp tips but they are available with a wide variety of cross-sectional shapes in their points. When sewing leather or plastic a cutting point needle will modify the set of the stitching and therefore the appearance of the seam. The reason for this is that the other difference between sewing sheet materials and textile materials is that in a sheet material the sewing thread remains essentially in the same position in which it was inserted into the material, because it is held in the cut hole. In a textile material the tension of the sewing thread in relation to the mixture of fibres and spaces allows, in most cases, for a bedding-in effect, a redistribution of the combination of fabric yarns and sewing thread to give a line of straight stitching. This effect is made use of in the sewing of leathers and plastics by having a variety of shapes of needle point which create particular decorative effects in the way that they cut the hole and insert the thread into the seam, as well as creating seams of the necessary strength. Three examples of cutting points are shown in Figure 3.57, along with the shape of incision produced when used in a machine with the commonest threading direction, that is, from the side. In a machine threaded from the front, the direction of the incisions would be at right angles to those shown. An indication of the appearance of the thread in a seam sewn with each needle point shape is also given.

The narrow wedge point cuts at right angles to the seam direction and allows a high stitch density to be achieved while leaving enough material between the needle holes to maintain seam strength. On soft leathers, stitch densities as high as 12 per cm are possible. It is the most frequently used point form for stitching uppers in the shoe industry. The thread is raised on the surface of the material.

The narrow reverse twist point produces incisions which lie at 45 degrees to the seam direction and produces a seam where the sewing thread is turned slightly to the left on the surface of the material. After the wedge point, this is the point form most frequently used. Again, threading direction is important since the narrow twist point, if used instead of narrow reverse twist with the same threading direction, would produce seams where the stitching is relatively straight but not very even. In addition the incisions would not be completely filled by the sewing thread.

The narrow cross point creates incisions along the line of the seam and requires a large stitch length with these incisions spaced as far apart as possible if there is not to be total perforation of the leather. Heavy decorative seams can be produced where thick sewing threads are used at large stitch distances. The stitches have a straight appearance.

With points such as these, care must be taken with needle insertion

Fig. 3.57. Cutting points. (i) Wedge point. (ii) Narrow reverse twist point. (iii) Cross point.

since, if a needle is replaced during sewing, a variation of as little as 5 degrees in the angle of the needle will affect the appearance of the seam. Thread size is also important as a thread which is too small for the holes will give an untidy appearance. Too thick a sewing thread however, although completely filling the incisions, will be subject to excessive friction during sewing, thus causing thread breakage.

A number of other point types is available for the variety of leathers, seams, sewing machines and strength and appearance requirements that arise. These include triangular cross sections, for multi-directional sewing.

The sewing of sheet plastic materials is similar to that of leather but with the added problem of possible damage if the needle becomes hot through friction against the material. If overheating does occur and the edges of the stitch holes become melted, the needle tends to leave a horseshoe-shaped mark corresponding to the shape of the groove in the blade of the needle. Many materials, especially in the synthetic shoe industry, consist of a plastic covering layer on some kind of textile material base. Provided the base is not too densely woven and the yarns are not strongly twisted, they are unlikely to be damaged by a cutting point needle, whereas if the material is sewn with a cloth point needle, excessive friction is likely to occur between the needle and the coating. On closely woven coated fabrics such as are used from time to time for raincoats, the coating is normally sufficiently thin for the material to be sewn with a conventional cloth point needle.

Cloth point needles, as their name suggests, are used for sewing textile materials rather than the sheet materials already described. The points have a round cross section as opposed to the various cutting shapes of the leather needles previously described and the tip at the end of the point can vary in shape to suit the particular material being sewn. The main division in material types which requires different treatment in terms of needle penetration is that between woven and knitted structures.

Knitted fabrics consist of yarns with spaces between them and if a yarn in a knitted fabric is broken the knitted structure may begin to unravel. This yarn breakage can happen in two ways, either by the needle directly striking the yarn and damaging it or by the needle entering a knitted loop which is not large enough to accommodate it and where, for reasons of machine speed or lack of flexibility of fabric, the loop is not able sufficiently quickly to draw in extra yarn and become large enough to take the needle. This situation is generally referred to as 'needle damage' but it is not the result of the needle itself being damaged but of the point type and fabric combination being unsuitable. Thus the requirement in sewing knitted fabrics is for a needle which will slightly deflect the yarns and enter the spaces, but one which is not itself so deflected that it fails to form the stitch properly, a needle of as small a size as possible consistent with needle strength and sewing thread size, and finally a fabric which is sufficiently lubricated that it has flexibility in relation to the movement of the needle. The shape of the tip of the needle point which best achieves this deflection is a ball shape and the needle is referred to as a ball point needle.

Woven fabrics consist of yarns, which can have greater or lesser amounts of twist, interlaced with each other at various degrees of density. Thus woven fabrics may have quite sizeable spaces within the structure if loosely woven from low twist yarns or they may be extremely dense if high twist yarns have been packed closely together. In either case there is no need for the needle to seek the spaces, if they exist, in the fabric, as there is little difference in effect whether the needle goes between the fibres of a single yarn or between the fibres of adjacent yarns. What matters is that the needle does go between the fibres and does not strike and break them. The shape of the tip of the needle point which best achieves this penetration between the fibres has the appearance of being slightly cone shaped. It is usually referred to as a set point needle as the tip has been set, or ground, and polished at a broader angle than the main section of the point. This construction strengthens the point and reduces the possibility of damage at the tip.

Both ball and set point needles are available in a number of types, illustrated in Figure 3.58. If any needle could be regarded as the general purpose needle in no-problem sewing situations it would be the medium set point. It is widely used for sewing a variety of woven fabrics and in some cases can be used for knits as well. In special cases a very acute set point is needed, for example in blind stitch machines where the curved needle has to hit the fabric almost at a tangent and must pick up a small part of the fabric without bouncing off it. In sewing dense combinations of materials such as shirting fabric and interlining in collars and cuffs, where for the sake of appearance a very straight line of stitching is needed, needles with very acute set points must be used in order to avoid an uneven, wandering seam due to the needle being deflected by the hard yarns in the fabric. The increased danger of damaging the fabric can be minimised by using the smallest possible needle size. At the other extreme,

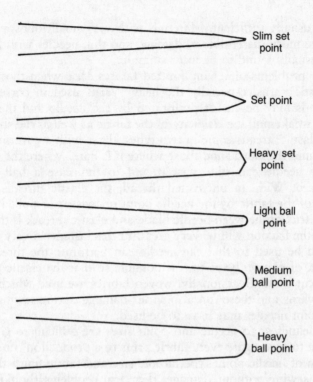

Slim set
point

Set point

Heavy set
point

Light ball
point

Medium
ball point

Heavy
ball point

Fig. 3.58.   Cloth points.

a heavy set point or stub point can be used for button sewing so that the button can be safely deflected slightly into the correct position so that the needle passes through the holes. However, the use of stub point needles when buttonsewing on some fabrics may lead to fabric damage and it is preferable that operators using buttonsew machines are encouraged to insert the buttons straight rather than crooked in the clamp so that the needle will not strike the button and break either itself or the button.

Ball point needles are available with a light, medium or heavy ball and each of these is available on different sizes of needle. As the needle size decreases, the radius of each ball point decreases proportionately. To maintain the proper tip bluntness, the heavier ball points may be needed for the smaller needle sizes. In general, needle damage is limited by using the smallest possible needle size but there is a limit to the use of thinner needles. They have a higher chance of breaking and are deflected more easily than thicker ones, possibly causing faulty stitches and an irregular seam.

The sewability of knitted fabrics depends on the type and size of yarn, on the density, size and regularity of the loops and on the nature of the finish applied. Open-mesh knitted fabrics can usually be sewn without difficulty as the yarns tend to be so thick that they can even be pierced by the needle without being damaged. In these cases medium set point needles are usually sufficient. Materials with very small loops made of a thin yarn are more susceptible to damage and thin needles with light ball points are usually found to be most suitable.

Particular problems of sewing knitted fabrics arise when those fabrics contain elastic yarns, especially the heavy yarns used in corsetry. The elastic threads may be cut or perforated by the needle and the threads then break, weakening the elasticity of the fabric as well as the strength of the seam. Elastic threads come in two types, those with a covering thread wrapped round the elastic and those where it is bare. Where the thread is covered the needle can slide past it and in this case a ball point is normally used. With an uncovered thread, the elastic threads may be pushed out of the fabric by the needle point or twisted or pulled out as a loop by the friction between needle blade and elastic thread. If the needle is too large the friction will be very great. In this instance a very acute set point would be used so that the needle can perforate the threads. The needle must, of course, be as fine as possible so that the elastic thread is not totally cut by it. Occasionally, woven fabrics are used which contain fine elastic yarns and these can also suffer damage during sewing. In this case, ball point needles may have to be used.

Firm guidelines as to needle and point sizes are difficult to give but if care is taken to investigate every fabric prior to a production run to find a combination of needle point type, needle size and fabric finish that gives satisfactory sewing without damage, then few problems should arise in production.

Where dissimilar fabrics are sewn together the problems are even greater, in proportion to the differences between the fabrics. It is sometimes necessary to sew woven corset satin to heavy knitted elastic net. The satin requires a fine, set point needle; the elastic a thicker needle with a heavy ball point. If the combination is sewn with the heavy ball point needle, untidy seams would result on the satin, whereas if sewn with the thin needle it would be deflected too much and possibly cause skip-stitching. There is always a tendency for ball point needles to produce slightly irregular seams because they push the fabric threads aside and in sewing difficult combinations of fabrics, the necessary investigations to determine needle size and point type would have to take place, as always, prior to production.

The names used here for the various types of needle point, namely cutting point and cloth point, with the latter divided into set point and ball point, are those which best describe the nature of the points and they are the names which are used in many sections of the industry. It should be pointed out, however, that needle points are sometimes divided up and labelled as cutting points and round points, thus describing their cross sectional shapes, with the term cloth point used only for the further sub-division that is here called the set point. Since the ball point needle is also used to sew textile materials, i.e. cloth, this seems less logical.

The final feature of a sewing machine needle which can vary is the surface finish which is given to it. Needles are made from steel and in the final stages of manufacture they are polished, especially in the area of the eye. In many cases they are then electroplated to give corrosion resistance, resistance to mechanical wear, reduction of friction during sewing and a good overall appearance. The materials used for plating are chromium or nickel. One requirement of the surface finish of needles is that they should not easily pick up any particles of synthetic fabric or synthetic sewing thread which they may have caused to melt as a result of excessive friction-generated heat. It has been found that chromium-plated needles resist the adherence of melted synthetic residues rather better than nickel-plated needles do, despite the fact that chromium-plated needles actually develop higher temperatures during sewing than do non-plated or nickel-plated needles.

(E) SEWING THREADS

If seams are to have satisfactory appearance and performance, a prime contributory factor is the sewing thread used. Correct selection of sewing thread requires consideration of its performance properties during sewing as well as its performance in the completed garment under conditions of wear and cleaning. It also requires consideration of its appearance in the sewn seam, which is both its appearance as sewing thread and the effect it has on the appearance of the materials being sewn, this last factor being also partly connected with thread performance.

As with other textile materials, sewing threads are composed of a fibre type, a construction and a finish, each of which may influence both the appearance and the performance of the thread. A wide variety of sizes is also available and the choice of size relates not just to the requirements of the materials being sewn but also determines the size of sewing machine needle used.

Fibre type, construction and finish

The simplest division of sewing threads is, in terms of materials, into those made from natural fibres, those made from man-made fibres and those made from a mixture, and, in terms of construction into those spun from staple or short fibre lengths, those made from continuous filaments and those which are a combination of the two.

Fibre types

A variety of natural and man-made fibres is used in the production of sewing threads although some have only limited uses. *Linen* was once used much more than it is now for making strong, rather stiff threads for heavy seaming and also for button sewing but it has been largely superseded by synthetic threads. *Silk* is available both as the continuous filament that is extruded by the silkworm and as broken filaments spun into a yarn. It has good appearance and performance but its high cost restricts its use mainly to couture and bespoke tailoring. Its only common use in higher volume manufacturing is as the thread used in short lengths for pick stitching the edges of men's jackets and, in more expensive garments, for machine buttonholes.

The natural fibre in commonest use is *cotton*, spun into yarns from fibres with an average length of around 35–40 mm and diameter 0.02 mm. Untreated cotton fibres have a flattened, ribbon-like appearance with frequent convolutions. Cotton threads in general provide good sewing performance but their strength and abrasion resistance are inferior to synthetic threads of equal thickness. Cotton threads are more stable at higher, dry temperatures than synthetic threads and are therefore less affected by hot needles during sewing unless special lubricant precautions are taken with the synthetic threads. In the version sold as soft cotton the fibres receive no other treatment than bleaching or dyeing and the application of a low-friction lubricant. Soft cotton threads generally have a high wet shrinkage which may cause pucker in seams after washing. In mercerised cotton threads the thread is treated under tension in a solution of caustic soda which causes the fibres to swell and become rounder in cross-section. The result is a thread with increased lustre and higher tenacity (strength related to thickness). Glacé cotton threads are produced from soft cotton threads which have been consolidated and protected by the application of a special surface coating. This produces a stiffer thread with a smoother surface and better resistance to abrasion than soft cotton. Sewing threads made from cotton used to be by far the commonest in use, for the reasons already given and because they sew well on poorly adjusted machines. In recent years there has been a major decline in demand for them and a great upsurge in the use of synthetic or mixture threads which do not rot and which give greater strength for their size and lower shrinkage. However, recent developments in the dyeing of whole garments rather than colour matching the materials separately has recreated a small demand for cotton threads for sewing cotton fabrics.

Under the heading of reconstituted fibres, a limited number of sewing threads are made from *viscose*. They do not have the strength or durability of synthetic fibres and they have low elasticity and low strength when wet but their great advantage is their high lustre for use in embroidery. Most commonly available in continuous filament form which has greater lustre than the spun form, their low abrasion resistance and strength is not a major disadvantage in embroidery machines. Garments incorporating them should not undergo repeated washing.

Synthetic sewing threads are made mainly from *polyester* and *polyamide* (nylon) with a small amount of aramid (e.g. Du Pont's Nomex) and polytetrafluoroethylene (PTFE). All synthetic fibres start life as continuous filaments. Various filament sizes are possible according to the size of the spinnerette holes from which they are extruded but polyester and polyamide are generally made about twice the diameter of cotton fibres. The filaments are then stretched to orientate the molecules within the material and produce high tenacity filaments. They are processed to ensure low shrinkage in washing at 100°C (between 0 and 1 per cent) and also in dry heat treatments up to 150°C (generally between 0 and 2 per cent). Beyond this, special threads may be needed as polyester and polyamide fibres begin to soften at about 230°C and melt at about 260°C. Low shrinkage is essential to avoid pucker in the seams on minimum care garments.

Synthetic threads are not significantly affected by rot, mildew or bacteria. They have high tenacities, especially in continuous filament form, and also have high resistance to abrasion. Polyester and polyamide possess good resistance to chemicals in general with polyamide being most resistant to alkaline conditions and polyester to acid. Both are degraded in strength by prolonged exposure to sunlight. Polyamide is affected by both the visible and the ultraviolet components of sunlight, as also is cotton, but polyester is only sensitive to near ultraviolet light. In tropical sunlight, polyamide may degrade faster than polyester though it has the higher initial tenacity.

The filaments may be processed to become sewing threads directly or a number of the fibres may be brought together into a tow or rope-like structure which is drawn or crimped to produce a better frictional surface. The tow can then either be cut into a suitable regular staple length or stretch-broken to produce a longer, more variable fibre length. These are then spun together in ways similar to those used with the natural staple fibres to produce yarns. The filaments of both polyester and polyamide used for the production of sewing threads generally have circular cross-sections and a smooth surface, making them more lustrous than natural fibres. Polyester is considered the best fibre for most sewing thread applications, having low cost, high strength, good chemical properties, favourable elastic characteristics and good dye fastness. Polyamide has the high strength to fineness of polyester but not such favourable extension characteristics. Its higher elasticity makes it unsuitable as a general purpose sewing thread as it tends to stretch during sewing and relax afterwards, thus causing puckered seams.

All these fibres have been described in terms of being used on their own in a sewing thread but one of the most commonly used threads nowadays consists of a mixture of polyester and cotton in the form of a continuous filament polyester core with cotton fibres spun on the outside. This type will be described further.

Threads made from the *aramid* or aromatic polyamide fibres such as Nomex are expensive but have important uses in fire-resistant garments. They have a high melting point followed by charring rather than dripping like other synthetic fibres. They are combustible but are self-extinguishing when withdrawn from the source of heat. This type of performance is not required by the flammability regulations covering nightwear but in items such as racing drivers' suits where the garment material would also be aramid fibre, such threads are essential so that the garment remains intact for as long as the fabric withstands the heat. PTFE sewing threads are also very expensive but they have a few specialist industrial uses where their complete non-flammability, non-melting, and high resistance to chemicals makes them important.

(2) Thread constructions

The creation of sewing threads from the natural and man-made fibres already described can take a variety of forms. Where the fibres occur naturally in short lengths or have been cut or broken into short lengths, they must be twisted together, initially into a single yarn, and then that twist must be balanced by applying a reverse twist as two or three such yarns are combined to form the thread construction. The twist in the single yarn consolidates the strength and flexibility provided by the fibres themselves. Without the reverse twist, known as finishing twist, a conventional thread could not be controlled during sewing. The individual plies would separate during their repeated passages through the needle and over the sewing machine control surfaces. Twist is defined as the number of turns inserted per cm of yarn or thread produced. If the twist is too low the yarns may fray and break; if too high, the resulting liveliness in the thread may cause snarling, loop knots or spillage from the package of thread. There are two possibilities of twist direction, as shown in Figure 3.59.

The frictional forces acting on a thread during its passage through a sewing machine also tend to insert some twist, predominantly in one direction. In a lockstitch machine, during normal straight sewing, the needle and hook tend to insert some Z twist to the sewing thread. A thread with a correctly balanced finishing twist reaches equilibrium as it resists further tightening up of the twist. A thread with an S twist becomes untwisted by the action of the machine and then frays and

Fig. 3.59. Thread twist.

breaks. Because the lockstitch machine type is the most severe in its handling of thread, the majority of threads intended for use in machine sewing are constructed with a finishing Z twist. There are only a few machines, such as flatlock, for which this is not suitable and special threads with S finishing twist are available for these. In most sewing threads, two, three or occasionally four component yarns are twisted together to form 2, 3 or 4 ply thread. Subsequent twisting operations may be used to produce heavier or 'corded' threads, with the direction of twist reversing each time.

The thread construction procedures described so far would apply to cotton and to silk, polyester or polyamide which had been cut or stretch-broken into short lengths. Polyester which has been cut is spun in the same way as cotton. Silk is normally broken and the process of spinning it into a yarn is referred to as Schappe spinning. When polyester is broken rather than cut the fibres are longer and more variable in length than when they are cut and the yarn produced is also referred to as Schappe spun. Polyamide which has been cut and then spun does not make a general purpose sewing thread because it is highly elastic and is not suitable as a needle thread. It is however useful in linking, the joining operation in fully-fashioned knitwear, and in other high stretch applications such as bottom threads in sewing swimwear. Threads made from spun yarns have good sewing performance, good dimensional stability and good stitch-locking properties in the seam due to their fibrous surface. Their abrasion resistance varies, depending on the fibre, and is about four times as great for synthetics as for cotton. Abrasion resistance is important in relation to the durability of threads to abrasive forces in the sewing operation.

When threads are made directly from continuous filaments, as in polyester and polyamide, a wide variety of different constructions is possible. The very simplest is hardly a thread at all, being just one filament of polyamide of a larger size than normal. It is called *monofilament* and is only of limited use. It is harsh on the machine and rather inflexible because the cross-sectional shape never varies as it would with multifilaments. In addition, the cut ends are harsh on the wearer. It has virtually no seam grip and stitches tend to unravel easily. Its great advantage is a translucency which reduces the need for shade matching and the three tones of natural, light and dark grey adapt to suit the limited range of applications for which the thread is suited. It tends to be used for blind felling and overedging at the lower quality end of clothing manufacturing and for upholstery and household textiles.

More conventional constructions of continuous filament thread are in *multifilament form*, either in *singles* or *plied* or *corded*. Where flexible threads are required the filament yarns are twisted, set, dyed and lubricated only. Where optimum sewing performance and abrasion resistance is required, the plied threads are treated with synthetic polymer which bonds the individual filaments and yarns together. In polyester, they give higher strength with fineness at a lower price than a similar spun thread, and with good loop-forming properties they give reliable stitch formation. Their fineness enables larger thread packages to be used, thus saving operator time changing them, and in particular they enable more thread to be wound on the bobbin of a lockstitch machine. In polyamide, the bonded threads give the highest strength and abrasion resisance of all the mass-produced threads and for this reason they are popular in the shoe and leather industry. For low fault rates and a consistent, even thread, these multifilament threads are the most satisfctory. They are less expensive than some of the others but there is a limit to the amount of stretch in them because of torque effects and snarling. Care must always be taken to secure the seam ends to prevent run-back.

Other types of thread which are made from continuous multifilaments of polyester and polyamide are those generally classed as *textured*. Texturing is a term used to describe modifications, obtained by various means, to the appearance and surface characteristics of straight synthetic filament yarns. Depending on the application for which the thread is intended, the degree of crimp rigidity (bulk) can be varied. In fine sizes these threads are useful as needle threads in overedge and chainstitch machines but their commonest use is in larger sizes where their soft handle and spreading properties provide good seam cover when used in the loopers of overedge and covering stitch machines. With appropriate stitch size and thread tensions, almost complete cover of the fabric can be achieved which adds greatly to comfort in garments worn next to the skin and to appearance in a fabric which frays badly. The degree of stretch in these threads can also be used when a fabric of moderate stretch must be sewn with a lockstitch and in this case they are used in the bobbin. Such threads are commonly refered to as *bulked* though the preferred term is *crimp textured*, their structure having been achieved by twisting, crimping, and untwisting again.

A relatively recent development of general purpose sewing thread is the locked filament polyester, also known as 'air entangled'. Continuous filament yarns are treated by means of air jets to have the characteristics and performance of threads produced by conventional spinning and twisting processes. The threads have high uniformity and freedom from imperfections and suit a variety of uses. An advantage of thread such as this which is constructed without twist is that it has a multi-directional sewing performance and can be used in sewing with the type of automated stitching jigs described later.

It was stated earlier that the sewing action in a lockstitch machine can insert or remove twist from a thread, depending on the twist direction. Z twist thread is normally used for forward sewing in a single needle machine but problems can arise in twin needle machines equipped with two hooks rotating in the same direction because the thread is pulled off the needles in opposite directions and one untwists and gives a different appearance from the other. Problems can also arise with some automatic machines such as those sewing round jigs where sewing can be in any direction. An untwisted thread would not vary in appearance or performance with varying sewing direction. For inexpensive thread production with very low fault rates, threads made by this process would seem to have great possibilities though at the present time there is some uncertainty about their versatility. For real success they must sew well in high speed lockstitch machines; in particular, they must withstand the high level of abrasion suffered by threads in this situation. Their development may well rest upon the level of price pressure put on the threads at present in common use which give very good sewability.

Yet another fundamentally different type of thread construction is that known as *corespun* where a continuous multifilament core is wrapped around with a sheath of spun fibres, two or three of these yarns then being plied together. This is the construction of the threads referred to earlier that can be a mixture of natural and synthetic fibres, the majority of these corespun threads consisting of a polyester core and a cotton cover. The continuous filament core produces high tenacities and excellent loop forming characteristics through the sewing machine needle. The thread lubricant is retained well by the surface fibres and, combined with the effect of air carried to the needle during sewing, results in good sewing performance. The thread strength and loop formation are well maintained in multi-directional sewing and on automatic machines. These threads also have a satisfactory amount of stretch and low shrinkage. A major objective was to create a thread which did not suffer damage on contact with a needle heated by friction against the fabric and the cotton cover fulfils this function extremely well. A difficulty with the polyester and cotton combination is that the thread must be dyed twice and this adds to cost.

Developments in thread lubricants in recent years have allowed totally synthetic threads to achieve much greater heat resistance than hitherto and less problems need now be experienced with hot needles against synthetic thread. Accordingly, many of the advantages of the corespun construction are now being achieved in threads which are 'poly poly corespun' that is, a polyester filament core with a spun polyester covering, and these do not need the double dyeing process. There is also a strength contribution from the polyester sheath which is not obtained with cotton although, with the type of high tenacity polyester used for the cores of these threads, strength is already very high. Sewability remains at least as important as strength and the cotton cover may continue to give this more successfully. Corespun threads in general enable clothing manufacturers to sew with finer threads and still achieve adequate seam strength. This is an important advantage with fine fabrics because the finer the thread, the less it will tend to cause pucker in the fabric. This also matches up with the use of finer needles to reduce needle damage.

From a situation where cotton threads formed a large part of the market a couple of decades ago, the synthetics and corespuns have made great inroads. Polyester/cotton corespun now has over 50 per cent of the market in Britain, especially in high volume, quality-conscious manufacture where the demands of thread performance in sewing and

Fig. 3.60. (i) Spun and (ii) corespun threads.

wearing are very great. Spun polyester is the dominant thread in the high volume area of underwear production where large quantities of white are used and it is also used in fashion manufacturing. Spun and corespun threads are illustrated in Figure 3.60.

(3) Thread finishes

The final aspect of thread construction to be studied is that of surface finish, the most important type of finish being *lubrication*. The requirement of a lubricating finish applied to a sewing thread is that it should produce a regular level of friction and that, for synthetic threads in particular, it should provide protection from needle heat. Without a controlled amount of lubrication applied to threads, unacceptable damage would be inflicted on them during the sewing process which would result in thread breaks during sewing and seam breakdown in wear. In a lockstitch machine, for example, each portion of thread may travel at least forty times through the eye of the needle, in repeated cycles of flexing and abrasion, before receiving a last impact from the needle eye as it becomes a stitch. A series of tension peaks occurs as a lockstitch machine goes through its stitch cycle. These occur as the stitch balance is set, as the needle punches the thread through the fabric, as the rotary hook picks up the loop of the needle thread and as the thread is pulled off the rotary hook at its lowest position. Thread must withstand these stresses and, even in fine sizes, retain enough of its initial strength during stitching to give adequate seam strength.

The nature of the lubricating finish is the result of considerable research by the thread companies to fulfil a number of requirements. A lubricant must not clog the needle eye nor cause staining, it must allow the thread to unwind evenly from the package and it must reduce friction with machine surfaces but without creating too much slippage. It must reduce fibre to fibre slippage in spun threads which could lead to loss of strength, it must not react adversely to high temperatures and it must be relatively inexpensive and easy to apply to the thread during manufacture.

Different threads need different amounts of lubricant according to their end use. Corespun and spun polyester threads must often withstand high temperatures when used as needle threads and thus need a high level of lubricant. A continuous filament thread would not generally need so much to perform well. The type of lubricant would vary between natural and synthetic fibres. Occasionally, where there are still stitching problems with excessive needle heating despite the use of a suitable thread, it may be necessary to add extra lubricant. In certain circumstances, the thread may be run between two felt pads soaked in the correct lubricant in a specially designed box which confines the lubricant to the thread and keeps it from soiling the rest of the machine. This should only be done on the advice of the thread maker as in many cases the problem can be overcome by correct choice of needle and thread, by further investigation of the fabric itself which may be poorly lubricated, and by checks on thread storage in case this is unsuitable and the natural moisture and the lubricant on the thread is becoming dried out. Spraying or soaking the thread package is generally messy and unsuccessful and should be avoided, as should the use of incorrect lubricants such as sewing machine oil.

Despite the discussion of the problems of needle heating which has been given here, and the further discussion which will be included later under the general heading of sewing problems, it should be stated that it is by no means as serious a problem today as it was when synthetic fibres were first used in any quantity. There was a time when many factories had needle coolers, in the form of jets of compressed air, attached to virtually all their sewing machines but their use now is far less common. Progress in fabric and thread lubricants, as well as the use of finer needles, have combined to reduce the problem to more manageable proportions.

Other finishes for sewing threads have been developed for certain threads for particular end uses. Synthetic threads are naturally resistant to *rot* and *mildew* but if cotton threads must be used, especially on items which will be kept in hot and humid conditions, then specially treated threads are available.

Another special demand is for threads with a *water-resistant finish*. Sewing waterproof or water-repellent clothing creates difficulty along the seams, which tend to allow water to enter the garment. Where a garment has to be totally waterproof the seams must be sealed by means of taping or welding over the needle holes but in the more everyday showerproof fabrics such as those used for raincoats, choice of seam type and positioning of seams in the garment, especially in the shoulder area, will assist in preventing too much water ingress and suitable thread can help in addition. Traditionally, cotton threads were used and the swelling of the fibres when wet helped to block up the needle hole. Unfortunately this swelling also caused a displacement of the fabric yarns which contributed to pucker in the seams and gave a poor appearance. A cotton-covered corespun thread can also achieve the swelling effect but eventually the water begins to wick along the thread and passes rapidly to the inside of the garment. Wicking is the crucial factor in keeping rainwear seams dry and water-repellent threads are available which reduce the problem. The thread no longer swells to block the needle hole, but this is less necessary once wicking has been reduced and less swelling is beneficial in terms of reducing pucker. The water-repellent finish must be fast to washing and dry cleaning although if the garment has to be reproofed at any stage this will benefit the thread as well. Lubrication of these threads must be done with care as some lubricants can diminish the effect of the water-repelling agent. The finish tends to darken the thread shade which must be borne in mind when shades are matched. In order to prevent shading of thread within a garment, the whole garment may be sewn with the treated thread.

Another matching of fabric and thread finish which is sometimes needed is in the area of *soil release*. Much workwear fabric is treated with a soil release finish and, unless the thread is similarly treated, the dirt washed off the fabric is redeposited on the seams, thus spoiling the appearance of the garment. A soil release finish is now available on some spun polyester and polyester and cotton corespun threads.

A specific legal requirement is that relating to the Nightwear (Safety) Regulations 1985 which cover the *flammability* requirements of the materials used in children's nightwear and also require that seams should come up to the same standard of performance. These requirements are that synthetic nightwear materials melt before they burn and extinguish themselves by the falling away of any burning, molten material. If a seam in one of these fabrics is sewn with cotton or cotton covered thread or even with a totally non-flammable thread such as Nomex, the seam will support the adjacent burning material and even act as a wick to encourage burning.

In sewing flame-retardant fabrics, thermoplastic threads must be used and 100 per cent polyester is the only one recommended as it shrinks away from the flame and does not support combustion. In sewing chemically treated fabric, the seam would probably be extinguished, regardless of its fibre type, by the deoxygenating gases which the fabric releases when burnt but it would seem sensible to aim for the highest standard of fire resistance possible by using spun polyester thread for sewing all nightwear. In some markets a flame retardant finish is required, particularly to neutralise any effects of the thread lubricant on the flame resistance of the finished seam, but many difficulties arise in developing satisfactory finishes which will last the lifetime of wearing and washing of the garment. It should be remembered that the choice of stitch and seam type is also important so that no more thread is present than necessary, consistent with good seam performance and satisfactory appearance.

In discussing the requirements of seams it was said that a seam must maintain any particular properties of the material under construction. It can be seen here that a particularly important contribution to most of these properties comes from the sewing thread.

Thread sizing

Numerous references have been made to fine and heavy threads without, as yet, any indication of these as relative sizes or any indication of the methods or units of measurement. All types of textile yarns can be produced in different thicknesses and the relationship between the length and weight of a specific yarn is known as its yarn count or grist or size. There are many traditional count systems which are either fixed weight systems which show the number of unit lengths that give a fixed weight, or fixed length systems that show the weight of a given length. The latter system is simpler in that it gives a higher figure to a thicker yarn or thread, which is more logical than the other way round, and it is easier to weigh a fixed length than to measure a fixed weight. As it happens the systems of measurement in common use for sewing threads in the UK are fixed weight systems and sewing threads are thus denoted by smaller numbers as they become thicker.

The commonest system and the one used for synthetic and corespun threads is the *metric ticket number system*. It is derived from the number metric (Nm) yarn count system which refers to the number of 1,000 m hanks which weigh 1 kg, or, effectively, the number of 1 m lengths which weigh 1 gm. Thus, a single yarn is labelled as being of count Nm 60/1 if 60 m of it would weigh 1 gm. Two singles yarns of this size plied together would be written as Nm 60/2 and in this case 60 m of the yarn would weigh 2 gm. Similarly, a thread given as Nm 120/3 would be constructed from three yarns, each of which would weigh 1 gm for a 120 m length. 120 m of the complete thread would weigh 3 gm. Thus the figures in the metric yarn count system relate to the sizes of the singles yarns used to form the final yarn.

The metric ticket number system for sewing threads is based on a threefold equivalent of the Number Metric system and relates its number to the finished thread rather than to the single yarns from which it is made. The ticket number is calculated via the resultant count, recalculated into threefold terms whatever the number of plies of yarn twisted together to form the thread. Resultant count is the length of a plied yarn which would weigh 1 gm, which means that a thread expressed in number metric system as Nm 120/2 (i.e. 120 m would weigh 2 gm) would have a resultant count of 60 (i.e. 60 m would weigh 1 gm). The metric ticket number of this thread, based on a threefold equivalent is then three times that, i.e. Tkt. 180. This means that 180 m of this thread would weigh 3 gm and shows that the figure quoted for thread size in the metric ticket number system is the length that would weigh 3 gm. The thread could be made from a single yarn or from two, three or more plied yarns. Other examples are: a thread of Nm 80/2 is Tkt. 120, Nm 30/3 is Tkt. 30, Nm 20/1 is Tkt. 60, Nm 60/3 is Tkt. 60, Nm 40/2 is Tkt. 60 etc. This shows that the same ticket number, in this case 60, can be used for three or more different thread constructions but to the user the size of the final thread is the same, i.e. 60 m lengths would weigh 3 gm. The inverse nature of this measurement system is demonstrated by the fact that Tkt. 60 is twice as coarse as Tkt. 120.

Cotton sewing threads are sized on the *cotton ticket number* system which works on the same principle but the figures do not denote the same size in terms of diameter. The basis of it is the cotton count which is written as, for example 3/60 Ne, meaning that the thread has three singles yarns, each of which would need 60 hanks of 840 yards to weigh 1 lb. The cotton ticket number is the threefold equivalent of the cotton count and is the number of 840 yard hanks that weigh 3 lb. A six cord construction of cotton yarns of count 60 Ne has a total resultant count of 10 and therefore a Tkt. No. 30 (equals 3 × 10). A construction of three plies of count 60 Ne has a total resultant count of 20 and therefore has Tkt. No. 60. Tkt. No. 30 is twice as coarse as Tkt. No. 60.

If it is required to make comparisons between thread sizes in the two systems, the conversion factor is that cotton count is equal to 0.59 times the metric count, i.e. Ne = 0.59 × Nm. The ticket number of a cotton thread which would be roughly equivalent in size to a synthetic thread can be determined by multiplying the synthetic ticket number by 0.6. For example, a Tkt. No. 60 synthetic thread is equivalent in size to a Tkt. No. 36 cotton thread. Conversely, a Tkt. No. 60 cotton thread is equivalent to Tkt. No. 100 synthetic thread. The comparison relates only to the actual size of threads and does not allow for the greater strength/fineness ratio of synthetic threads which must be taken into account when thread selection is made.

It should be clear from these figures that it is quite wrong to maintain the same ticket number when changing from cotton thread to synthetic. It is not even appropriate when changing from one type of synthetic to another. The choice depends on many factors including seam strength, fabric weight and type, stitch type, seam type, needle size, end use and many others.

The only other system used for sewing threads is the denier system. This is a fixed length system and the denier count or Td is the weight in gms of 9,000 m of thread. In sewing threads it is generally only applied to polyamide, particularly to monofilaments.

Methods of sizing other than those quoted here are available for use with sewing threads and other yarns. Such systems are the Tex and the related Decitex systems. These systems are described in standard works on textiles and conversion factors exist between all the systems if they are needed.

A particular thread type only comes in certain discrete sizes and only covers a size range appropriate to the intended end uses of the thread. While it has already been made clear that a great many factors determine the choice of thread size, it may be helpful at this stage to give a brief indication of the sizes available in the commonest types of thread and their likely end uses. This is given in Figure 3.61.

Thread packages

In order that thread should sew well, it must be presented to the machine in a satisfactory way. It must be possible to purchase it in economically large or small quantities, while still having the right number of separate

Spun polyester or polyester/cotton corespun

Metric Tkt. No.	Typical uses
180 & 150	Neatening and general seaming of lingerie, shirts and blouses
120 & 70	General seaming of underwear, knitwear, foundationwear, shirts, blouses, dresses, tailoring, jeans, workwear
60 & 15	Jeans, workwear, decorative stitching, buttonsewing and buttonholing

Fig. 3.61. Typical thread sizes and uses.

packages available for use on multi-thread machines. It is sold by length rather than by weight and is sold in a variety of types of package appropriate to the thread type and its end use.

Spools are the smallest packages and are flanged bobbins, once made in wood but now always made in plastic. Although used to a small extent on slower industrial machines, especially in footwear and leather goods manufacture, they are largely used for domestic sewing. A relatively short length of thread, usually 100 or 500 m, is parallel wound onto the bobbin. Spools are not suitable for delivering thread to high speed industrial machines, nor for textured threads.

Cops are small, cylindrical, flangeless tubes onto which thread is cross-wound for stability. The lack of flanges facilitates regular offwinding from the top on industrial sewing machines, mainly lockstitch, their small diameter making them less well suited to the faster thread offtake of machines such as overedgers. They usually contain lengths of 1,000–2,500 m of thread and are a popular size in fashion manufacturing where production runs in any one colour are short. They are suitable for cotton, spun polyester, spun nylon or corespun threads but not for glacé finish or fine filament threads where spillage from the package would be a problem.

Cones contain 5,000 m or more of soft or mercerised cotton, spun polyester or corespun thread, crosswound for stability and good offwinding performance. They give trouble-free thread delivery at intermittent or continuous high speeds and this, combined with their long length capacity, makes them ideal for use on class 400, 500, 600 and combination stitch machines where stops for rethreading need to be minimised. Cones are the ideal package for conventional sewing threads in situations where thread consumption is high and production runs are long with limited shade changes. They are also well suited to automatic machines.

Vicones are parallel tubes or low-angled cones with an additional base in the form of a raised flange which may incorporate a small lip. They contain polished or continuous filament thread and are designed to contain any spillage which may occur in offwinding these smooth threads with no snagging or trapping when the slack thread is taken up.

Large packages for use on overedge and cover stitch machines can hold in excess of 20,000 m of spun or corespun thread wound on large cones or tubes.

Containers are constructed to handle lively monofilament threads which would be difficult to control on standard packages. An exceptionally large spool of thread is held within the container which can incorporate an extra lubricant applicator at the thread draw-off point.

Cocoons are self-supporting, i.e. centreless, thread packages, specially designed for insertion in the shuttle of multi-needle quilting machines and some types of embroidery machines.

Pre-wound bobbins are precision-wound thread packages which can replace metal bobbins on a variety of lockstitch machines. Conventional bobbins in these machines are inconvenient and inefficient as time is lost in starting up an empty bobbin on its winder after removing a full one, thread tensions and lengths are variable and faulty build-up of thread on the bobbin may cause jamming in the bobbin case. They also inhibit overspin during stitching, a particular problem on zig-zag machines. Prewound bobbins generally contain more thread and the length is guaranteed. Thus in cases where bobbin runout must be avoided, the number of seams which can be sewn with each bobbin can be determined and the almost empty bobbin changed in time. Bobbin changing time is considerably reduced and smoother unwinding results from the initial

Spool   Cop   Cone   Vicone

Pre-wound bobbin

Container   Cocoon   Large package

Fig. 3.62. Thread packages (not to scale).

precision winding. This improves efficiency and quality of production. A variety of thread types is available prewound and in a variety of sizes to fit most lockstitch machines. From some manufacturers, these packages are self-supporting and have no metal, wood or paper support.

Examples of thread packages are shown in Figure 3.62. Choice of package is important if sewing is to be trouble-free and thread handling by the operator is to be minimised. Where a number of machines are involved in manufacturing a style and shade of garment, enough thread packages of suitable size must be available without excess stock of thread being required. Thus, a small contract for which only a small quantity of thread is needed, may present problems in supplying enough packages to run safety stitch machines which require five threads, especially since thread is normally purchased in boxes of, say, six or ten packages. One answer is for a company to make use of a thread winding machine which enables them to rewind cones as smaller cops which can then be spread around more machines, especially when stocks are running low.

Thread costs

An important consideration in selecting thread, after performance and appearance have been settled, is the cost. Thread costs only represent a very small proportion of the material cost of an item such as a garment but manufacturers are nevertheless tempted in some cases to try to cut these costs and use cheap threads. If threads are purchased separately from the other materials used in garment production, the overall thread bill for the year may be studied rather than the cost per garment and in this situation it may be tempting to economise.

Total thread costs are made up of the thread that is actually used in a production run of garments, the thread that is wasted during sewing (e.g. by chaining off excessively on overedge machines), the thread stock that remains unused at the end of a contract, and last, but by no means least, the costs which can arise in production or during the subsequent use of the garment because the thread was faulty. It is these last costs which can increase dramatically if low quality thread is purchased in an attempt to cut the obvious costs of actual thread purchase.

In the publication *Productivity in Sewing Operation* by Grills and Brown, which demonstrated that only about 20 per cent of an operator's time on a conventional machine was spent in sewing, it was also shown that, on average, about 4 per cent of the operator's time was spent rethreading the sewing needle after a thread break. This means that about 20 minutes each day is being spent on the unproductive task of making good a fault incurred in the sewing operation. This time could be considerably increased if the operator has to unpick the seam back to the beginning so that a join does not occur in a visible part of the garment, or if working on a multi-needle operation or on a machine where rethreading is a more complex process. It is not difficult to estimate the

Stitch type	Thread usage, in cm, per cm of seam
301 lockstitch	2.5
101 chainstitch	4.0
401 2-thread chainstitch	5.5
504 3-thread overedge stitch	14.0
512 4-thread overedge	18.0
(401.504) safety stitch	20.0
606 flatlock	32.0

Fig. 3.63. Thread consumption ratios.

cost involved here at current labour rates. Estimates from the thread manufacturers suggest that the cost over a day of rethreading a single needle lockstitch machine could be twice the total cost of the thread consumed by that machine in the day. A small increase in the price paid for the thread to obtain more consistent, fault-free thread would be a good investment.

It is possible to estimate the quantity of thread which will be consumed in manufacturing a certain style of garment, either by measuring the seam lengths sewn in each stitch type and calculating the total amount from published ratios of thread usage, or by unpicking and measuring the thread used in a sample garment. The latter is more accurate because it allows for fabric thickness and stitch density. Approximate net thread consumption ratios for typical seams sewn in one or two plies of fabric at 7 stitches per cm are shown in Figure 3.63.

It will be seen that the more complicated stitch types use large amounts of thread. Tables of likely thread consumption for different types of general garment are also published by the thread manufacturers, based on their experience of actual consumption by customers. These show figures varying from 5 m of thread to make a tie to 280 m to make a raincoat. In the latter case, thread cost has been estimated at around 22 pence per garment in a raincoat with a wholesale price of about £30. This is a typical order of magnitude of thread cost in relation to total garment cost.

Published estimates of thread consumption by thread suppliers usually include a 5 per cent allowance for wastage. Some wastage is inevitable though it can be reduced where machines are fitted with automatic thread trimmers. Extreme situations of thread wastage occur where operators working on overedge or safety stitch machines keep the machine running constantly for long spells as they feed garment parts into them. A long section of thread chain will join the garment parts and where seams are short, e.g. blouse shoulder seams, wastage could easily exceed actual usage. If waste thread is collected and weighed on an accurate balance, some surprising figures may be obtained.

Not only does thread wastage cost money, it may cause a manufacturer to run out of thread before the completion of the contract for which it was purchased. In many areas of clothing manufacturing where long runs of a garment style used to be the norm, styles are changing increasingly rapidly in response to retailing demands. Thread quantities required for these smaller contracts must be more accurately estimated than hitherto if enough is to be available, in the correct size and number of packages, and if stocks are not to be left over at the end. Lack of control over thread wastage makes such estimates extremely difficult.

Thread properties and seam performance

Having analysed the general nature of sewing threads, it is appropriate at this stage to summarise their particular properties, most of which have already been introduced, and to consider how they relate to the more general requirements of seams. Although thread is by no means the only factor which determines the value of the properties of seam strength, elasticity, durability, security and comfort, identified at the beginning of this chapter as relevant to seam appearance and performance, or helps maintain the special properties of certain fabric types, it is one of the most important ones. The others are the type of stitch, seam, needle and feed mechanism, which have now been studied, and the nature of the material being sewn. Thus, in summarising sewing thread properties, it is appropriate to return to the subject of overall seam appearance and performance. The important but purely visual aspect of thread, namely its colour properties, will be discussed in Chapter 5.

Seam strength

Because of the different nature of woven and knitted fabrics, it is necessary to discuss seam strength separately for each.

When two pieces of woven fabric are joined by a seam, and an increasing force is applied to the assembly at right angles to the seam line, rupture ultimately occurs at or near the seam line and at a load usually less than that required to break the unsewn fabric. Since every seam has two components, namely the fabric and the sewing thread, seam failure must result from the breakage of either the fabric or the thread or, in rare cases, both simultaneously.

In the case of a fabric break, two different mechanisms are possible. The fabric may actually break, perhaps as a result of being weakened by needle damage, and the seam will rupture, but a more common occurrence is the situation where the seam opens up due to the phenomenon known as seam slippage. This happens in fabrics woven from slippery yarns, especially if rather loosely woven, and it is the result of the yarns parallel to a seam, and within the seam allowance, sliding over those at right angles to the seam when the seam is stressed transversely. It shows on the outside of the garment, close to the stressed seam. For a distance of as much as 5 mm from the stitching, there are no yarns in the fabric parallel to the stitching, only the yarns at right angles to the stitching that have pulled out of the seam allowance. It gives an unacceptable appearance long before the seam actually breaks down, which happens when the yarns at right angles to the seam pull completely out and the yarns parallel to the seam in the seam allowance fall off on the inside.

Increasing the seam allowance and neatening the edges may help, especially if there is an additional problem of seam edges fraying, perhaps on the inside of a garment on a lining edge, and an increase in stitch density, up to a certain point, does have a useful effect. A change of seam type from a simple superimposed seam to one such as a lap felled seam can help considerably but only at the expense of a more bulky seam. In practice, many fabrics are unsuitable for making up into tight-fitting garment styles. Examples would be fabrics for trousers in a closely fitting style or jackets which are a close fit across the back of the shoulders. Fabrics should be investigated at the garment design stage by means of the standard tests for seam slippage and by wearer trials. Fabrics have on occasions been rejected for garment use without having been worn after trial garments failed at the seams during wash testing for reasons of seam slippage. Garment failure due to fabric breakdown is more common than that due to thread breakdown and it is usually seam slippage that is the cause. In commercial terms, the seam has failed once it has visibly opened up although the seam may still be a long way from complete breakdown.

When woven fabrics are seamed, the absolute seam strength is not, in the majority of cases, of paramount importance, providing it is reasonably high. Knitted fabrics are normally more extensible than woven fabrics and, in some instances, much more extensible. Care is needed in the selection of stitch types so that when a seam in a knitted fabric is extended along its length, the extension limit of the sewing threads is not reached before that of the seam, with seam cracking possibly resulting. Thus, the behaviour of seams under longitudinal, rather than transverse stress, is of much greater importance in knitted fabrics than in woven ones. This point will be discussed further.

Seam failure in a woven fabric which is due to thread breakage could be said to be less of a problem than that due to fabric failure because it can at least be repaired, though causing much consumer dissatisfaction. Several thread properties are connected with seam failure due to thread breakage, most of which have already been introduced.

Tensile strength is the tension at which a thread breaks. It will vary slightly according to the conditions under which the thread is broken, i.e. humidity, temperature, rate of applying the load and the length of thread being tested and for this reason any testing of it must be carried out in a laboratory in a temperature and humidity-controlled environment. Tenacity is the relative strength of a fibre, yarn or thread and is obtained by dividing the tensile strength by the thickness. It is obvious that a thick thread will be stronger than a thin thread of the same type, but the usefulness of tenacity or relative strength is that it is independent of thread size and can therefore be used to compare the strengths of various fibres and thread constructions. The conventional measure of linear tensile stength is useful as a quality control check in thread production but bears little resemblance to the breaking point of a thread in a stitch.

The majority of thread-breaks in a seam occur at a looped part of a stitch and the loop strength of a thread is more closely related to stitch strength than is linear tensile strength. Loop strength is the load required to break a length of thread which is looped through another thread of the same length and it is influenced by stiffness, fibre or filament type, ply and twist construction and the regularity of these factors. The measure of thread strength which most closely relates to stitch strength is minimum loop strength—the strength of the weakest loop in a series, tested in a continuous length of thread. A measurement of this nature is difficult and tedious to do in practice but it has been found that the strength of a thread into which has been tied a simple overhand knot or a figure-of-eight knot is very close to the figure for loop strength. The same situation obtains, namely that the thread is bent sharply round its own diameter as well as being strained longitudinally.

For minimum knot strength, a series of knots can be tied in one length of thread which can then be tested. The work of Burtonwood and Chamberlain demonstrated that it is possible to calculate the strength of a seam under conditions of failure due to thread breakage simply from the stitch density and the minimum knot strength of a thread after sewing into and recovery from a seam. (Measurement of unsewn thread strength would not allow for the loss in strength which inevitably occurs when thread is sewn.) The calculation applies to lockstitch seams but, since chainstitch seams were found to be slightly stronger, the same calculation can be used and a safety margin gained. It applies specifically to simple superimposed seams but it was found that in seams with multiple rows of stitching, the strength increases proportionately to the number of rows of stitching.

Synthetic threads have higher loop strengths than cotton threads and technical developments have increased even these so that finer synthetic threads can now be used which have the same strength as coarser threads of a few years ago. The stretch and regularity of the material being sewn influences seam strength, even when it is the stitches that break before the material. For this reason the mean loop strength is only a guide and sample seams should be compared in critical cases.

Other factors affecting seam strength must also be considered. Variations in stitch density affect seam strength and, if other factors remain unchanged, then seam strength normally increases with stitch density up to a point where the concentration of needle holes starts to weaken the material. After this, a stronger thread should be used at a lower stitch density. This will require a larger needle size with all the attendant problems of possible needle damage, emphasising again the need to use the strongest possible type of thread so that the finest size of thread and consequently of needle can be used, consistent with other sewing properties. The effect of stitch type on seam strength relates to the greater loss in strength which affects needle threads, especially in lockstitch machines, during the sewing process, and to the stitch geometry which puts more strain on the needle thread in a lockstitch than in a chainstitch or overedge stitch. Thus chainstitch 401 and overedge 504 are slightly stronger than lockstitch 301 though 504 is limited in its uses because of its narrow bight. Variations in seam type can also affect seam strength with improved strength obtained in some of the lapped seams which have additional rows of stitching. For the full benefit to be achieved, care must be taken to set the thread tensions the same in each row.

Seam elasticity

When knitted fabrics are being considered, the questions of seam strength and seam elasticity are difficult to separate because the majority of problems of seam breakdown arise from thread breakage when a seam is stressed longitudinally and stretches in excess of the amount that the stitch type and the stretch in the sewing thread can accommodate. With comfort stretch fabrics stretching up to 30 per cent and action stretch fabrics stretching 100 per cent or more, it is necessary to create seams which will stretch and recover in excess of this so that they do not restrict the flexibility of the garment or break at their limiting extension.

Choice of stitch and seam type is very important. Both lockstitch 301 and chainstitch 401, if carefully adjusted, will give adequate stretch for sewing comfort stretch fabrics when used with superimposed or lapped seams. In experimental conditions, figures as high as 80 per cent have been obtained for seam stretch. With lockstitch, there is a limit to the extent to which the stitch tensions can be loosened to increase stretch and still obtain a satisfactory stitch formation. With chainstitch 401 it is possible to set the stitch looser but only at the expense of an increase in seam 'grinning', a temporary appearance of the stitch opening up in the seam when stressed transversely. A small amount of grin is normally acceptable and 401 stitch can thus be used where a little more stretch is needed. This feature has given 401 the reputation of having higher stretch than 301 but it must be remembered that this is only in circumstances of increased grinning. To achieve maximum stretch with this stitch, a ratio of needle thread to looper thread length in the seam should be of the order of 1:3. Seam grinning can itself cause problems since each time the seam gapes in wear, the sewing threads themselves are pulled through the fabric as it distorts in the neighbourhood of the stitch. They return again when the strain is removed but this sawing to and fro of the sewing threads must eventually tend to cut through the yarns in the fabric and lead to seam breakdown.

For action stretch fabrics and for cut-and-sew knitwear, it is not possible to achieve high enough stretch in a seam using stitch types 301 or 401. Fortunately, in many garments, a class 500 overedge stitch is acceptable, despite the bulky seam it inevitably produces. The 504 three thread overedge stitch provides the maximum attainable extensibility. The length of the looper threads in the class 500 stitches, together with the compressibility of the enclosed fabric edges, enables these seams to extend to over 100 per cent without cracking. In garments such as corsetry and swimwear, use is made of lockstitch zig-zag stitches to give high stretch as well as high seam security but, as was shown previously, limited seam constructions are then available. In appropriate fabrics, class 600 covering stitches can also be used to sew flat seams with high stretch and low bulk. Since the stitching shows on the surface of the garment, this is generally used on underwear garments or where the seam can be used as a decorative feature.

Increasing stitch density helps to increase seam stretch but only up to a certain point. In lockstitch seams, an increase in stitch density actually reduces the proportion of thread lying on the surface of the fabric and available for direct extension with the seam, unless thread tension is adjusted at the same time as the stitch is shortened. If the tension is adjusted so that the amount of grin with the higher stitch rate is the same as with the lower stitch rate, instead of being less, then the expected increase in stretch with a higher stitch density will be achieved. It is these kinds of adjustment which are necessary in order to produce stretch figures in lockstitch seams of 70–80 per cent. Stitch densities of at least 8 st per cm are needed. With overedge stitches, increasing stitch density will increase seam stretch but a limit is reached when the fabric becomes jammed between the crowded stitches. The seam extension is then limited and the fabric edge cannot relax completely after stretching. Too many stitches may also weaken the fabric and cause failure under transverse stresses.

Thread extensibility has a part to play in achieving seam extensibility but with conventional needle threads it is not the overriding factor. Cotton threads typically have extensions at break of 6–8 per cent, synthetics threads in medium sizes have 15–20 per cent or up to 25 per cent in heavier sizes, yet still with good sewing performance. This extra extensibility of synthetic threads will only increase seam stretch by 10 per cent over what can be achieved with cotton threads. If a dramatic increase is required, use can be made of spun polyamide threads which have extensions up to 30 per cent. However, because of their specially engineered high stretch properties, none of these can be sewn as efficiently as needle threads. Although when 401 chainstitch is stressed it is the needle thread which breaks first because of the greater amount of looper thread which is present in the seam, the use of a high stretch thread in the needle would just result in poor sewing performance. When used in the loopers of chainstitch or overedge machines, with standard synthetic sewing thread in the needles, these more elastic threads stretch first, allowing the maximum extension to be obtained from the needle threads to suit the most demanding situations. An improvement in the stretch performance of a lockstitch seam can also be achieved by a similar combination of threads provided the stitch is unbalanced. A balanced stitch is normally required to give maximum stretch but with a highly extensible thread in the bobbin, the sewing tension can be adjusted to hold the needle thread loop under the fabric as in a chainstitch. The bobbin thread should also be wound with the minimum tension so that it is relaxed as it comes off the bobbin. This helps to realise the full stretch potential of the seam and prevent creep-back and pucker.

Seam durability is the third aspect of seam performance originally identified as necessary to satisfactory seaming. The length of life of a seam in a garment should be as long as that of the other materials and both should be appropriate to the required end use of the garment. The seam can be considered to have failed in durability terms if either the thread or the fabric in the seam fails at an early stage. (An immediate failure of the thread would be regarded as a failure of seam strength or extensibility.) Jeans and workwear garments, underwear, schoolwear, etc., all suffer considerable abrasion in wear and seams must be designed to resist this abrasion as effectively as possible.

The first abrasive act to be overcome is that of the act of sewing itself and the problem of loss of strength in needle threads during sewing has already been discussed. The durability of a thread in a seam depends on a number of factors which include the stitch type, stitch balance, stitch tightness, seam type, thread type and the nature of the material being sewn. The critical factor is the extent to which the thread beds into the material. Investigations by thread manufacturers have shown that the exposed surface of a balanced lockstitch has much better abrasion resistance than the exposed underside of a chainstitch and seams sewn at high tensions are much less susceptible to damage than those which are sewn at low tensions. Also, the life of the looper threads in a chainstitch increases if the stitch balance is adjusted so that the needle thread to looper thread ratio is approximately 1:1. This is because the stitch loops are spaced out instead of being concentrated at each stitch hole. All these effects are concerned with the improved bedding in of the thread into the material, affording a degree of protection.

As would be expected, seams sewn in a densely woven or coated material cannot bed in and are therefore more quickly abraded than those sewn into softer materials. A typical area of a garment where abrasion may be experienced is on the inside leg seams of denim jeans. The traditional strong jeans seams consisting of a lap felled seam with two rows of 401 chainstitch does not always perform well in this position because the stitching suffers considerable abrasion, a heavily built wearer adding to the problem. Superimposed seams sewn with safety stitch are more commonly used, preferably sewn such that the needle side of the chainstitch row is worn against the skin with the chain underside protected by the seam allowance.

A different problem of seam durability and abrasion can arise with denim jeans when they are subjected to stonewashing. In this process they are severely abraded to produce a worn and faded look. Careful thread selection is required to prevent damage to seams requiring immediate repair or damage which shows later and shortens the life of the garment. A satisfactory result can be obtained with polyester/cotton corespun thread and an even better result with the new type of locked filament polyester thread though the latter has poorer initial sewability.

A stitched component of a garment which is both functional and decorative and is subject to much abrasion is the buttonhole, especially when the button is being undone. Synthetic threads give greatly superior performance to cotton threads and spun polyester and cotton- or polyester-covered corespun give both good durability and good appearance. Of relevance to the life of a buttonhole is the thread with which the button is sewn and this should also be a spun thread. The use of continuous filament button thread may significantly shorten the life of a spun fibre buttonhole thread by its abrasion.

Seam security is another important seam performance factor but at this point it will become clear that these various factors are not independent. If seam security is regarded as including seams which do not break down as a result of thread or fabric breakdown or seam slippage then all the factors discussed above are important in this context. Seam security has further implications, though, such as those of stitch security due to stitch type and due to stitching quality in an individual case. In earlier discussions on stitch types, three possible ways were given for threads to pass each other in a stitch, namely interlacing, interlooping and intralooping, and it was said that this has an effect on stitch security. Particular stitch types were also described as having various levels of security.

The securest of stitches, lockstitch, is formed, as its name implies, by the interlocking of the threads together. If a thread breaks in a lockstitch seam, the stitches may run back for a short distance, depending on the longitudinal and transverse stress applied to the seam, the stretch in the fabric and the surface nature of the thread used. There is, however, no tendency for the stitch to continue undoing along the seam, nor any loops of thread which can be snagged and pull the stitches undone further. Additionally, the stitches can be backtacked at the end of the seam which makes the seam even more secure.

The least secure stitches of all are the single thread chainstitches in class 100. This is because they are formed by intralooping where each loop of the thread is secured by the succeeding loop of the same thread. Such a simple construction contains very little friction within it, especially in the blind felling 103 version which is often sewn with a fine multi-filament thread for minimum visibility. If the last stitch is not properly locked, if a thread is broken, or if a stitch slips because the machine is improperly adjusted or it sews over a thicker section of fabric, it will run undone very easily. In the case of slip-stitching, a loop of thread is left which is particularly likely to become pulled. Since much of the blind felling, buttonsewing, buttonholing and multi-needle stitching which is used on bulk production garments today makes use of this stitch, and since it is inherently insecure there is much customer dissatisfaction with garments where the stitching fails to last the lifetime of the garment. However, the machines are fast and there are many of them in use. They could be replaced with other, more modern machines using different stitch types but only at considerable expense in capital investment and slower production. Other modern machinery goes part of the way to improving the situation by automatic condensation of stitches at the ends of seams on stitches which cannot be backtacked. Careful thread selection can also increase friction within each stitch and reduce the tendency to run back. As consumers generally become more quality and performance conscious, they are likely to become more aware of the problem of seam insecurity. They may be willing to pay more for more secure stitching but unfortunately this willingness is not normally transmitted to those who purchase machinery.

Intermediate in security between the two already described are the chainstitches in classes 400, 500 and 600. Here the threads are interlooped – that is, needle threads are looped through one or more loops of one or more other threads. Although run-back is still possible, the greatly increased friction within each stitch, subject as always to smoothness of thread surface, ensures that in many cases tangling of the thread in the stitch occurs before it has run very far. The most likely to run is the simplest, 401, and as with 101 just described, it can run from the end, from a break in the thread, or because there is a slip-stitch at some point along the stitching. The latter leaves a loop of thread which is easily caught and pulled.

In dealing with insecure ends of stitching, careful thought must be given to the overall method of construction of a garment and particularly to the sequence of the various stages, to ensure that weak ends of seams are not left and those where sewing across is necessary do actually receive it. In many cases, there is no alternative but to bar-tack the chain end of thread back into the seam.

Where seams become insecure because of thread breaks, the problems are usually those of seam strength and stretch described earlier. Thus the stitch type used influences the initial likelihood of a thread breaking in a seam and also the extent to which the stitching will further unravel. The type of seam break familiar to many consumers is that of a hem which comes undone as a result of catching in it the heel of a shoe or the zip tag of a knee-high boot. Most of these problems can be avoided by care on the part of the wearer but, nevertheless, the garment tends to be given the blame.

Slip-stitching arises as a result of a failure of the bobbin hook or the looper to pick up the loop in the needle thread. Thread elongation and recovery properties are very important in determining the thread loopforming properties. Threads which form large, consistent loops are much more safely picked up by the looper, even if the timing is imperfect or the needle is badly deflected in passing through heavy material. Other causes of slip-stitching are bent needles, incorrect needle size or type for the thread size or type, incorrect thread tensions or poor material control arising from a large throat plate hole or poor presser foot control. If presser foot and needle hole clearances are too great the fabric may move up and down with the needle. This keeps the sewing thread taut in the needle instead of it being held by the fabric as the needle rises, thus allowing the loop to form. A typical needle deflection problem can arise on a jeans waistband, commonly attached with 401 chainstitch, where there are belt loops and zip tapes to be sewn across in addition to the thickness of the body of the garment and its waistband.

Comfort is the last of the five seam performance factors previously introduced. Comfort is rarely a conscious sensation but discomfort certainly is. Seams may be locally tight against the body, they may present a ridge or roughness to the skin because of an unsuitable choice of stitch, seam or thread, or there may be local discomfort because of such things as thread ends or label corners. All may be aggravated by poor garment fit.

If a seam is tight against the body it suggests that the extension in the fabric is greater than that in the seam which in turn suggests that seam cracking is a strong possibility. An alternative stitch type may be more suitable. If a seam forms an uncomfortable ridge it is likely to be because it is a closed overedged or safety stitched seam which is more bulky than an open seam would be. Unfortunately the alternative open seam is considerably more expensive to make and the stitch types which can be used on it may have insufficient stretch. Any seam which is likely to be rough against the skin can be softened by the use of a crimp textured thread in the loopers of the overedging or cover stitching that is used to neaten the raw edges. Particular problems of discomfort are associated with the use of monofilament polyamide threads. If used in places such as hems, the long ends which must be left to prevent unravelling, along with the cut or melted end of a rather substantial filament, can cause considerable discomfort.

Investigations into comfort sensations of garments in general have recently shown that there is a high level of complaint as a result of the types of labels used in many garments and the methods of attaching them. Many of the less expensive labels are printed on fabric made from thermoplastic fibre and cut and sealed to narrow widths. They may then be cut and sealed again to the short length that is needed to insert into the garment. For economy, many labels are simply folded and inserted into a row of overedging or even just lockstitched close to the sealed edge. Sharp corners abound and while a lockstitch-attached label might be easily removed, though possibly with the loss of any care instructions, labels inserted under overedging or cover stitching must be regarded as permanent. This might not appear to be a problem of seam performance but it is certainly a common cause of dissatisfaction with garments. Greater care in choosing label positions, in deciding how to sew the seam which attaches them, and in covering over the cut edges with a textured thread, will produce more satisfactory garments.

The other seam properties mentioned earlier relate to the maintenance of specialised properties of a fabric. The particular ones which can be spoiled by incorrect choice of seaming are the properties of waterproofing and water resistance and of flame retardance. These have been discussed when considering sewing thread finishes.

SEWING PROBLEMS

All through this chapter, the emphasis has been on correct selection of the various factors of stitch, seam, feed system, needle and thread which together determine seam appearance and performance. At the same time, mention has been made of particular sewing problems which can arise and how one or other of these factors relates to each problem. It is necessary now to draw this information together by studying the range of problems that can arise, their causes and the various solutions available.

The problems which arise when materials are sewn vary in their seriousness, with some causing only minor appearance problems, negligible in low price garments, whilst others cause damage to the material which it would not be economic to repair even if it were possible.

The problems are most conveniently divided into:

(1) problems of stitch formation which give rise to poor seam appearance and performance;
(2) problems of fabric distortion known as 'pucker' which also give rise to poor seam appearance;
(3) problems of damage to fabric along the stitch line.

Problems of stitch formation

The main problems which arise from the actual stitch formation are

- slipped stitches
- staggered stitching
- unbalanced stitches
- variable stitch density
- needle, bobbin or looper thread breakage

Slipped stitches arise from the hook or looper in the machine not picking up the loop in the needle thread. In a lockstitch, a slipped stitch will create a small gap in a seam or a poor appearance in topstitching but it will not cause seam failure. In a 101 or 401 chainstitch, it produces a weak point in the stitching that will run undone during use of the garment. The causes of slip stitching have been discussed under the heading of seam security.

Staggered stitching can be caused by yarns in the fabric deflecting the needle away from a straight line of stitching, giving a poor appearance. In some hard, woven fabrics, really straight stitching will only be achieved at a slight angle of bias.

Unbalanced stitches in lockstitching can reduce the potential for stretch in a seam in a knitted fabric and, as explained earlier, lead to seam cracking. Bobbin tension should be adjusted until a full bobbin in its case will just slide down the thread when held by the end of the thread. Needle thread tension should be adjusted so that the threads interlock in the middle of the fabric, unless different colour threads are being used, for example, in topstitching, when a slight imbalance towards the underside may be needed to prevent the colour of the underneath thread showing on the top. Where maximum stretch is required in a lockstitch seam, careful adjustments of the type described earlier may be needed.

Variable stitch density arises from insufficient foot pressure in a drop feed system, causing uneven feeding of the fabric through the machine. It can occur particularly with materials with sticky or slippery surfaces. Pressure must be adequate to enable even feeding but it will be realised from previous sections that with many fabrics and sewing situations, specialised feed systems are necessary to achieve even feeding of all the plies of the material.

Breakage of needle, bobbin or looper threads arises largely as a result of normally smooth metal surfaces in the machine becoming chipped or otherwise damaged and then causing damage to the thread. The guard over the hook in a lockstitch machine can become chipped, as can the needle hole in the throat plate, as a result of needle deflection. Thread breakage during production is time-consuming for the operator, especially if a join in the stitching is not acceptable and she must unpick it and start again. Both the cause of the damaged machine parts and, if appropriate, the cause of the needle deflection, must be investigated.

Problems of pucker

The main problem which arises which is solely one of appearance is that of pucker. To describe it like that is not to say that it is unimportant, for it can produce some very unsightly seams, but it does not actually cause any damage to the material being sewn.

Pucker is a wrinkled appearance along a seam in an otherwise smooth fabric. It generally appears as if there is too much fabric and not enough thread in the seam; as if the thread is drawing the seam in. For this reason the sewing thread is often blamed for causing the problem but there are several factors which contribute to pucker including fabric structure, seam construction, needle size and feeding problems, as well as incorrect thread tensions and unsuitable thread. Pucker may show itself when the garment is first sewn or it may not appear until later when the garment is pressed, wetted or washed. It may show itself in all the plies of material which have been sewn together or only in some. It can also arise from more than one cause at the same time, which can make elimination extremely difficult. It could be said that there is pucker present in all sewn seams because it is impossible to introduce stitches into a fabric without it suffering some distortion, but in practice there are many fabrics of loose construction from soft yarns which show no visible pucker at all. By contrast, many of the modern smooth, fine, synthetic fabrics are almost impossible to construct without pucker. Indeed, so accustomed do people who work on these fabrics become to seeing some level of pucker at all times that they forget what a smooth seam looks like and may gradually accept a lower and lower standard.

The earliest detailed investigations into the causes of pucker are those by Dorkin and Chamberlain, who described five main causes which they felt covered at least 90 per cent of pucker they found occurring in practice. Their descriptions are still relevant today.

(a)   Seam pucker due to differential fabric stretch

In discussing sewing machine feed mechanisms, it was said that the prime requirement of a feeding system was that it should move the plies of fabric past the needle and that all the plies should move together. The variety of feed mechanisms which were described have all been developed because the simple feeding systems do not move the plies together. Thus one of the prime causes of seam pucker is differential fabric stretch caused by the feeding mechanism, often referred to as differential feeding pucker or just feeding pucker. If two fabric plies are being sewn together in a lockstitch sewing machine, fitted with a drop feed mechanism, the feed dog rises up, presses the fabrics onto the underside of the presser foot against the spring pressure of that foot, and, ideally, carries both fabrics with it for the required distance, sliding them over the underside of the presser foot. The lower ply is engaged positively by the feed dog and moves with it by the same amount. For the upper fabric, the lower fabric effectively acts as a feed dog and exerts a frictional force tending to move it forward. The friction between fabric and fabric is never as great as between fabric and feed dog and in some cases is quite low. The upper fabric, being in contact on its upper side with the lower side of the presser foot, is subjected to a frictional force tending to impede its forward movement. Thus, as far as the feed mechanism itself is concerned, the amount that the upper fabric moves, relative to the lower, will be determined very largely by the balance between two frictional forces, one between upper and lower fabric tending to move the upper fabric forward, and the other between upper fabric and presser foot tending to hold it back. In general, therefore, the upper fabric would tend to be moved forward, but by an amount always less than the movement of the lower one.

The situation is also further complicated by local distortions which take place during sewing between the actual stitch line and the areas each side where the feed dog operates. These cause an extension of the upper fabric, in the plane of that fabric, immediately in front of the needle and a compression of the lower fabric in the same position. The relative amounts of extension and compression suffered by the upper and lower fabrics respectively is governed entirely by the relative extensibility and compressibility of the two materials. If, for example, the upper fabric is a readily extensible material like elastic net, and the lower is a relatively incompressible one like polyester satin, most of the distortion will appear as extension of the top fabric and when the seam leaves the machine the lower fabric will be puckered by the contraction of the upper. In general, the compression and extension may be shared between the two in any proportions, subject to the fact that extension occurs more easily than compression because compression of the fabric in its own plane would require an increase in thickness which would be opposed by the presser foot pressure.

In order to ascertain, in a particular case, whether the observed pucker in a seam is due to the presence of differential fabric stretch introduced by the feed mechanism in the manner described above, a simple test may be applied. Two strips of fabric should be cut from the warp direction and two from the weft direction of the fabric, about 10 cm wide and long enough to be marked with 25 marks at 1 cm intervals at right angles to the long edge. Each pair of fabrics is placed together with the marks face to face and in register and pinned at the starting end so that the register is not lost as sewing commences. The strips are seamed down the centre line, starting from the pinned end, removed from the machine and opened out. If differential stretch has occurred, the marks on the two pieces of fabric will gradually lose register along the line of the seam and the seam will be puckered to a greater or lesser extent. Half a mark gained in 25 indicates a differential extension of 2 per cent which is sufficient to cause noticeable pucker in some fabrics.

The methods of overcoming pucker due to differential stretch are those of specialised feeding systems and operator handling described earlier.

(b)   Seam pucker caused by differential fabric dimensional instability

The essential feature causing differential pucker is the relative change in dimensions of upper and lower fabric after the seam has been made. In the case discussed so far, this change is due to elastic forces brought into play by differential action of the sewing machine feed, but in general, any relative alteration in the dimensions of the two fabrics after the seam is made will produce a comparable effect. Such changes can occur if one of the fabrics is dimensionally unstable whilst the other is not. In such cases, the seam may be perfectly flat and unpuckered as it leaves the machine but on subsequent washing one of the fabrics may shrink more than the other so that a differential pucker appears.

Differential pucker due to dimensional instability may be suspected when the two fabrics being joined are markedly different or when one shows noticeably more pucker than the other. The fabrics should be tested for dimensional stability by marking up sections of fabric and subjecting them to the washing process that the garment will undergo, or in the case of raincoat fabric to a simple wetting and drying process. Several washings may be needed as some fabrics shrink progressively. If the two fabrics show a difference in dimensional change of 2 per cent or more, then pucker due to differential dimensional change may be expected to occur in finished garments after comparable treatment.

(c) Seam pucker due to extension in the sewing threads

In sewing a seam on a lockstitch sewing machine, two sewing threads are used and both are subjected to tension forces which tend to stretch them. The needle thread operates at a much higher tension than the bobbin thread because during the making of the stitch the upper thread has to snatch the lower thread up from below the fabric to form a loop midway between face and back of the seam and this requires considerable force. All sewing threads have some extensibility and they are thus extended by the action of the tension devices and pass into the seam in an extended state. When removed from the machine they will tend to contract. Provided the fabrics contract by the same amount this will have no visible effect but if the sewing threads are particularly extensible and continue to contract after the fabric has reached its original unstretched length, pucker will result.

It is possible to test, in a particular case, whether pucker is due to the extension of the sewing threads. A seam is sewn joining two test pieces of fabric, using the thread in question at the tension previously used. If this seam shows pucker, it is resewn with a sheet of paper on top of it, sewing through the paper as well as the fabric and after sewing the paper is torn away along the needle holes. The paper ensures that extra thread is fed into each stitch and when this paper is removed the extra length is released into the seam. If the pucker previously was due to sewing thread extension, this seam should now be free of pucker. This only identifies the problem, of course, as it would not be practical to construct garments by sewing each seam through paper. Another test which can be used is to sew a seam in the normal manner, though with a larger stitch than usual, and then to cut every stitch on the face and back of the seam using very fine scissors, without disturbing the thread ends in the fabric. The tension in the sewing thread is now zero and if that was the cause of the pucker it will have disappeared.

Where thread extension is proved to be a cause of puckered seams, consideration must be given to the type of thread being used and to the tension settings on individual machines as these can cause the level of pucker to vary from machine to machine. Equipment is available which will measure thread tensions in sewing machines and enable an attempt to be made to set all machines to the same, satisfactory, level.

(d)   Seam pucker due to sewing thread shrinkage

This type of pucker was not included in the original work by Dorkin and Chamberlain but it should be mentioned here as the effect is exactly the same as the last situation described but it does not appear until the garment has been pressed or washed. Cotton sewing threads increase in diameter and shrink in length when wet and these distortions may cause pucker in sensitive fabrics. Synthetic sewing threads have negligible wet shrinkage and should always be used for such fabrics. When selecting sewing threads for a fabric, it is important to match performance rather than fibre content. Thus, a non-shrink cotton fabric should be sewn with synthetic or corespun thread.

For dry conditions, synthetic threads are generally stabilised so as to have negligible shrinkage up to 150°C but if there is to be any processing of a garment at a higher temperature than that, such as in a permanent press treatment, then special threads may need to be requested.

(e)   Seam pucker due to structural jamming

Having considered the types of pucker directly attributable to distortion in one or other of the seam components, whether caused by the mechanical action of the feed dog and presser foot on the fabric, the action of the tension devices on the thread or the shrinkage of the thread itself, there is a third possibility to be considered. The presence of the seam itself may introduce a distortion, in no way dependent on the action of the sewing machine, but inevitably appearing as soon as the seam is formed. If a woven fabric has been constructed so as to be close to the practical weaving limit, that is, with very little space left between the yarns either warp or weftways, it may be extremely difficult to force in any more threads in either direction.

For example, a fabric might be constructed with 45 warp yarns per cm and 24 weft yarns per cm, of a size such that there is no space within the construction of the fabric. If that fabric is then seamed on a lockstitch machine at 5 st per cm, five holes will be made in a line, for each centimetre of fabric, and into each hole will be inserted side by side two threads whose diameter may be about the same as that of the yarns in the fabric. Along the line of the seam, instead of 24 picks per cm, an attempt is being made to insert 34. As the fabric already has as many picks as it is possible to cram into it, or very nearly so, there is not room in the structure for the insertion of sewing threads. In consequence, the fabric along the line of the seam must be extended, although on either side of the seam and at a short distance from it no such extension occurs. The extension along the seam line must be accommodated by the fabric along the seam line assuming a buckled or puckered configuration. The term 'structural jamming' is given to this type of pucker because it results directly from the act of jamming extra threads into a structure which is already too closely set to accommodate them.

It is commonly the case when sewing fabrics which suffer from structural jamming pucker that the problem is more pronounced in one direction than the other. An important feature of the fabric which seems to relate to this is the crimp in the yarns. In a construction such as a poplin the warp yarns do all the bending while the weft yarns are nearly straight. As a result, the warp yarns can move sideways along the weft yarns with no crimp to prevent them but the weft yarns cannot move in the same way over the warp yarns because the sharp crimp of the warp yarns locks them and prevents such movement. In stitching a seam parallel to the weft, the space necessary for accommodating the sewing threads can be provided by such sliding of the warp yarns. When stitching parallel to the warp such accommodation is not possible and, if sewing threads are inserted, the necessary space can be found only by extension of the warp, with consequent pucker.

An important point about structural jamming pucker is that it is entirely independent of the mechanics of the sewing machine and entirely inherent in the fabric structure. If the seam was made by hand, using the same sewing thread and the same stitch rate, the same pucker would appear. It is therefore essential that structural jamming pucker is correctly identified when it is present so that effort is not wasted in making adjustments to sewing machines in a vain endeavour to eliminate it.

Identification of structural jamming pucker, out of the other possible causes of puckered seams, requires following a sequence of steps which eliminate some of the other possibilities. Where two plies of the same fabric are being seamed, differential fabric stretch can normally be easily eliminated since it would show more on one ply of fabric than the other. Structural jamming pucker normally shows on both plies when they are the same fabric. If a seam is stitched through paper and the paper torn away, then if the pucker disappears it was caused by sewing thread tension. If the pucker remains, it is likely that the problem is one of structural jamming. Finally, a seam should be stitched at a lower stitch density than usual, about 2–3 per cm, and the stitches carefully cut on both the front and the back without disturbing the thread in the fabric. The pucker will remain, despite the removal of any possible thread tension, and will only finally disappear when the cut ends of thread are removed from the fabric with a pair of tweezers. This proves that the pucker was jammed into the seam by the inserted sewing threads, whose removal unjammed the structure and allowed the fabric to return to its original flat state.

It is clear that prevention of this type of pucker is a matter for the fabric designer rather than the garment manufacturer and where there is a choice of fabric it may be possible to prevent the problem. The worst types of fabrics are plain weaves constructed from hard yarns of a size similar to the size of the sewing thread. If the fabric is made from thicker yarns then not only will there be relatively more room for the much finer sewing threads but the whole fabric will be much more stiff and rigid and pucker will be less likely on both accounts. The other problem is fabrics which are set close to the practical weaving limit, such fabrics showing a high level of pucker whereas the more open ones would not show so much. Constructing a slightly more open fabric however may not be acceptable as it will have a poorer appearance and less opacity. A different construction of fabric, away from a plain weave, will also improve matters providing the appearance is acceptable. Unfortunately, the opportunity to make radical changes of this sort to a fabric will only be possible in a situation of long-term fabric development or where it is possible to find alternative fabrics from stock which are also satisfactory in other respects.

When a garment maker has no choice in the matter of fabric, measures have to be taken in the design of the garment and the sewing of it to minimise the problem. The only step which can be taken which will always produce a perfectly sewn seam is to sew the seam on the bias, that is, at some definite angle to the warp or weft. A seam sewn on a 45° bias angle will only encounter 70 per cent of the yarns it would meet if it were sewn on the straight grain. It is unlikely to be necessary for the bias angle to be as high as 45°, and in most cases 15°–20° is sufficient.

In garment design terms, of course, it may not be possible to angle the seams in this way without giving problems of drape or uneven hems or without giving production problems of fitting pattern pieces into a marker. On the other hand, the amount of flare on some garment seams may be enough to help and some totally straight grain seams might be avoided if extra fabric could be used so that the seam can be eliminated altogether. When there is no choice but to make the garment up in a fabric and style that gives problems, it is unlikely that the problem can be completely eliminated though it may be possible to reduce it. Synthetic threads have become stronger for their size in recent years and this enables finer sizes to be used while still producing satisfactorily strong seams. The types of fine fabric which are often a problem used to be sewn with Tkt. 120 thread but there are Tkt. 180 threads now with the same level of strength which will cause less pucker. This will also enable a finer needle to be used so that there is less distortion of the fabric during sewing. The use of a lower stitch density may help but there will be a limit to how large a stitch gives an acceptable seam appearance.

So far it has been assumed that seaming was by means of a lockstitch machine. If a chainstitch could be used instead there would be no intersections of thread within the fabric in the way that there are with lockstitch and thus less bulk inserted into the fabric. Alterations in seam type might effect an improvement if less layers of fabric are sewn. An example would be the change in a shirt side seam from a lap felled seam to a superimposed seam sewn with safety stitch. This normally gives an improved appearance in terms of pucker but goes away from the traditional construction of an expensive shirt.

Finally, the elimination of topstitching can reduce pucker and on garments such as workwear this is often done for reasons of appearance as well as cost but it is unlikely to be possible on garments where topstitching is a design feature.

(f) Seam pucker due to mismatched patterns

Situations will occasionally be seen in a made up garment where there is pucker on some seams but not on others. If the patterns are carefully checked it will be found that there is a discrepancy between the lengths of the stitching lines on the pattern pieces that go together in that seam and consequently a difference in the length of the cut parts which the machinist is sewing together. An experienced machinist will attempt to ease in the longer ply and if successful in doing so the garment parts will appear to go together satisfactorily in the sense that the seam ends are level but the seams will have a puckered appearance on one ply. How much the problem shows depends to a great extent on the nature of the fabric, since, to quote an extreme contrast, a wool jersey would accommodate a considerable mismatch whereas a pre-shrunk cotton poplin would not accommodate anything at all. If deliberate ease has been built into patterns designed for use with soft wool fabrics then these patterns must not be used for more rigid fabrics without adjustments being made to them to achieve the required shape of garment by means of pattern shape along a seam rather than pattern length.

The above discussion has made the assumption that having made the patterns, accurately or not, the materials are then cut out correctly to that shape and size. Instances of random pucker on seams may well occur as a result of inaccurate cutting of garment parts which are then eased together.

In discussing these causes of pucker, ways have been suggested for identifying each of them out of the various possibilities. If this identification is carried out as an investigative process prior to production, it is possible to predict the extent to which pucker might be a problem in sewing a particular style and fabric and take steps to eliminate or at least minimise it before it happens. These simple test procedures can be carried out on new materials to indicate whether or not making up problems are likely to be encountered and, if so, of what nature and severity. In addition to these simple procedures, very sophisticated instruments have been developed recently to assess the likelihood of such problems prior to production. These are described in the last section of the chapter.

It was suggested earlier that it is often difficult to assess the level of pucker that is present in garment production, particularly in a situation where it is almost impossible to eliminate it entirely and consequently those working with it become accustomed to accepting a lesser or greater amount of it as normal all of the time. Whether a small amount of pucker is acceptable or not, it is essential to be able to grade puckered seams as objectively as possible.

For this purpose, a set of photographic standards has been produced by the American Association of Textile Chemists and Colorists which shows five standards of pucker in a seam from class 5 = no pucker to class 1 = very badly puckered. This 1–5 classification is similar to many others used in textile testing. In using the photographic standards, three test seams are compared with the standards by three observers under standardised lighting conditions. The use of three observers helps to level differences of opinion to which these types of assessment are liable. Attempts have been made over the years to develop instruments which could make a quantitative assessment of pucker in a seam but none is yet commercially available. However, research is currently being undertaken into the problems of pucker, making use of computerised equipment which has not been available until recently. Such work may, in the future, provide instrumental methods of testing for pucker and for reducing or eliminating it.

Problems of damage to the fabric along the stitch line

The problem of damage occurring during sewing as a result of the use of unsuitable needles or of sewing unsuitable fabrics, or a combination of both, has already been outlined. It has also been mentioned many times in discussing needle points and thread types since the reason for so many of these being available is, to a great extent, to overcome these kinds of problems. Sewing damage is a serious problem in garment production, leading to poor seam appearance and performance and, in a severe case, to complete breakdown of the seam. It remains now to summarise the basic needle damage problems which arise, to consider their causes, and to attempt to offer solutions.

It is worth stating again that the term 'needle damage' is used here because it is the terminology conventionally used in the clothing industry. However, it is not really the ideal term to describe what happens. The question of needles which actually become damaged has already been discussed as a straightforward problem with a simple solution. It is inevitable that damaged needles will damage the materials that they sew and the main problem is to establish the reason for the damage occurring and prevent its continued occurrence. The real problem is that a new and apparently perfect needle can cause damage because it is itself inappropriate in point type for the material being sewn or because the combination of other factors, to do with the nature of the fabric and the speed of the machine, is such that damage occurs. The problem is especially serious in knitted fabrics because they will ladder if damaged and because the damage is often not apparent when first sewn. It only becomes evident when flexing in wearing and washing causes the damaged or broken yarn to run back and become visible.

The problems which occur in sewing can be divided into those of mechanical damage and those of needle heating damage.

(a) Mechanical damage

The ways in which needles can strike and break fabric yarns and burst the loops in knitted fabrics have already been described and the appropriate set and ball point needles suggested as suitable for the sewing of woven and knitted fabrics respectively. It has also been suggested that needles should always be as small as possible.

Unfortunately the needle is not the only contributing factor to the problem of mechanical damage. a major problem is that the combination of the machine speed and the nature of the fabric prevents the yarns from moving out of the way of the needle sufficiently fast to avoid damage. Reducing machine speed is often effective in reducing the incidence of mechanical damage but it is not a popular solution since it affects production levels if machines run more slowly. However, if a problem is not discovered until garments are actually in production, it may be the only possible action. Since sewing normally only takes place for about 20 per cent of an operator's working time, a reduction in machine speed will not have as much effect as it would if sewing took place for the whole of the time.

A further difficulty if sewing speed is reduced to overcome a problem of sewing damage is that the machine may always be working on the borderline of damage recurrence. If damage is found and an incorrect needle is being used, changing the needle type may bring about a complete removal of the problem. The slowing down of a machine is more likely to bring about a gradual improvement to the point where damage is negligible, but there will always be the possibility that a machine which runs slightly faster than expected or a needle which is not absolutely perfect, will cause the damage to reappear but perhaps go undetected. In many cases it is necessary to unpick the stitching in a seam and examine it with a magnifying glass to detect the damage but it is precisely this level of damage which will begin to show after wearing and washing. While damaged garments are always a problem, those which are not detected until they have been worn and washed are a more serious problem because of the quantity that could have been made and sold up to the time of discovery. The problem could still be happening in production.

The other approach to enabling the material to move out of the way of the needle more effectively is to ensure that the fabric is adequately lubricated at the finishing stage. Many fabrics have resin finishes applied to them and that, especially on a tightly woven fabric, additionally fixes the yarns tightly in the structure so that they cannot readjust to permit free passage of the needle. A level of lubricant of only 0.5–1 per cent is needed but it makes the fibres more mobile within the fabric structure and, in the case of knitted fabrics, enables the yarns from one loop in the fabric to move into the next loop during sewing so as to prevent bursting damage. If a problem such as this is not found until the garment is in production, and if measures such as the slowing down of the machine are unacceptable or ineffective, then it may be necessary to try a lubricant spray on the fabric ahead of the needle. This can give staining problems and, as with attempting additionally to lubricate sewing thread, it is potentially messy while not being nearly as effective as correct lubrication of the material beforehand. In an emergency, however, it may help.

The only real solution to the problems of mechanical damage is that all sample lengths of fabric should be tested for sewability, that any necessary finishes should be specified before the bulk fabric is ordered, and that bulk fabric should be tested before production to ensure that finishing treatments have been effective. Tests for sewability should be incorporated into the same testing programme which checks such properties as shrinkage and colour fastness. Unfortunately this assumes that materials are ordered other than from stock and that while the materials are being made these treatments can be included. In fashion manufacturing where purchasing is usually from stock and lead time is short many problems of sewability can arise. In high volume bulk production where the highest standards of seaming are required, there is usually time to get these matters right provided there is concern to do so.

(b) Needle heating damage

Needle heating occurs as a result of friction between the needle and the fabric being sewn. In high speed sewing of dense materials temperatures as high as 300° or even 350°C can be reached. At these temperatures it is possible that the needle may suffer damage and lose its hardness. Natural fibres in a fabric or thread can withstand these temperatures for a short time without serious effect although some finishes or coatings may melt and spread to the needle surfaces, increasing friction, and thereby producing higher temperatures. With synthetic fibres the position is more critical since PVC fibres melt at around 100°C, polyamide and polyester soften at about 230°C and polyacrylics will only withstand temperatures up to about 280°C.

Overheated needles can therefore soften the synthetic fibres in a fabric, weakening them and producing rough seams with harsh stitch holes. Melted fibres stick to the surface of the needle, increasing its friction and clogging the eye and grooves so that eventually no thread will sew because of breakage or skipped stitches. Before this state is reached, damage to the sewing thread by melting or abrasion may have produced weak seams.

Different approaches to the problem of needle heating are possible, namely preventing the heating occurring, cooling down the needle as it heats, and preventing the heated needle from damaging the fabric or thread.

Since the heating is the result of friction, reducing the heating requires reducing the friction. One method is simply to reduce the sewing speed, but, as was the case with mechanical damage, this is unpopular because of its effect on production. Reduction of friction can also be achieved by either changing the shape or surface of the needle or by changing the material it rubs against. Needles were described earlier which have a reinforced shoulder area and a bulged eye, both of which open up the needle hole in the fabric to allow freer passage of the main part of the needle blade. The extent to which the blade is reinforced is limited by the size of needle hole which is acceptable, since it can give a poor appearance in fine fabrics. The amount of reinforcement normally used enables an increase in stitches per minute sewing rate of 15–20 per cent above that which could be used with an ordinary needle without causing damage. The application of a roughened surface to the needle has also been found to reduce friction and heat development and also to resist the accumulation of any melted debris that does form. In fabric terms, there is the same need that there is with mechanical damage to enable the yarns to move away from the needle easily and the application of a lubricant to the fabric is again the answer. The length of seam sewn in a garment also has an effect on the temperatures built up in the needle. If long seams are sewn, high temperatures will be generated and if there are only short time intervals between seams there will not be much opportunity for the needle to cool down. By contrast, short seams such as shoulder seams can be sewn at high speed without so much build-up of heat.

In order to cool down the needle, if it is accepted that heating is inevitable, by far the most effective method is the direction of a jet of compressed air down it. This may be from a separate compressed air line if the factory has one, or by means of a small piston acting within the needle bar. Temperature reductions of as much as 70°C have been found to be possible. With a separate air line, it should be set up so that air is only blown when the machine is actually stitching. This will reduce the cost in terms of compressed air and also reduce the potential annoyance to operators for whom the air jet can be uncomfortable.

The sewing thread has a part to play in needle cooling with spun or corespun threads being the most effective. All threads cool the needle to some extent but if there are fibres on the surface they carry cooling air past the needle and also transfer more lubricant to the needle surface. If a thread break occurs for any reason there is an immediate rise in needle temperature and if sewing conditions are near to, but not quite critical, this hotter needle may produce damaged holes. Thus a section of fabric may become damaged in the distance it takes the operator to notice that the needle thread has broken and stop the machine. If the needle has picked up any molten fibres from the fabric at the same time, when the needle is rethreaded these deposits will produce higher needle temperatures and damage will continue until a new needle is fitted.

In terms of preventing the heated needle from damaging the fabric or thread, there is not a great deal than can be done to protect the fabric, the main action being needed in the areas already described. To protect the thread from damage, the use of corespun threads with a cotton covering ensures that the synthetic part of the thread is not exposed to the heat of the needle. As has already been explained, the development in thread lubricants is such that all threads, including those which are 100 per cent synthetic, have much greater resistance to high temperatures than they used to and the choice of threads which will not suffer from needle heating damage is now much wider. Needle heating can occur with any fibre type but it is, of course, only a problem with synthetics. Thus many natural fibre fabrics are sewn without risk of damage to the fabric but they are in many cases sewn with synthetic or corespun threads in order to achieve the necessary seam strength and minimising of pucker which these provide. Care must therefore be taken over thread selection and needle cooling so that no loss in strength occurs in the seams as a result of damaged thread. The production of jeans in cotton fabrics is typical of a situation where high speed machines are used on a natural fibre fabric and where considerable needle heat can be generated, particularly on the long seams. Corespun threads are normally used to achieve both strength and heat resistance.

The problems of fabrics becoming damaged during stitching have been described in detail here because the possibility of fabric damage is always present and it is essential to know how to overcome it. Even more, it is essential to investigate fabrics prior to production to find out if damage is likely with that particular fabric. However, it should be said that the practical problems of damage experienced in sewing factories are not nearly as great as they used to be. Improvements in fabric finishes have made a great contribution to improved sewability, especially where needle heating is concerned, as have improved needles and threads, and whereas some years ago it was normal for many factories to have cooling air lines on virtually all their machines, many engineers find nowadays that it is rarely necessary.

Testing for sewability and tailorability

The question of testing materials prior to production for what is termed tailorability, largely pucker, and for sewability, i.e. mechanical damage and needle heating damage, has been mentioned several times. Testing for such properties should be as automatic as testing for other aspects of materials' performance which will affect a garment during making up, wearing and cleaning but it is not often so. This is why time has to be devoted to palliative measures in the face of these problems when they are found to be occurring with garments that are already in production. There are two instruments which have been available for some years for investigating sewability and two more recent instruments which have been developed to investigate tailorability.

(a) Sewability testing The Hatra Sew is used in conjunction with a sewing machine and it measures the temperature reached in the sewing machine needle when sewing a particular fabric, making use of an infrared detection device.

The L & M Sewability Tester operates independently of a sewing machine and measures the force required to push a needle through a fabric.

Both instruments enable the information obtained to be related to actual damage experienced during manufacture. Other test methods have been developed by companies for their own use. These involve sewing a piece of the test fabric with a specified machine, needle size and type, at a specified speed, through a specified number of thicknesses in a particular shape which includes sewing in various directions on the sample. The sample is then inspected closely for damage.

(b) Tailorability testing The Kawabata Evaluation System for fabrics (KES-f) was originally designed to measure a range of mechanical and physical properties of fabrics which were related to the handle of a fabric. The system consists of four instruments which between them measure the tensile, shear, compression, bending and surface properties of fabrics. Recent research has shown that these properties can also be used to predict how easily the fabric will make up into a garment, i.e. the 'tailorability' of the fabric. Based on prior experience on the factory floor, control charts are constructed which indicate the allowable limits for each of the mechanical properties before problems arise in cutting, sewing, pressing or in garment appearance. This equipment costs several tens of thousands of pounds and requires skilled technicians to use it.

The FAST equipment (Fabric Assurance by Simple Testing) was developed by CSIRO in Australia specifically to measure the mechanical properties of woollen and worsted fabrics which were relevant to tailorability. The system consists of three instruments to measure tensile, shear, bending and compressive properties of fabrics. A simple test for the dimensional stability of the fabric is also included. The results are plotted on a chart similar to that used for the KES-f instruments, with upper and lower limits marked for each property. Fabrics whose properties lie within these limits should make up into garments without any problems. Where a fabric property falls outside a particular limit, the chart indicates the nature of the assembly problems that are likely to occur – for example, difficulty in setting sleeves or difficulty in obtaining satisfactory pleating. The FAST equipment can be obtained for about £15,000 and it is gaining increasing acceptance as a tool for assessing fabrics prior to manufacture.

The terms sewability and tailorability have been used here in the sense given above but it should be noted that researchers in this field do use the terms somewhat interchangeably, and especially use the term tailorability to cover broader issues of general garment appearance.

4

Sewing Machinery

The sewing machine types used in clothing manufacture can be classified into the following levels, with the quantity of machines in commercial use decreasing rapidly from the first level to the last.

(a) Basic sewing machines

These are of the types already studied under the subject of stitch formation. They consist of several elements: a stand, table, electric motor, a head normally offering one stitch type, a bed of various shapes and the means for the operator to control the speed of sewing, stitch density and presser foot position. A large number of additions are available for these machines in the way of work aids and attachments which can relieve the operator of some of the handling associated with sewing operations. Microprocessor systems are increasingly being applied to these machines to enable such things as presser foot lift, backtack, thread trim, fullness and numbers of stitches to be preset and controlled automatically.

(b) Simple automatics

Here the machine is usually cam-controlled, producing only one configuration of sewing. Examples of these are buttonholers, button sewers, bar tack machines, and label sewers. The shape of the sewing line is determined by the machine, hence achieving consistency, but the operator must still carry out all the handling both before and after sewing.

(c) Mechanised workplaces

These carry out many complex functions in addition to sewing. They make use of electric, electronic and pneumatic control and incorporate sophisticated conveyor and clamp technology. Examples are patch pocket setting on jeans and shirts, run stitching collars or flaps, long seam joining, making jetted pockets, serging trousers and sequential buttonholing. The operator still loads the machine and may remove the garment part after sewing but the machine controls the rest of the handling and all of the sewing. The operator is able to undertake various handling activities, depending on the type of machine, during the sewing cycle. Thus handling time is incorporated into sewing time and the machine utilisation can rise from the 20 per cent that is typical of a basic sewing machine to as much as 80 per cent. Each machine carries out one basic conformation of sewing but size or shape of, for example, collar or patch pocket, can be altered for different sizes and styles.

(d) Transfer lines

Here garment parts are loaded and a series of machines carries out a series of operations to a section of a garment. A current prototype assembles a three-part jeans pocket. This level of mechanisation, apart from sophisticated handling devices, requires extreme consistency of material characteristics and shape and extreme reliability of operation by the machines in the line. Transfer lines are not yet in commercial use for clothing operations. They will be discussed in the last chapter.

Each succeeding level in the classification means a large increase in capital cost, hence a large increase in the output necessary to sustain it. It also means a corresponding decrease in flexibility, because the machines produce one basic form of stitching, with few variations. The more variations the higher the cost. Only in the last few years has there been an attempt to develop 'flexible automation' through the adaptation of robotic devices to control the limp fabrics. These are only slowly coming into commercial use.

BASIC SEWING MACHINES AND ASSOCIATED WORK AIDS

The sewing mechanism of the lockstitch machine has already been discussed, along with the actual stitch formation of lockstitch and single- and two-thread chainstitch in their simplest forms. The extent to which the operator is responsible for everything the machine does and the quality of the work it produces has also been stated, along with the unacceptably low figure of 20 per cent as the average time one of these machines is actually sewing during a working day. The main purpose of this section is to study the variations which exist in the machines and the types of additions which can be made to them in order to speed up production and control quality standards.

Sewing machine shapes

In fashion manufacture the machines are still predominantly used in their basic forms but, for more specialised garments and those made in higher volume, variations in machine shape are available which enable easier movement of the materials around the machine. These variations primarily affect the shape of the bed of the machine, i.e. the part on which the materials rest. The best known version is the flat bed and the main alternatives are cylinder bed, post bed and feed-off-the-arm. The blind felling machine sewing stitch type 103 is also a special shape, as are the overedge machines which have no fabric space to the right of the needle. These are illustrated in Figure 4.1. Shapes (i) to (iii) occur in lockstitch and chainstitch machines, (iv) normally only in chainstitch.

The flat bed is used in the majority of sewing where a large and open garment part can easily be handled past the needle. It provides a suitable surface for much flat sewing and also facilitates the use of markers to control the position of garment parts, for example, a patch pocket on a shirt front. Cylinder and post bed are used where the parts to be sewn are

Fig. 4.1. Machine bed types. (i) Flat bed. (ii) Cylinder bed. (iii) Post bed. (iv) Feed-off-the-arm. (v) Blind stitch. (vi) Overedge.

small, curved or otherwise awkward in shape, a particularly common situation in sewing footwear. The feed-off-the-arm machine is used where a lapped seam has to be closed in such a way that the garment part becomes a tube. They are common in jeans production where the outside leg seam is normally the type known as lap-felled and it is joined after the inside leg seam in the sequence of construction. The operator wraps the part to be sewn around the machine bed and it is fed away from her, off the end of the bed, as she sews.

The requirements for work aids

The additions which can be made to basic sewing machines are many and they come under the general term *work aids*. The typical sewing operation has been analysed into the stages of separate and pick up, orientate, mate, control through sewing and dispose. The term handling is normally used to describe those of these elements that are not sewing and it is this handling, along with that of dealing with garment bundles where they exist, plus various aspects of machine attention and personal needs, that make up 80 per cent of the time spent working by most sewing machinists. In the search for improvements in the ratio of time spent sewing to time spent handling, some elements of the sewing operation offer more scope than others. Thus the nature of clothing materials makes the stage of separate and pick up difficult because the materials are limp and they slip or cling. What is difficult for a machinist is, in this case, also difficult to mechanise. Orientate, mate and control through sewing are greatly slowed in some operations because of the need to pause repeatedly to realign the parts or to fold them into position. Disposal may include severing the sewing thread as well as stacking the garment part. Sometimes threads must be cut close for neatness while on other occasions a stitch type requires an end to be left. The stacking of completed parts by one operator not only takes time but may affect the next operator as well.

Slowness, however, is not the only problem. While machinists are matching up fabric edges in order to sew them together to the correct width or turning up double rolled hems, not only are they working slowly but they are also trying to achieve the required quality standard in their work. Depending on the standards required in relation to the operators' level of skill and the nature of the fabric and the sewing operation, this will in some cases be very difficult. Achieving accurately controlled stitching at speed with operators without a high level of skill is greatly to be desired. A further drive for economy arises from the fact that there are some seam constructions where the final effect can be achieved in more than one way, typically in several stages of sewing with perhaps some pressing in between, or in just one stage by using a device that folds the fabric, along with a multi-needle machine. Finally, in this justification of machinery development, machinists are required to change the operation that they do from time to time, and it is in the interests of efficient production that they are quickly able to gain proficiency in the new operation. Thus machinery is needed which will minimise the training time required on a new operation but without that machinery being too restricted in its flexibility.

All these factors point to the need for work aids in as many applications as possible in relation to the use of conventional sewing machines. Work aids are devices which are built into machines, added to them afterwards, attached alongside or made use of in whatever ways a resourceful engineer can devise to improve productivity, improve or maintain quality standards, reduce training time and minimise fatigue for the operator. In some cases it is difficult to distinguish a work aid defined in this way from aspects of machinery which are an accepted part of modern development such as microprocessor control. It is not proposed to be too pedantic in this matter, simply to indicate the opportunities that are available for the application of technology. If a broad enough definition of work aid is used, it will be seen later that certain types of interlinings can even be included, rather than it being a name reserved solely for machinery. It will probably long remain the case that garments made for the fashion market will be made with the minimum of additions to the basic sewing machine so as to maintain maximum flexibility of style while those made in high volume in limited styles will make use of every device available.

Types of work aid

The work aids that are used during sewing operations can be categorised in a number of different ways and they vary in the aspects of their overall purpose that they emphasise. Some offer greatly increased speed of working in a situation where quality is already satisfactory. Others give very little improvement in productivity but great accuracy of sewing. In terms of their function the commonest ones are used for guiding or folding materials, for trimming threads and other components from garments and for stacking the work after sewing. Least common are those which assist the initial picking up of the parts to be sewn. In terms of their method of working some are purely mechanical, some operate pneumatically, some are photo-electric and some are electronic. Some are built into the machine such as a special motor, some are a variation of a normal machine part such as a special presser foot, and some are a completely separate added part.

Guides are used where sewing must take place in a certain position on a garment, usually a certain distance from a raw edge as in a conventional superimposed seam, where a narrow item such as a lace or braid must be correctly positioned on a garment and where one garment part must be correctly placed on another such as a patch pocket on a shirt, skirt or pair of trousers.

In their simplest form they are *edge guides*, forming some kind of physical barrier to the edges of the fabric being joined together. Instead of

Fig. 4.2. Edge guides. (i) Straight. (ii) Curved.

the operator having to match two fabric edges together and sew the correct distance from that edge by eye, an upright section of metal is screwed to the machine bed and each of the fabric edges is butted up to it. For accuracy on a sharply curved seam the edge guide can also be curved. Examples are shown in Figure 4.2.

Edge guides enable seams of accurate width to be sewn, giving more accurate garment sizing and allowing the operator to work faster. On an overedge machine an edge guide can be set so that the amount trimmed off by the trimming knife is that intended by the pattern cutter rather than an amount which will cause the garment to be too large or too small. In some sewing situations it is important for the neatness of the finished garment that the seam turnings contained within it are uniform in width and without frayed edges. An example would be the outer edge of a tailored jacket, where the facing is joined to the main garment. Such neatness may not be achievable by an edge guide alone if the edges have frayed during handling of the garment parts. Lockstitch machines are available with a trimming knife attached which trims the seam turning during sewing to an even width which is narrower than could be sewn but which will give the correct amount of bulk in the finished garment.

The function of edge guiding can be performed in some circumstances by a special presser foot called a *compensating foot*. In general, presser feet can be used as specialised work aids, in addition to their normal function of holding the materials against the feed dog, when the scale of the situation is within the small size of the foot. Thus an edge guide to give a line of stitches at 2 cm from a fabric edge can only be a separate guide attached to the machine bed. Where the requirement is to sew at 1 or 2 or 5 mm from an edge, such as when topstitching a shirt collar, the guide can be contained within the presser foot which is able to carry out its normal function as well. The compensating foot comes in a variety of forms according to the configuration being sewn and the width of stitching needed but the basic principle is of one or more fixed toes and one or more which can move up and down vertically on a spring. Two types are illustrated in Figure 4.3. The one on the left could be used for

Fig. 4.3. Compensating feet.

(i)   (ii)

(iii)

Fig. 4.4. Applications of compensating feet (i) Topstitching a seam. (ii) Closing down a shirt collar. (iii) Sink stitching to close a waistband.

topstitching a shirt collar at 5 mm from the edge, the one on the right at 1 mm from the edge.

A compensating foot can be used in any situation where there is a difference in height to the left and right of an edge and stitching is required a specific distance from that edge. Thus they are not only used for topstitching round garment edges, where there is fabric to one side only of the edge, but they are also used for attaching and for topstitching patch pockets and topstitching raised seams which have been created by turning the seam allowance to one side. These could be such things as topstitching a lengthwise seam on a skirt or pair of trousers or the lower edge of a waistband. A conventional edge guide cannot be used in these circumstances as there is no exposed edge of garment for it to run up against. In addition they are used for closing seams such as the inside of a shirt collar or the lower edge of a waistband where sink stitching is required. Diagrams of these seams are shown in Figure 4.4.

The stitching known as sink stitching is shown in Figure 4.4(iii). As its name implies it is stitching which sinks in under a turned edge of fabric. It is also referred to as stitching in the seam shadow. Accurately sewn, it is almost invisible.

In some circumstances an operator can make use of a combination of a compensating foot and an edge guide. When a garment style requires two rows of topstitching round the edges, such as on a raincoat sewn at 1 mm and 6 mm from the edge, this could be done on a twin needle machine. However, if there are any corners to be turned the machine must be equipped with a split needle bar whereby, at the touch of a lever, the two needles are separated and the outside one sews round the corner while the inside one remains stationary until they are level again. This machine would use a compensating foot on its own but if a twin needle machine in the split needle bar version is not available, the sewing would have to be done in two stages, using a compensating foot for the outside row and an ordinary edge guide for the row which is further from the edge.

In all these instances the operator is able to work quickly and accurately as far as the actual sewing is concerned and skill can be concentrated on aspects of the job which it is less easy to mechanise. If a particular sewing operation includes some stitching where there is not any difference in height to the right and left of an edge the presence of the compensating foot does not present any problems since the spring on the lower toe enables it to be used equally well with all the toes on the same level.

Other types of *specialised presser feet* can also be used in guiding situations. If a piping has to be attached to a garment in the manner shown in Figure 3.6, a specially shaped foot will control the position of the piping in relation to the needle so that the stitching is always close to the piping. When sewing zips into garments the stitching must often be closer to the teeth of the zip than a standard presser foot would allow. A half foot enables this to happen, or alternatively two very narrow toes give the same result but with improved fabric control. These feet are illustrated in Figure 4.5.

In the special case of setting an invisible zip, used frequently in ladies' wear to give a neat and unobtrusive fastening, a specially shaped presser foot is essential. On these zips the teeth are turned inwards and join together on the inside of the garment. If the seam is not to gape on the outside the fabric must be sewn very close to these teeth. The zip is attached unfastened from the inside and the special foot rolls the teeth upright as shown in Figure 4.6, giving the seam type indicated. The stitching can only go as far as the opened slider at the bottom of the zip and the zip is sewn in before the seam is joined. When the seam is joined at a later stage, the stitching overlaps the zip stitching by about 1 cm and a half foot is used so that the stitching can be as close in as possible. Since the zip cannot be sewn in right to the bottom, and the stitching of the seam then overlaps this stitching, there is a loss in operating length of these zips and they require to be at least 2 cm longer than conventional zips. The spare length of zip at the lower end is secured by sewing the zip tape to the seam turning on each side. The advantage of invisible zips lies not just in their appearance but in the simpler handling and hence lower level of skill required to attach them compared with a conventional zip.

Yet another type of edge guide can be used to ensure an accurate stitch

Fig. 4.5. Special presser feet. (i) Piping foot. (ii) Half zip foot. (iii) Narrow toed zip foot.

Fig. 4.6. Invisible zips. (i) Presser foot for invisible zips. (ii) Seam diagram as sewn. (iii) Seam diagram as worn.

Fig. 4.7. Stitching jig for sewing a pair of pocket flaps.

line in relation to an edge of fused interlining in a garment part. In the sewing of shirt collars, an accurate collar shape is required and the best appearance is obtained if the stitch line is uniformly close to the edge of the interlining without actually sewing through it. Interlinings can be cut very accurately using dies and the use of the outer edge of the interlining as a stitching guide gives the correct sewing line. The device which enables this to be done is a small toothed wheel alongside the presser foot with which the operator follows the edge of the interlining.

Another type of work aid which is in wide use where accurate stitching lines are required is the *stitching jig*. Using an edge guide to achieve accurate sewing assumes accurate cutting and for many garment parts this cannot be adequately achieved. Collars must have two identical points, patch pockets, cuffs and other small items such as epaulettes and tabs must be perfect pairs and revers and front edges of formal jackets and raincoats must match. The only way to ensure this where die cutting is not possible is to control the sewing line in relation to the pattern shape of the garment rather than the edge of the cut material and this is what stitching jigs achieve. The simplest type is illustrated in Figure 4.7. It shows a jig for sewing a pair of pocket flaps.

The jig consists of two layers of a rigid material such as aluminium or plastic which are joined together by a hinge. A slot is cut out of both layers of material which conforms to the exact sewing line of the garment part and the bottom layer carries a shaped guide close to the hinge to which the edges of the garment parts are aligned. This would be the neck edge in the case of a collar. The lower section is normally also covered with a non-slip material so that the fabric plies are firmly held. The two pieces of the garment part are laid into the jig, along with the interlining if a sew-in interlining is being used, and the jig is closed to hold them firmly. If fullness is needed on the top ply to give a piped effect on a part such as a pocket flap, a fulling bar would be included in the jig between the two plies. This ensures the inclusion of extra length in the top ply so that the lining cannot show on the right side of the finished part. The operator then sews round the slot on a machine with a specially adapted presser foot and feed dog. There is no conventional feeding system as the operator needs to move the jig in every direction while sewing. The lack of a feeding system also means that there is no control over stitch size other than the rate at which the operator handles the jig past the needle.

Careful training and control are required if stitches of lengths of 5 mm or more are not to occur on the longer edges of a garment part. Another disadvantage of the jig as a work aid is that a larger seam allowance round the outside of the garment part is needed so that the fabric edge does not become pushed down into the stitching slot but remains firmly held during sewing. This extra fabric is costly and it must be trimmed off, often by hand, afterwards. An advantage may be that the outer edge of the collar need not be accurately cut. The use of hand-controlled stitching jigs such as those described here achieves quality rather than productivity. Separate jigs are needed for every style and size and consequently they are only used for long production runs. A minor change of pattern shape can require a costly new set of jigs. As will be seen later, the process can be fully automated to give greater improvements in productivity as well as quality.

Another situation where a guide is needed is when a lace or braid or binding is attached to a garment part. It is not usually satisfactory for the operator to unroll the reel on which the material is wound and then lay the material freehand onto the garment as it would be impossible to position it accurately. In this instance a guiding system usually known as a *rack guide* is needed in addition to the edge guide which will still be needed to obtain the correct position for the fabric. The rack guide ensures that a material of narrow width is presented flat to the needle and in a position such that the stitching will be in the correct place on it. It usually consists of a series of linked bars the width of the trim to be attached and, if the trim is being attached on top of the garment fabric, it is mounted above the presser foot and carries the trim downwards from a reel mounted above the machine. If the trim is being attached below the garment fabric, the reel would be mounted below the machine table and then carried up onto the machine table and through a series of bars to the presser foot. Where bias trim in the form of a binding is attached to a garment it is normally fed in at right angles in the manner shown in Figure 3.43. If a ribbon is being attached to a garment it is likely that a twin-needle machine, either lockstitch or chainstitch, would be used and the guide would ensure that the ribbon was presented centrally between the needles. If a lace is being attached by means of a 406 bottom cover stitch the lace would be guided such that the edge of it projected just above the left hand needle and the use of an edge guide as well for the cut edge of the garment part would ensure that the raw edge was maintained between the two needles of the stitch.

The third situation described above where a guide is needed is when one garment part is positioned onto another. When a patch pocket is added to a shirt front there are several ways of ensuring that it is in the correct position but some of them are slow or inaccurate. One method is to drill holes for the pocket corner positions when the material is cut but drill holes frequently occur out of position. Even if they are in the correct position there may be problems in covering them with the pocket corner and its stitching. Another method of positioning pockets is to lay a pattern-shaped template over the garment part and mark the required position with tailor's chalk which melts when pressed or with special ink which shows up under an ultraviolet light which would be placed over the machinist's work area. This kind of marking is extremely time-consuming though virtually unavoidable in circumstances such as the positioning of buttons and buttonholes on double-breasted garments.

For a shirt front, a skirt panel or a trouser back where the pocket is normally attached to the flat garment part, guides can be set up on the machine bed for the position of the part to which the pocket is being attached. These are really edge guides, though often far removed from the needle, and at least two would be needed so that the part is correctly positioned in two dimensions. The guides would be made of a material such as Perspex and they would be a few millimetres thick, enough to form a barrier edge to the fabric but not so high as to be in the way of the rest of the sewing. Once the garment panel has been positioned, the pocket is then correctly placed by putting the top right hand corner under the point of the needle.

If the pocket is being sewn parallel to a garment edge as it would be on a shirt it is usually possible for the operator to set the pocket straight by eye. If there is no such reference as there would not be on the back of a pair of jeans, there can be a further guide on the bed of the machine which the operator can feel through the thickness of the fabric, and match up with the centre back seam. The machine would be fitted with a compensating foot to determine the stitching width on the pocket itself. A guide system for a shirt pocket is shown in Figure 4.8.

Once a flexible attitude is developed towards the use of guides, a great variety of possibilities can be seen in a variety of sewing situations, especially where positioning is needed well away from the garment edge. To give just one more example, if a seam is being joined in which an opening must be left of the right length for the insertion of a zip, a guide the correct distance behind the needle, to which the edges of the garment part are put, will ensure that sewing commences the necessary distance down the garment. A second edge guide will, of course, also be needed to ensure correct seam width.

Where garment parts must be positioned without reference to outside edges, increasing use is being made of *lights as guiding systems*. On both sewing and pressing equipment, narrow beam light sources can be set up so that the garment part is positioned with a seam or a dart aligned with the light markings. For very accurate location, fibre optics can give very fine points of light. In some cases where the marking of garments using a

Fig. 4.8. Guides for positioning a shirt pocket.

template is unavoidable to ensure correct positioning of such things as double-breasted fastenings, if pencil or other visible marks are used they often remain visible on the finished garment. Markers are available which are invisible in ordinary light but which show up under ultraviolet light and such a light over the needle enables the operator to see the position needed.

Folders are used, as their name implies, in situations where fabric must be folded prior to sewing. They vary from the simple fold which could be achieved by an operator alone, though only slowly and perhaps untidily, through to extremely complex combinations of folders which enable constructions to be achieved in a fraction of the number of stages that it would take without the folders, and indeed enable some to be achieved that would not otherwise be possible at all. In most cases they are separate devices attached to the machine except that, in a similar manner to guides, where the scale of the folding job is very small the folder can be contained within the presser foot. Folders are frequently used on machines having more than one needle.

Folders enable great increases in productivity to be achieved along with a high standard of control over the quality of the finish obtained. They are made from highly polished metal over which the material will pass smoothly and they can either be purchased from specialist suppliers or made by skilled factory engineers. They must be made to take particular materials so that they are held firmly enough to remain under control but not so firmly that there is a risk of them jamming. The demand for folders in a company will depend to a large extent on the type of garment they make: lingerie, corsetry and children's dresses offering particular scope for combining economy with decorative effects by their use. Their use is only justified in moderate and high volume production and brings with it its own limitations. Although some folders are easily loaded with fabric and indeed must be loaded afresh with each garment, many add another

(i)

(ii)

Fig. 4.9. Hem folders. (i) Narrow hem folder. (ii) Wider hem folder. (Not to the same scale)

section of material or trim to the garment and are much more quickly used if that section is in continuous form rather than short lengths. Where self-fabric is involved this means that enough garments must be made to make it worth cutting fabric into straight or bias-cut strip on a long roll. It also means that control of colour must be good enough between pieces of cloth that the use of such strip will not introduce shading into garments. The sequence of construction of the garment may also have to be altered since a section of a continuous strip can only be applied from an edge to an edge and not in a circle.

Folders are of many types but can be roughly divided into *those which fold a part of a garment piece*, commonly an edge in a seam of class 6 but not always so, *those which join garment sections together* and *those which add a section of self-fabric or other material to a garment*. The latter type usually create bound seams of class 3 or seams of class 7. In addition many class 8 seams require folders.

Examples of folders which operate on a garment part without any additional materials are shown in Figure 4.9.

The *narrow hem folder* makes a double rolled hem of the type used on scarves and handkerchieves and a folder to make a hem as narrow as this is easily contained within the space of a presser foot. Indeed, since it is a requirement of folders that they keep the materials being sewn under control right up to the needle point, it would be difficult to site a separate folder close enough that such a small hem did not become unrolled before it was sewn. Once a hem as wide as 5 mm is required, a *separate folder* would be needed and this could look like (ii). Many widths of hem can be sewn, up to at least 40 mm but a different folder would be required for each. They could be used on such items as dresses, shirts, skirts and linings and the stitch used would probably be either 301 lockstitch or 103 chainstitch. The use of 401 chainstitch would require that the hem be folded down rather than up which, though possible, is less easy to handle. The nature of the hem may also require back-tacking. On more expensive garments the bulk of a double rolled hem may be unacceptable and in this case the edge would be neatened with overedging and the hem would only be folded up once. A folder would probably still be used although with some materials the operator might handle the garment sufficiently quickly and accurately freehand.

The main concern is that hems often develop a roping or ringing appearance as the fabric twists on being sewn down. This tends to be worse if the hem is wide and particularly if the garment is very flared as there is then more hem edge than the length of garment it is being sewn to and the grain direction changes as the operator sews around the hem. Folders are a great help in achieving good quality hems, especially when used in conjunction with specialised machine feed systems, but in a double rolled hem it may only be possible to obtain a high enough standard if the hem is very narrow. Where a single turned hem such as on a dress is used it may be helpful to ease the fabric slightly onto the overedging by means of a suitable feeding system, before blind felling, so that there is no extra length of fabric in the edge of the hem compared to the part of the garment to which it is being sewn.

Where the garment is open at each end of the hem a fixed folder can be used and the fabric can be introduced to the folder at the beginning and run right through to the end. On many garments, such as shirts and dresses, the beginning and end of the hem is bulky because of the presence of a placket front of some kind. In this case the start of the hem might need to be turned up freehand and a swing out folder of the type shown in Figure 4.9(ii) swung into place after that section had been stitched. This type of folder would also be used where an item such as a lining hem had already been joined into a complete circle by the time the hem was sewn, the starting and finishing points of the hem again being made freehand.

Other hem-type effects which are used on garments which also require folders are those shown in Figure 3.15(iii) and (iv). The first one requires a second row of stitches after being sewn with the folder, the second one is done in one step with a folder and a twin-needle machine. It is common on the buttonhole side of men's shirt fronts but would not be suitable for garments in more bulky materials because of the difference in thickness between the two sides of the placket effect.

Another situation where folders are increasingly used is in the production of shirt collars which give an appearance of being a two-piece

Fig. 4.10. Construction of mock two-piece shirt collar.

collar when they are actually only one-piece. Shirt collars were traditionally constructed from a separate neck band and collar and the additional curvature which could be put into the collar compared with the neck band allowed an extra good fit to be achieved. Such collars are more expensive to construct and are rarely seen nowadays. The joining of the curved shapes is difficult to automate but equipment does exist to join a collar and separate neck band without additional shape along the seam and this is in common use in the production of men's shirts because it still gives a higher quality appearance than a one-piece collar. Women's shirts rarely have a genuine two-piece collar and it is here that the mock two-piece is often seen. The use of special fusible interlinings enables a sewn down pleat, giving the appearance of a seam, to be incorporated into the top collar only. Two types of fusible can be used. One has lines of adhesive resin along the fold lines, the other has slots cut out. Either reduces bulk and enables the collar to be folded easily by the operator where required, to create the pleat. The collar does not, of course, have the shape advantage of a genuine two-piece collar but a good break-line is achieved at moderate cost. The construction is shown in Figure 4.10.

Of the folders which join major garment parts together, the commonest one is that already mentioned for jeans construction, the *lap fell folder*, shown in Figure 4.11.

As stated previously, twin needle 401 machines are used for this seam to avoid problems of bobbin run out. The folder would be used on a flat bed machine or a feed-off-the-arm machine, depending on the configuration of the part of the garment being sewn.

Many folders are available which add further items of self-fabric or other material to a garment and of these, many come into the category known as *binders*. Fabric edges are frequently bound, either as a means of edge neatening or to create a decorative effect or both. Indeed, one of the great advantages of the use of this type of work aid is the scope that is offered for modifying the methods of garment construction so that stitching which is a necessary part of the garment also provides the decorative effects.

Fig. 4.11.   Lap fell seam folder.

The simplest types of bound seam can only be constructed with a material such as a braid which does not have raw edges and a double fold is necessary where self fabric is used. A folder of this type was shown in Figure 3.43, along with its associated rack guide. Most situations require the binding to lie smoothly round a curved fabric edge and for this reason bias cut binding is most often used. While straight cut binding is easy to make, requiring only that a roll of cloth is sectioned off to the required width with a power saw, bias cut strip is initially made by unrolling the cloth, folding it in half and seaming it into a tube. The open end of the tube is then rotated past a knife blade which cuts through one ply at 45 degrees to the grain direction, the bias fabric thus created emerging from the machine at 45 degrees to the original fabric direction to be re-rolled. The re-rolled cloth can then be sliced through to the required width. A result of this procedure is that bias stripping always has joins in it at intervals and there may be problems over the acceptability of these joins, depending upon where they appear on the garment and the requirements of the market for which the garment is being made.

As always, it is necessary that the folder maintains total control of the fabric right up to the point of sewing and with many folders a conventional presser foot would not allow for this. Accordingly, the presser foot and also the feed dog can be cut away to enable better positioning of the folder and these three items together make a package which is needed to sew that particular bound seam. On concave curves the binding is stretched slightly as it is sewn on; on convex curves it is fulled or eased. In all cases the garment part must be fed fully into the folder or the binding may slip off it.

A wider, straight grain version of the type of binding shown in Figure 3.43 is used for waistbands on jeans and on some trousers and skirts. A twin needle machine is used and the seam type achieved is that shown in Figure 3.11(iv). The fabric for the waistband normally has an interlining fused to it, it is cut longer than required and a number are joined in a long length, often by fusing them to a continuous strip of interlining, to avoid repeatedly loading the folder. Twin needle 401 chainstitching both attaches and topstitches the waistband but the speed and quality advantages of this method of construction are to some extent offset by the fact that the ends must be turned in and sewn down separately. This separate operation can be facilitated by a compressed air jet which can be activated during the binding operation to blow the needle thread away from the looper so that there is a short gap in the stitching at each end of the waistband. Without this extra work aid, the stitching must be unpicked sufficiently to allow the ends to be tucked in. Apart from the time this would take, it could lead to insecure stitching at the finishing end.

Other common types of bound seam are those which were shown in Figure 3.11(i), (ii) and (iii) when discussing seam constructions. These also require fabric to be cut into long strips but as they are always constructed in knitted fabrics for underwear type garments, the fabric has adequate stretch when cut straight across in the course direction. More than one folder may have to be put together to achieve these seams.

The type of fabric folding which the bias binder achieves is similar to that used on single sections of fabric to make items such as belts. Two possibilities for belts were shown in Figure 3.18(ii) and (iii). In (ii), the belt must be seamed inside out with a space left in the stitching for it to be turned through to the right side. Pressing it is then slow and difficult and following that it must be topstitched. If the seam is offset slightly as in (iii), the main part of the belt can be run through a folder after the ends have been bagged out. A swing out folder would be needed. Not only is this quicker to sew but the pressing of the finished and topstitched belt is quick and easy compared with one which has been totally bagged out. If the topstitching is not to be on the edge of the belt, the seam must be offset. If there are to be four rows of stitching on the belt the seam could remain on the edge. With lower priced garments it may be acceptable to make a belt where the ends are not bagged out but are just turned back and sewn down. The belt could then be run through the folder from end to end.

A commonly used seam from class 8 is the lengthwise fold of fabric which makes a belt loop for jeans, raincoats etc. Folders are available for use on stitch type 406 bottom cover machines which not only fold the fabric to the required shape but which can accept scrap pieces of fabric of various shapes and widths. A pair of cutting knives in front of the folder trims off waste fabric so that the folder is presented with the correct width. The operator feeds successive pieces of fabric into the folder with a small overlap when a join is needed. When the belt loops have been cut to length, any which contain a join are thrown away.

The examples given here of folders, combined with machines of particular stitch types and numbers of needles, are just a sample of the opportunities available to construct garments quickly and accurately, provided enough of the style is to be made to justify the purchase of the necessary equipment. In small volume manufacturing garments will be made in many more stages with many separate rows of sewing and a need for much more pressing. Thus the actual methods of construction of apparently similar garments may vary a great deal according to the quantity of a style that is made.

Slack feeding and elastication

The work aids described so far are static, mechanical devices. The only movement that occurs is the simple motion of the swing out folder, moved by the operator as needed. Most of the other work aids to be studied are dynamic and the next ones which must be considered are those which help supply materials to the needle point. Rack guides have already been mentioned but supplying lace or braid in a flat state to the needle or to a folder is not the only requirement. Many braids are slightly stretchy and in order to roll them onto some kind of reel they will have been put under some tension. If this tension is not allowed to relax, it will be sewn into the garment and relax and cause pucker later. Such materials are often just pulled off the reel and left to relax but tension may again be introduced into them as they are pulled by the machine or the operator into a rack guide.

The device known as a slack feeder enables narrow materials to be presented to the needle point in a completely relaxed state. The device consists of a small motor and a set of rollers through which the material passes. From the rollers, the material hangs in a long, slack, loop down to the sewing machine. A small tension on this loop, such as occurs when all the slack has been sewn onto the garment, causes the motor to drive a further section of material through the rollers and this then hangs in a relaxed state ready to be sewn.

Many other items are added to garments which are deliberately highly elastic such as the stretch braids, laces and plain elastics which are used a great deal in lingerie and corsetry. Although in the past elastic was inserted into a casing sewn to the garment, nowadays it is almost always sewn to the fabric in a stretched state, all along its length, giving uniform gathering all round the garment. Some method must be adopted which will stretch the elastic by just the right amount so that the garment part will have the correct relaxed and stretched sizes. Several different ways are available to generate this stretch. The simplest is by means of a screw-down bar which clamps the elastic a short distance before it arrives at the needle. It is held stretched from the clamp to the point of sewing and relaxes and draws up the garment immediately behind the needle. The screws are adjusted until the correct measurements, both stretched and relaxed, of the garment part being sewn are achieved.

Another method consists of a set of metering rollers in front of the needle, driven from the machine and metering out the right amount of elastic for each revolution of the machine, with a puller feed behind. The elastic is maintained in a stretched state between the rollers and the puller feed and the fabric is sewn flat to it while it is in this state. This method is frequently used for wide elastics sewn down with four needles such as are used in the waists of pyjama trousers and short, casual jackets. Fabric can be folded round the elastic by means of a folder if necessary.

The methods described so far for stretching elastic can only provide the same amount of stretch all along and can only be used when sewing from one edge of a garment to another rather than round in a circle. Computer-controlled methods are available now which will allow both intermittent elastication and sewing in a circle, thus allowing much greater flexibility of both design and construction methods of garments. For intermittent elastication, an electronic motor is used which can either be pre-programmed or it can be operated by the machinist using a knee press. When elastication is required, the motor meters the elastic to give the right amount of stretch. When a flat section, i.e. no elastication, is required the motor speeds up and runs in enough of the elastic material that there is no stretch in it at all. A typical use would be in the waistband of sports shorts and in the non-elasticated sections, the unstretched elastic would act like an ordinary waistband interlining.

Cutting of threads, elastic, tapes, etc.

When the sewing of a seam has been completed, the machinist needs some means of separating the work from the machine, preferably without the time-consuming act of picking up a pair of scissors and cutting it away. In a limited number of instances, the operator 'chains off' the parts, that is, sews continuously from one to the next and leaves them joined by the thread, to be cut apart later with scissors or even presented to the next operator in a ready-to-sew form. In the majority of cases, however, the threads must either be cut close, normally the case with lockstitch sewing, so that the garment is neatly finished and so that thread ends are not sewn into subsequent stitching, or else a safe length of end must be left, usually at least 1 cm in the case of the various chainstitches. In many factories thread ends are left on all the stitching at the time of sewing and those which have not been subsequently sewn across and trimmed off by the time the garment is finished will be hand-trimmed at final inspection. This is time-consuming and some of the ends may be visible but difficult to remove and, given that the machinist has to separate the material from the machine anyway, it is better if it can be done in the minimum of time and with the correct length of thread left.

A simple method which may be used on lockstitch machines is a metal edge behind the needle bar which is sufficiently sharp that a thread pulled tight across it by the machinist will be cut. It is quicker to use than scissors but the thread ends will vary in length. It would not be suitable for use with chainstitching as the pull that is required to sever the threads would be too great and might cause them to unravel.

Among the more complex systems are several which provide for a knife to cut the thread behind the presser foot and these are available for most machine types. The actual knife operation is pneumatic, i.e. by means of compressed air, the use of which will be described later. The differences between them are largely in their method of activation which can be a knee press operated by the machinist when the material has passed beyond the knife or a photo-electric or infra-red detector which senses the presence or absence of fabric. During the time that the material is being sewn, the sensor on the bed of the machine is covered and the knife inactive. When the edge of the garment part is reached, the sensor is uncovered and the knife cuts the thread. Suitable knives can be used which will cut through reinforcing tape, elastic or other materials if necessary. Such cutters, often known as impact cutters, not only save time but also materials.

On lockstitch machines, the most satisfactory thread trimming mechanism is the one known as an underbed thread trimmer which is usually combined with another work aid which is a needle positioner motor. The underbed thread trimmer severs the threads below the machine throat plate and no thread ends show on the top side of the stitching. It is activated by the operator 'heeling back' on the treadle controlling the machine. The needle positioner motor operates such that each time the machinist stops without activating the thread cutter, the machine stops with the needle in the down position. This enables corners to be turned or work to be readjusted before continuing sewing. When the thread cutter is activated, the needle is automatically raised. The savings in time for the sewing operator are considerable and there are no threads to be trimmed at a later stage. Machines must be purchased with the needle positioning and underbed thread trimming facility already fitted but the extra cost is well worth it and they are increasingly common in all sections of the industry.

It is perhaps appropriate at this stage to mention another time-saving device related to thread trimming and that is the *latch-back device* used on overedge machines. In the construction of the kinds of leisurewear and underwear made from lightweight knitted fabrics that can be overedged together, it is not always possible to sew across every seam to secure the chain end of thread from that seam. They cannot be trimmed close or the seam will unravel and in many cases there is no alternative to a separate lockstitch tack or bar tack securing the thread chain to the seam turning just before the end of the seam. This is time-consuming and could be avoided if the thread chain could be secured as part of the seam. A device known as a latch-back is available which is able to secure the thread at the starting end of the seam. More than one version exists and they begin operation at the end of the previous piece of sewn work.

At the same time as a chain end is left on the end of the previous seam that was sewn, one is also left extending away from the operator from the chaining off finger on the machine. This will be the starting-end chain end on the new seam. In one system, a jet of compressed air blows the chain towards the operator and, as she begins to sew the new seam, the thread chain is laid along under the looper threads of the new seam. This is sufficiently secure and no further tack is needed. In many cases the sequence of construction of a garment can be arranged so that all seam ends are either latched-back or sewn across. An example would be a tee shirt where the side seam and the sleeve seam were each sewn from the

Fig. 4.12. Start and finish latch back on an overedged seam, stitch type 504.

hem edge which could then be latch-backed and the setting of the sleeve on the round was used to secure the other end of both seams.

Latch-back devices for the starting ends of seams have been available for some time but more recently it has become possible to latch-back the finishing end as well. In this case an accurate sensing device detects the end of the seam and stops the machine immediately. The operator turns the garment part over and sews a short distance back along the seam. Correctly set up, no loop of thread is left at the turn. The appearance of the starting and finishing latch back on an overedged seam is shown in Figure 4.12.

Another work aid of the cutting variety is that used to cut items such as belt loops to the required length. Separate machines have long been available which can take a reel of any such narrow material and cut it into the necessary short lengths, heat sealing the ends where appropriate on a synthetic material. More recently developed is the means to determine the lengths of sewn seam by microprocessor-controlled stitch counting rather than physically measuring the length. In a machine such as the one described earlier where random pieces of denim are fed past trimming knives to a folder making belt loops for jeans, it is possible to equip the machine with a *stitch counter operating an impact cutter* which cuts the sewn strip to the required length.

Although very useful in this last situation, stitch counting is not universally applicable for measuring sewn distances. Over lengths greater than a few centimetres, and especially on a fabric with any stretch in it, operator handling could cause the length measured by stitch counting to vary considerably. The solution to such measuring problems is to combine the use of stitch counting with photoelectric or infra-red sensing. For example, in topstitching a shirt collar, it is possible to programme in a number of stitches to give the correct size for the stitching at the end of the collar band, along with photoelectric or infra-red detection of the collar point so as to stop the machine at the right position, with the needle down for long enough for the turn to be made. Such sensors can also detect different thicknesses of materials such as occur between a patch pocket and the garment panel it is being attached to. Thus the machine can be set to stop automatically at the pocket corner for the operator to move the garment around.

Other activities which the machinist must do as part of the sewing job are such things as raising the presser foot and, on a lockstitch machine, backtacking at the end of a seam. These activities can also be programmed into a microprocessor-controlled machine, along with needle positioning and thread cutting, so that the operator has only to depress the foot pedal for the initially required cycle – raise presser foot to allow insertion of material, lower presser foot, commence sewing with a backtack, and sew forward – to occur. A similar cycle is activated at the end of the sewing cycle by heeling back on the foot control.

These programmable machines are often referred to as integrated sewing units or ISUs. The various facilities described above, including such details as exactly how many stitches a backtack will consist of, are entered by pressing buttons on a box on top of the machine, the result being visually displayed. Different levels of facility are available at different cost but the advantages to the operator in a typical short cycle, repetitive sewing operation of just the backtack, needle position and thread-cut facility are considerable. Once the programme has been set for a particular operation, such as attaching a rectangular label or top-stitching on a patch pocket, all aspects of the stitching cycle are operated by the foot control, leaving the operator free to concentrate on the amount of handling that unavoidably remains.

Compressed air itself can effectively be a work aid, assisting the quantity and quality of a machinist's work. One such application overcomes the problem of single jersey fabrics which curl at the edges, especially when given a light pull as they are handled through the machine. If two plies are being joined on an overedge machine the amount of the edge which curls is just that which should be under the stitching and if attempts are made to sew inside the curl it will result in excess fabric being trimmed off by the knife on the machine. Often, the two edges are curling away from each other and a jet of compressed air above and below the fabrics will flatten them sufficiently so that they can be joined with the correct trim-off. Another rather similar use of compressed air overcomes the untidy effect often associated with sewing hems on fabrics which fray badly. Where hems are double rolled and lockstitched up on garments such as blouses the edge has often frayed considerably by the time the garment reaches that stage in its construction. The frayed ends often remain partly out of the seam even when it has been sewn with a folder. A jet of compressed air can be directed towards these ends and into the fold of the hem so that they are secured tidily inside.

The applications of compressed air in clothing manufacture have become so widespread that it is impossible to describe them all but a brief description of how it works should give an idea of the possibilities. When introduced in the early 1970s, it was expected to provide a wide range of low cost automation. In practice, the applications have generally been restricted to two main areas: where a company already uses compressed air to operate pressing machinery and has already accepted the capital costs of the system, and where bulk staple manufacture gives opportunities for considerable workplace engineering.

The air is normally supplied at a pressure of 5.5 bars. The main features of a compressed air system are the compressor, a storage vessel to act as a reservoir, an air cooler to maintain a constant temperature (because changes in temperature affect pressure), a main air filter to clean the air, pipework (usually in the form of a ring main to provide constant pressure), drains in the pipe to remove moisture, and flexible tubing to carry the air to individual workplaces. Clean, dry compressed air at each workplace is produced by a filter to clean the air, a regulator to maintain pressure and a lubricator. As has been described, a jet of air can be used alone for moving fabric edges and for cooling overheated sewing machine needles, but its main use is as the power source to move machine parts or ancillary equipment. At the point of application, a valve, opened by an electric signal from a switch or sensor on the operator's machine, admits air to a cylinder. This drives a piston to the end of the cylinder. The movement of the piston carries out the work required which may be to depress an impact cutter behind the presser foot to cut threads or tapes, to raise the presser foot or to operate a stacker.

Stackers

The work required for an operator to dispose of the garment at the end of the sewing cycle depends to a great extent on the size of the garment or part and on the method of handling of the garments or parts between operators.

In many factories, garments are transported in tied bundles or in boxes and they must be formed into some kind of stack as they are worked on. Where small parts such as collars and cuffs are being sewn, off-loading devices are available where each part is passed off the machine table into a box which will confine all of them in a stack and which adjusts its height so that the top of the stack is always level with the machine table surface. When sewing larger garment parts, the operator passes the piece off the back of the machine over the horizontal bar of a stacker. Pneumatic operation then moves this bar away from the machine so that the garment part falls astride it and the bar then returns to its former position to await the next garment.

In companies where hanging transport systems are used, there are many sewing operations where the machinist does no more than reach sideways for the garment without taking it from its hanger or clip. When the section of the work is completed the garment is released and returns to its hanging position. The operator pushes a button on the machine table which moves this garment on and presents another one ready for work. There is a considerable saving in handling time, as well as a reduced amount of capital tied up in bundles of partly assembled garments in the line, but the capital cost of the installation is high. The requirement for pick up or stacking devices is nil but other work aids, as described, would still be used.

In more recent developments in production organisation and garment handling, a style of team working has been introduced where the operators in a production line work standing up at machines on higher pedestals. Each operator is multi-skilled and can do several operations in the sequence of construction of the garment. Thus they move along several machines, taking a single garment through these several operations, until they meet another operator ready for work, when they pass the garment on and return to an earlier machine to begin working on another garment. Again, no pick up or disposal mechanisms are required, and in this case there is no investment in garment handling equipment between operations, but investment in sewing machines may be higher because the production line usually contains more machines than operators. There is very little work in progress and throughput is very fast. This is the main aim of the system as it enables a fast response to be made to demands for style change but it also improves skill levels amongst operators and gives opportunity for greater job satisfaction. Machines are specialised to each operation, with all appropriate work aids, and are generally slowed down to improve machine reliability and the operators' control of their work.

SIMPLE AUTOMATICS

There are machines which sew a short, automatic cycle such as a buttonhole, bar tack, button sew or label. The machine only sews one stitch type and changes in the stitching configuration are limited. As is the case with the plain machines just described, more possibilities are available with the advent of microprocessor control.

Buttonhole machines

These come in a variety of types according to the type of buttonhole needed on the garment. The simplest buttonholes are used on shirts, blouses and other lightweight garments and the more complex ones on the heavier tailored garments. The variables in buttonhole machines are the form and size of the buttonhole, the stitch type (lockstitch or single- or two-thread chainstitch), the stitch bight, the stitch density, whether the buttonhole is cut before or after sewing, and the presence or absence of a gimp.

Buttonhole machines may form a simple circle, where the stitches radiate from the centre of an eyelet hole; two legs on either side of a straight cut with a bar tack at both ends as in a shirt or blouse; a continuous line of sewing up one leg, round the end and down the other without a cut, as in the sham buttonholes on the cuffs of jackets; a buttonhole similar in form but larger in length and bight, with the hole partially or wholly cut and a separate bar tack closing off the end as on the lapels of jackets; a buttonhole with two legs and an eyelet hole at one end, with a separate bar tack closing off the other end, as on the fronts of jackets and overcoats; a variation in which the second leg is sewn over the first stitches of the first leg to close off the end, as frequently on knitwear; and an eyelet ended or lapel type buttonhole, the edges of which are lightly oversewn, known as 'cut and serge', which does no more than provide a firm edge to receive a hand-sewn buttonhole, now increasingly rare.

The choice between cut before and cut after machines applies principally to buttonholes in tailored outerwear. The advantage of cut before buttonholes is a neat appearance with the thread covering the raw edges of the hole effectively. The disadvantages are that once the sewing cycle has begun the position of the hole cannot be altered and that with the fabric flagging slightly at the edge of the hole the regularity of stitch formation may vary (which tends to restrict cut before buttonholes to relatively densely woven, well-milled fabrics). The advantages of cut after buttonholes are that the edge of the fabric gives some protection to the thread, the fabric is more stable during sewing and repositioning is possible after the machine cycle begins if an error is detected. The main disadvantage relates to the finished appearance of the buttonhole, with the cut ends of fibres protruding between the stitches; the worst appearance is on the fronts of jackets with a dark coloured outer fabric and a light coloured interlining. This style of buttonhole is also used on denim jackets and jeans of the type which are laundered before sale to give a worn look. In this case the cut before buttonhole is preferable as the severity of the laundering process causes a very untidy appearance on cut after buttonholes.

Gimp is a stiff thread positioned at the edge of the buttonhole under the stitching when the finished buttonhole requires reinforcement to preserve its shape and bulk to raise the purl effect of the stitch proud of the surrounding fabric.

The choice between lockstitch and chainstitch is affected by the security requirements of the hole, the finished appearance required and the relative costs involved (both capital and operating costs). In general, buttonholes on tailored outerwear make use of a two-thread chainstitch of the 400 class, the chain effect giving an attractive purl appearance to the buttonhole. The simpler shape of a buttonhole on shirts and other lightweight garments is often sewn with single thread chainstitch, and in some cases the sewing is done inside out on the garment so that the purl side of the back of the stitch is on the right side. Increasing use is being made of lockstitch buttonhole sewing to give greater security on these types of garment. For shirts, where the garment shape remains the same and the fronts can be buttonholed before assembly, sequential machines are available which sew all the buttonholes on the front, moving the garment part along by the correct amount between each and stacking it at the end. These will be referred to again when describing automatic machines.

Buttonsew machines

The variables in buttonsew machines are the size and shape of the button which determines the design of the button clamp, the number and disposition of the holes, the form of stitching where there are four holes (this may be crossover or parallel – known as 'swiss kiss') and whether the button has a sewn shank or neck, the stitch type (lockstitch or single thread chainstitch) and the number of stitches. Buttons may be flat with two or four holes or they may have a shank on the back. Where they are flat, a thread shank may be required so that there is space behind the button for the thickness of the garment when fastened. This can be created by means of a spacing 'finger' over the button during sewing. In the case of the shank button, it is clamped on its side during sewing and the needle passes alternately into the garment and then into the hole in the shank and into the garment. The advantage of lockstitch buttonsewing is security but its disadvantage is an untidy look to the stitching on the other side of the fabric from the button. A chainstitch buttonsewer gives a cleaner appearance at the back but less security.

For tailored garments, machines are available sewing stitch type 209 and giving the appearance of a hand-sewn button. The machine sews the button, wraps the thread shank, and secures the stitching by passing the last few stitches through the thread of the shank. The front edge of the garment is presented folded to the needle so that the minimum amount of stitching appears on the reverse side. This increases security.

On the basic machines sewing two or four hole buttons with lock-stitch or chainstitch, the requirement for the operator to position the button in the clamp can be avoided, where long runs justify it, by using a hopper feed which automatically feeds the buttons to the clamp at the needle point. For standard garments such as shirts, the same type of sequential machines are available for sewing buttons as were described for buttonholing.

Bar tack machines

These machines sew a number of stitches across the point to be reinforced and then sew covering stitches over and at right angles to the first stitches. The variables are the number of tacking stitches and the number of covering stitches. Typical uses are closing the ends of buttonholes, reinforcing the ends of pocket openings and the bottoms of flies, and sewing on belt loops.

Label sewers

A variety of label sewers is available from those sewing simple zig-zag stitches to a predetermined length on one or two edges of a label to those which are programmable profile stitchers able to be set to sew round a wide range of shapes and sizes of label. A specially shaped cylinder bed machine is available over which the inside pocket of a jacket can be passed, enabling jackets to be labelled with a retailer's label after manufacture.

A variety of other short cycle machines is available which can be used for attaching hooks, bars, metal badges, motifs and many other decorative and functional garment parts. These increasingly take the form of programmable machines which can sew a variety of items provided an appropriate clamp is attached.

MECHANISED WORKPLACES

These are sewing systems which could be described as fully automatic and which offer the opportunity to raise dramatically the proportion of a sewing machine operator's time which is productive. In all the machinery that has been discussed so far, the operator must still undertake a significant amount of the handling. Despite the application of a wide range of work aids, the operator's pattern of activity is still:

handle – sew – handle – sew – handle etc.

The material must still be loaded into the machine and removed at the end and however much the section in between has been made more efficient it normally involves the operator in waiting while it happens. An operator's activities may vary from constant handling and attention to the job in the attachment of a complicated collar to intermittent spells of activity while a machine sews round a buttonhole. In each case, the productivity is low.

The principle behind mechanised workplaces is that the operator is able to undertake further useful handling while the machine is sewing and some at least of the handling time is incorporated into the sewing time. Such workplaces always contain a sewing machine but in many cases it is so surrounded by other parts of the total system that it is barely visible. The machine is normally equipped with any necessary folders and thread cutters, the latter automatically operated, but in addition the workplace has sophisticated positioning and guiding equipment operating before and during sewing and stackers which operate afterwards. Combinations of pneumatic and mechanical handling achieve the wide variety of fabric movements that are needed and consumption of services such as compressed air can be high. The space required may be the equivalent of several ordinary machines. The workplaces are extremely expensive, costing tens of thousands of pounds at a time when a basic sewing machine can still be obtained for about £1,000 and a fully programmable ISU for less than £2,000.

The mechanised workplaces, or 'automatics' as they are commonly called, are available in a variety of types to achieve particular sewing operations. Their modes of working can be roughly classified as follows:

(a) The machine sews continuously while the operator keeps it supplied with garments. An example would be a machine which turns up the cuffs on short sleeved casual shirts. The operator can pick up and position a garment part during the time the machine takes to sew the previous part. The parts are normally positioned onto a conveyor which takes them past the sewing head. Only a short space would be left between parts and the machine would automatically cut the thread between each part after sewing and stack them at the end. Thus the machine, in this case a lockstitch or a chainstitch, is utilised for a large part of the time (allowing for the short gaps between parts) until the operator has to stop and deal with a completed bundle and organise another one. The average utilisation of these machines is about 75 per cent.

Other operations which can be done by this type of workplace are attaching interlining to the front edge of blouses by means of an overedge stitch, with the interlining feeding from a roll cut to the correct width, or constructing the placket on the buttonhole front of a man's shirt. In the latter case, if the placket is constructed by folding the edge of the shirt front, a folder would be built into the workplace and the operator would still only have to load the front into the machine. If a separate strip is used to make the placket, the operator would have to load the strips as well as the fronts and the machine would normally pause between fronts while this is done. A photo-electric device would detect the end of one shirt front and stop the machine. Even allowing for these pauses, a utilisation of 65 per cent is achievable with these workplaces. Unfortunately, lack of uniformity of shade of fabric frequently prevents continuous strips of fabric being used for these plackets.

If H and S are taken to represent operator handling and machine sewing respectively, and – to indicate continuous operation, a diagrammatic representation of the operation of this type of machine can be as follows:

Operator   H – H – H – H – H – H   deal with bundle
Machine   S – S – S – S – S – S   pause

A large number of garments would normally be sewn before a pause would be necessary.

(b) The machine sews an automatic cycle which includes the handling during sewing which would normally be done by the operator. During the cycle the operator performs the considerable amount of handling which is needed to prepare for the next cycle of automatic sewing. An example would be the automated version of the stitching jigs described earlier. In this situation the machine, once loaded with a jig and started, controls the speed and direction of sewing round that jig. It stops automatically at the end, whereupon the operator removes the jig and replaces it with a new one which was loaded with garment parts during the previous sewing cycle. There is thus an overlap between the handling which is unavoidably the operator's, of unloading and reloading the jigs and presenting them to the sewing head, and that which the machine is able to do while sewing, of controlling the speed and accuracy of the stitching. As well as the sewing of small parts such as collars, cuffs and tabs, the same as can be sewn more slowly with the hand-held jig, the automatic jigs can also be used for large garment parts such as jacket and raincoat fronts. The additional seam turning which is necessary when using jigs is trimmed off by a knife immediately after sewing as the jig moves round. Utilisation with these machines is of the order of 75 per cent.

Another example of this type of operation is the workplace which makes gauntlet openings in shirt sleeves, traditionally an expensive part of shirt production. Only one sewing head is required but two loading stations are needed which separately create the type of fold used on a left and a right sleeve. One side of the opening in the sleeve is pre-hemmed and the operator then loads the sleeve and the gauntlet patch piece into the loading station for that side whilst the machine is sewing the previously loaded sleeve for the other side. Manually constructed gauntlet openings usually have a square end to the gauntlet section rather than the pointed end which is regarded as more desirable. The automatic machine is able to make the pointed shape which is actually easier for a mechanical folding device than the square shape. A representation of the operation of this type of machine would be as follows, the colon (:) indicating a brief pause on the part of the operator and the machine as each reaches the end of its cycle of loading or sewing.

Operator H : H : H : H : H : H   deal with bundle
Machine   S : S : S : S : S : S pause

(c) The machine sews an automatic cycle in which a difficult sewing job is achieved very quickly and accurately though the operator is not able to do much during the cycle time. An example would be the construction of a jetted pocket in a tailored jacket or the attaching of a patch pocket to a shirt front or a pair of jeans. Several parts have to be loaded into the machine but the sewing cycle is then short and of perfect quality. The utilisation with these machines is about 80 per cent.

In the attachment of patch pockets, the workplace incorporates a folding device which folds the side and lower edges on a pocket which has been hemmed at the top edge. The operator loads the pocket into the folder and the garment part onto the machine. The pocket is folded, placed on the garment part and sewn round. The stitching includes the required shape of reinforcement at the top, often a triangle. There is normally provision for the operator to intervene in the placing of the pocket so that, in the case of checked or striped shirts, the pattern can be matched. An example of such a mechanised workplace for attaching jeans pockets is shown in Figure 4.13(i). It includes a milling machine with which to make new pocket creasers when the pocket shape changes.

In the construction of jetted pockets, the jacket front, the fabric which forms the jetts and, if appropriate, one side of the pocket bag, are loaded into the machine. The sewing head sews two parallel rows of stitching of the correct spacing and length, a knife slashes the fabric along the middle and two further mitre knives slash into the corners. The pocket is completed by turning the jetts through to the wrong side, tacking the triangular sections left at the corners to the ends of the jetts, and attaching the pocket bag sections. A pre-made pocket flap can be incorporated if necessary. The machines will normally also do a single rather than a double jett. The size of pocket is easily adjusted. An example of this workplace is shown in Figure 4.13(ii).

A representation of the operation of this type of machine would be as follows, w indicating that the operator is waiting for the machine.

```
Operator  H w H w H w H w H w H     deal with bundle
Machine      S : S : S : S : S : S  pause
```

The workplace shown in Figure 4.13(ii) is available in several different levels, at different prices, and at the highest level the operator waiting time has been largely eliminated by clamp technology which allows the operator to begin loading jetts and flaps while the previous cycle of sewing is taking place.

(d) The machine sews a fairly long automatic cycle during which the operator would be idle between loading and unloading. To avoid this, more than one machine is operated, perhaps even three or four. An example would be the buttonhole and buttonsew machines referred to as sequential which can move the garment part, normally a shirt front not yet attached to the rest of the shirt, by the correct amount between each buttonhole or button until the complete set has been sewn. Automatic button feeding would, of course, be included. The sewing of six buttonholes on a shirt front can take around 0.35 of a minute and in this time the operator can easily load another machine and then another. The sewing of six buttons takes slightly less time but still offers scope for multiple machine operation. Balanced combinations of several button-holers and buttonsewers are possible with very little sign of hurry on the part of the operator. Indeed, since the machines are large, a constraint can be the time it takes for the operator to move from one to the other.

Another workplace type in this category hems tee shirts and underwear. The type of hem previously referred to as overlock welted which is frequently used on lightweight knitted garments such as tee shirts is extremely difficult to sew and operators require long training. On the

(i)

(ii)

Fig. 4.13. Mechanised workplaces. (i) For attaching patch pockets on trousers and jeans. (ii) For making jett, welt and flap pockets on tailored jackets and trousers.

automatic machine, the operator loads the lower edge of the garment, already joined into a circle, onto guides which move apart to place the garment under the correct tension. The edge is inserted into a folder and the complete hem sewn automatically. While this is happening the operator can operate a second machine.

Yet another example is the automatic serging machine which is often used on men's trousers. A machine can be set to sew three sides of a leg panel with automatic turning at the corners and during this time the operator can unload and reload two or three other machines. A representation of the operation of three machines could be as follows. The cycle time of each of the machines does not have to be the same.

```
Operator  H(1)  :  H(2)  :  H(3)  :  .....
Machine 1          S(1) ............
Machine 2                  S(2) ............
Machine 3                          S(3) ............
```

The operation of the machine for overlock welting described above is the only one mentioned which sews a garment in three dimensions rather than working on flat parts. Although there are some mechanised work-places which automatically sew these types of construction, they are few and far between because the control systems needed to handle fabric in three dimensions are very much more complicated than those needed for flat fabric. The limp nature of textile materials makes automatic handling difficult and the frequency of style change in most sections of the industry means that any automated systems which are built for them must be easily adaptable. This is not always easy.

The result of these constraints is that most of the fully automatic sewing equipment that is available has been developed for assembling the types of garment which are made in very large quantities with minimum style change and which have within their design a number of parts which can be sewn with the materials in a flat state. These garments are primarily shirts and men's jackets and trousers. On formal shirts, the operations of collar and cuff assembly and topstitching, label attachment to yoke, yoke attachment to body, folding of front edges, buttonholing and buttonsewing of fronts, patch pocket attachment and attachment of gauntlet openings to sleeves can all be achieved with mechanised work-places where the operator only loads the machine. When these stages have been completed, however, the ensuing three-dimensional activities of attaching sleeves to body, closing side seams, attaching collar and cuffs, and turning up the hem have to be undertaken by operators at more conventional machines, albeit fitted with appropriate work aids and pro-grammable facilities. On men's jackets and trousers the main opportunities for automation are in the construction of the varied jett, welt and flap pockets that most styles include and in the serging and joining of leg panels.

5

The Use of Components and Trims

The items and processes to be discussed in this chapter are those components, other than the main fabric of the garment, which are an essential part of the construction of the garment or which act as trimmings or fastenings of some kind.

As far as the separate items are concerned, no one term is in universal use to denote them. To many people, the word component includes the sections of main fabric which make up the garment as well as the additional items. The word trim tends to have decorative overtones, though many items are purely functional. Even that can change with fashion as the humble shoulder pad has shown, having swung with fashion from being a hidden support in tailored garments to being an ostentatious addition to a wide variety of garments. Many items are primarily fastenings but unless they are totally hidden they often provide decoration as well.

The total number of items available for use in garments in addition to the main fabric is extremely large and it is neither possible nor necessary to describe them all. Sewing threads are described elsewhere because their importance in terms of overall garment construction merits separate consideration. Interlinings are divided into those which are sewn into the garment and those which are fused and the technology of fusing is sufficiently important that it is also given separate consideration. For the rest, it is proposed to discuss a selection of those that are most important and most commonly used.

The aspects of these items which are important are the functions they serve, the materials from which they are made, the methods by which they become part of the garment – i.e. are attached to or applied to it – and the performance properties which they must have. Their materials and performance properties are only of importance in the current context where they are relevant to garment construction, being otherwise more appropriate to a separate study of the properties of all clothing materials.

However, a brief summary of the most important performance properties of these items will be given at the end of the chapter.

The selection of components it is proposed to discuss is as follows:

- labels and motifs
- linings
- interlinings
- wadding
- lace, braid and elastic
- hook and loop fastening
- seam binding and tape
- shoulder pads
- eyelets and laces
- zip fasteners
- buttons
- tack buttons, snap fasteners and rivets

The logic behind the selection and the sequence is to look first at those components which are purely textile, for which construction methods are akin to those for the rest of the garment, and then to consider some of the items made from non-textile materials for which special, non-sewing machinery may be required.

Labels and motifs

No garment can be sold without some kind of label attached to it. Labelling as to fibre content is mandatory, size labelling is clearly necessary and country of origin marking, though no longer required in every case, is likely to continue in extensive use. Care labelling is not a legal requirement in the UK but its use is on the increase as retailers try to ensure that garments do not fail the consumer as a result of incorrect action. Few manufactures or retailers would wish to sell a garment without including their brand name and, in addition, garments often carry information identifying the manufacturer who supplied the retailer and the date of manufacture. The term 'motif' is often used to describe a decorative addition to a garment but the use of motifs carrying a company's name, trade mark or logo is now so widespread that the subject of labels and the subject of motifs cannot easily be separated.

Labels

The majority of the items that are traditionally called labels are sewn into garments and the type of label and its cost are closely related to the type of garment and the level of the market in which it is selling.

The labels with the highest standard of appearance are *woven to a narrow width* with the necessary information woven into them as a jacquard design. They normally give the company's name and the

Fig. 5.1. Methods of sewing labels to garments.

garment size and fitting and they are used in men's and women's outerwear and tailored garments, especially at the more expensive end of the market. In made-to-measure garments the individual purchaser's name is sometimes embroidered on the label using a computer-controlled embroidery machine. These labels are usually sewn flat to a facing or lining, with the two raw edges turned in. Machines are available which will sew the required rectangle of stitching automatically with a lockstitch. Alternatively, a straight or zig-zag stitch may be used at both narrow ends.

The least expensive labels are *printed* on a large area of woven, thermoplastic fabric and *heat sealed to the narrow width* required. They can be delivered to the garment manufacturer as a roll of individual labels to be cut apart by hand, or already cut and sealed to length. As was mentioned before, these sealed edges are a frequent cause of discomfort when worn against the skin. These labels may be sewn flat onto a facing but are most often folded and inserted under the stitching of a superimposed seam or under the edge of a collar seam. They may be supplied ready folded. Examples of labels sewn to garments are shown in Figure 5.1.

Garments often carry a label in more than one position. A lady's coat, for example, may have a woven label giving brand name and size sewn flat to the facing and a further, printed label inserted into the side seam of the lining giving the fibre content and care instructions. A common compromise to reduce the number of labels is to use jacquard weaving for constant information and overprinting for variable details.

Small, woven labels carrying a maker's name or logo are frequently inserted into a seam on the outside of a garment and are designed to show. They are commonly used on jeans and other casual wear.

Motifs

Motifs are available in a wide variety of types, sizes and methods of attachment but the range will be limited here to small, decorative items which are attached flat to the outside of garments. The majority are either an all-over embroidery, or a section of fabric with some embroidery on it, or a section of fabric neatened or sealed in some way at the edges and carrying a printed design. Many have special threads woven into the back to make them suitable for attachment by ultrasonic welding, the method for which is described in Chapter 6. This gives a secure attachment while at the same time maintaining the slightly three-dimensional structure which is an attractive feature of embroidered motifs. Printed motifs are often designed to be attached by a heat transfer process for which a special small heated press is used. Motifs may be attached by sewing but to do it freehand is likely to be slow and is potentially inaccurate. For companies sewing large quantities of such items, lockstitch machines are available which can be programmed to sew the particular profile required.

As programmable embroidery machines become more readily available as well as faster and more flexible their use is tending to increase at the expense of attaching pre-made motifs. Direct embroidery on to the garment generally gives a more subtle and flexible motif with a higher quality appearance than sewing or welding on of a separate motif.

Linings

Linings are generally a functional part of a garment, being used variously to maintain the shape of a garment, to improve the hang and comfort by allowing it to slide over other garments, to add insulation and to cover the inside of a garment of complicated construction to make it neat. In many cases linings are selected to match the garment so as to be unobtrusive but in others they are chosen to add to the design of the garment and even as a subtle, identifying feature of the brand on an otherwise widely available style.

Linings are available as warp knits but they are predominantly woven and are made from polyester, polyamide, acetate and viscose for use where a slippery material is required and from cotton, polyester/cotton and wool or wool mixtures in plain or brushed versions where decoration or warm handle is required. Where non-slippery lining fabrics are used in garments they are generally only used for the body, the sleeve being lined with a more slippery material to make for easier putting on and taking off.

Lining material can be used for small garment sections such as pockets and for complete garments, either fully bagged out, i.e. sewn down all the way round, or sewn to the facing and open at the bottom.

For small sections such as patch pockets or pockets flaps it is necessary for the lining to remain hidden and it is in the construction of such parts as these that jigs with fulling bars as previously described would be used. For jackets, coats and raincoats the outer garment must not be constrained in any way by tightness in the lining and in these garments there is normally extra lining fabric in the body and the sleeve. In skirt and trouser linings, the stability of the outer garment in wear may be assisted by the lining being slightly smaller than the garment.

Linings made from polyester, polyamide or viscose can, in some constructions, be prone to the problem of seam slippage described earlier.

Since these fabrics also tend to fray easily, a loss of seam allowance by fraying can contribute to seam slippage and it may be necessary to neaten seam edges during lining construction even though the garment and its lining will be totally bagged out and the lining edges will not be seen. Where a coat and its lining are open at the hem it is common to neaten the lining edges. In practice, if safety stitch machines are available, linings can be joined and neatened simultaneously at no extra cost except for the thread.

Lining attachment

The actual method of attaching linings to outer garments depends on the garment type and on whether it is fully or only partially bagged out. It also depends on whether the entire construction must be machine-sewn or whether some part of it will be finished by hand. Where the lining is left unattached at the hem on a garment such as a raincoat, it can be machine-sewn to the body and sleeve facings and turned through. If it is required to close the garment at the hem as well, a gap in the seam of the sleeve lining can be left through which the garment can be turned. This gap can then be topstitched closed on a lockstitch machine and it will not show on the outside. On men's jackets the body lining is normally attached to the jacket and, separately, the sleeve lining to the sleeve at the cuff. After attaching of jacket sleeves to jacket, each sleeve lining is attached to the body lining and turned through a gap in the forearm seam or vent, these gaps then being topstitched closed.

Interlinings

Interlinings are used to support, reinforce and control areas of garments such as collars, cuffs, waistbands, hems, facings and the fronts of jackets and coats. They may be sewn into the garment or they may be attached by means of fusing, the technology of which will be described in the next chapter. Although fusing is now very common as a method of garment construction, there are many fabrics which are not suitable for fusing, as well as small manufacturers who do not have the requisite equipment. The complexity of interlinings used varies greatly between tailored wear, especially menswear, and other types of garments.

In the non-tailored garments often referred to as 'light clothing' – i.e. blouses, dresses, skirts, and lightweight jackets and coats – interlinings are sometimes laid into a garment section such as a collar or cuff and sewn around the edges when the part is constructed. They may also be joined to facings and waistbands when the edges are neatened and run into placket fronts via a folder. In all these cases they do not require to be stitched, other than in the seaming that will be part of the necessary garment construction. This is because, in general, they do not cover a very large area and consequently do not need attaching to the garment part they are to support other than at the edges. All that is necessary is to select an interlining which, by virtue of its weight, construction and fibre content, will perform satisfactorily in the wearing and washing or dry-cleaning of the garment.

In tailored garments, interlinings play a very important part in creating the shape of the garment and smoothing out the contours of the body. A man's jacket has an interlining all down the front which must be invisibly fastened into place, with others at hems, vents and sleeve heads, along with substantial canvases in the chest area.

Interlinings are available in a wide variety of weights and constructions to match the properties of the garment fabrics they will support. They can be woven or non-woven, both of which can be constructed to give a different softness or resilience in different directions.

Woven interlinings are, most commonly, plain weave construction. In the lighter weights they may have a cotton warp and weft, giving a soft handle in both directions, or a cotton warp and a viscose weft to aid crease recovery and retention of shape. More substantial constructions may include hair, wool and viscose blends. Finishing processes are used which may include a crease resistant finish to give good crease shedding properties as well as stability to shrinkage.

Nonwoven interlinings are made directly from textile fibres and are held together by mechanical, chemical, thermal or solvent means or by a combination of these. The fibres used can be viscose rayon to provide the harder handles, polyester to provide suppler handles, nylon to provide resilience and bulk, or some combination of these fibres to give specific physical and mechanical properties.

Nonwoven interlinings have different properties according to the way in which the fibres are laid in making the material. The fibres may be laid at random for all-round stability, parallel to give stability in one direction with extensibility in the direction at right angles, cross to give extensibility in both directions (making them suitable for soft outer fabrics) and composite to give combinations of properties for general purpose inter-linings. A variety of methods is available to bond the fibres together within the material and this also affects the interlining properties.

Wadding

Wadding or batting are the names given to the fibre fillings used in garments where warmth is required without great weight. They aim to simulate the warmth and lightness of down, but with the advantage of washability and speed of drying as well as lower cost. The fibre most commonly used is polyester though polypropylene is also used where a garment will not be subjected to the heat of dry-cleaning. For maximum insulation, as much air as possible must be trapped among or within the fibres which must be as light and resilient as possible. The fibres themselves are of various diameters and may be solid or hollow with the possibility of one or more hollow channels within them. Different weights and thicknesses of batting are possible as a result of different densities of fibre material, different thicknesses of fibre, and different densities of fibre within the batt. At some stage in the construction of a garment the batting must be quilted, that is, sewn to an outer fabric. Present fashion demands that this quilting, where it shows on the outside of the garment, should be as widely spaced as possible. The more closely-spaced traditional quilting does not require that the fibres in the batt are attached to each other in any way because they are held sufficiently in place by the quilting itself. The further apart the stitching is, the greater is the need for some kind of binding agent in the wadding, enabling the fibres to adhere together and not drop towards the garment hemline or the lower part of a stitched cube, box (the traditional diamond shape), or channel. The necessary bonding can be achieved in a variety of ways, mainly the addition of a resin or the use of heat bonding. Heat-bonded battings are softer and are the result of the inclusion of a proportion of fibres of lower melting point or the making of each fibre in a bi-component form.

With such a variety of waddings available, care is needed in their selection and in the choice of garment construction methods if the designer's intentions and the performance requirements of a garment are to be realised. The main factors governing the choice of wadding are the amount of bulk appropriate to the style, the amount of insulation which must be provided and the cost. Wadding is normally thinner around the limbs than the trunk. In terms of making up, the style may require the quilting to be visible on the outside or the inside or on both or on neither. Where the filling is sandwich-quilted, with garment fabric both sides as would be the case in some reversible garments, and where it is quilted before garment construction commences, extensive use is made of binding to neaten edges and seams, sometimes adding contrast decoration in the process. Where an outer or lining fabric is wadded and quilted but will then be made up with a further loose layer of lining or outer fabric, or where the wadding is just attached to the fabric of the garment part around the edges, awaiting quilting when it has been bagged out with a further layer of fabric, the wadding may require a surface bonding or a light non-woven backing to assist cutting and sewing. Loose fibre battings could clog the moving parts of the sewing machine, especially the feed dog. If sewing must take place with one side of the wadding uncovered, a large, unjointed presser foot adjacent to the wadding is likely to cause the least problems.

It will be clear that quilting may take place at various stages in the construction of a garment and may even be one of the very last stages. Large garment sections such as jacket backs may be made with the wadding attached to the outer fabric just at the edges and then bagged out with the lining. The sections are normally then quilted in large squares or rectangles before the garment seams are joined. Closely spaced quilting would be very costly if done at this stage as a multi-needle machine could not be used. The dimensions of the quilting will be determined by garment style and the requirement to support the wadding. Special feed mechanisms of the types previously described may be needed in order to overcome problems of creepage in sewing through such bulky materials. Compound feed is particularly useful for keeping the fabrics and wadding together without an excessive need for handling on the part of the operator.

When selecting fabrics to use with wadding it must be remembered that it has requirements similar to that of down in that, unless the correct kind of closely woven fabric is used over it, the fibre ends will work their way though the interstices of the weave and appear on the surface.

For showerproof garments the problem of water penetration exists where an outer fabric is quilted. This may be overcome with thin wadding by the use of stitchless quilting by ultrasonic welding in the kind of box designs normally achieved by sewing.

Lace, braid and elastic

The narrow trimmings generally referred to as lace and braid can be various natural and synthetic materials or mixtures but are predominantly polyester, polyamide, polyester/cotton, and cotton for the lace, and the same fibres plus wool and acrylic for the braid. They can also contain elastane fibres to give stretch and recovery. Their use is normally decorative although it may be functional as well. The term 'elastic' is here being reserved for those corded elastics and rubber strips used functionally in garments to draw in part of the garment in an elastic manner.

Lace

The term lace correctly refers to the type of open structure originally made by hand and now available in a variety of machine-made forms. Some are formed from twisted yarns, some are embroideries on net or more solid fabric and yet others are knitted. For present purposes the construction is important for the following reasons. Some types may be so open structured that stitch types such as 101 may not sew them satisfactorily. Some fray on one edge rather than being neat on both sides and these must be neatened during garment construction. This is common with the embroidered fabric known as broderie anglaise. Others have a scalloped edge and for maximum decorative effect must be sewn to the garment along the shape of the scallop.

Braid

Braids were originally braided fabrics, produced by interlacing yarns diagonally in a form of plaiting. They were either narrow flat fabrics or the type of narrow tube familiar as shoelaces. Flat braids of this type are still used and in wool and acrylic they make soft and flexible edgings for binding around medium and heavyweight garments. Since the edges do not fray, the simplest type of bound seam can be used. Corners on the garment would normally be rounded rather than square. The term braid is also used to describe other narrow fabrics which are woven or even knitted. In woven form they are similar to the many forms of ribbon available and in plain as well as jacquard constructions they are often used on children's garments, simply sewn flat with a twin needle machine of an appropriate needle gauge (spacing).

Although lace and braid would traditionally have been regarded as totally separate in appearance and function, they are available as both stretch and non-stretch materials and in their stretch versions they have a number of similarities. Thus the elastication and decoration of the edges of garments such as ladies' briefs is accomplished simultaneously by using a narrow stretch material that has either the open appearance of a lace or the more solid appearance of a braid. Attachment requires metering of the elastic material as previously described along with the bottom cover, top and bottom cover or zig-zag stitching in the versions also described earlier.

In the non-stretch version, lace is frequently used as a decorative edging on lingerie in a seam of class 7. If the lace is straight along the joining edge it can be attached with stitch type 406 or with 304, the former being necessary if the garment fabric is woven and on the straight of the grain as it would fray along the edge. In many cases it is a shaped or scalloped edge of lace that is attached to the garment and for maximum effect the edge of the garment needs to be cut away to match it. This would be slow and difficult to do by hand but machines are available which have a trimming knife operating below a plate adjacent to the needle. The operator joins the lace to the fabric with the lace above the plate and the fabric below and guides the machine to follow the shape of the lace, the knife trimming the fabric away just before they are sewn together. Stitch type 304, the lockstitch zig-zag, is normally used for flexibility of sewing shape. The shape of the seam is such that even on a woven fabric there is no significant fraying and no further neatening is necessary.

In virtually every case where braid, lace or elastic is applied to a garment it would be applied at a stage in the construction such that it could be attached to a reasonably flat section of garment from an open edge to an open edge. This assists the use of edge guides in positioning the item and enables it to be fed from a long length on a reel via a rack guide rather than handled in short lengths.

Elastic

Where elasticated effects are required locally on garments but without added decoration, corded elastic of various widths and even flat rubber strips are used. Corded elastics contain rubber or elastane threads which provide high stretch and recovery. Elastane is more common nowadays than natural rubber because of its greater durability. A typical use is on the waist of a loose fitting dress or at the wrist of a sleeve which ends in a frill. A 3 or 4 mm elastic would be used and it would most commonly be sewn using a 304 lockstitch zig-zag. This stitches across the whole width of the elastic which gives greater comfort than a straight lockstitch as it prevents the elastic rolling into a ridge. In addition, an alternating slightly pleated effect is produced on the outside of the garment which adds to the decorative effect of the elastication.

Flat strips of rubber are used to provide control on the edges of garments such as swimwear and men's briefs. On swimwear they would normally be attached to the fabric edge by overedging and then the hem would be turned up and secured by sewing with stitch types 304 or 406, depending on the appearance required. On men's briefs, the elastic would be inserted into the binding on the legs and waist as it is attached. This type of elastic can be supplied already joined into a ring of the required size for the hem, if the method of garment construction allows it to be used in that form, rather than open.

Hook and loop fastening (e.g. Velcro)

This item consists of two woven polyamide tapes, one covered with very fine hooks and the other with very fine loops. When pressed together they adhere securely to each other. They are very strong against the kind of shearing forces present in a simple lapped join yet they peel apart easily when required to be undone. Each side is joined to the garment part simply by sewing close to the edge with a lockstitch machine.

Hook and loop fastening is used in only a limited number of garment applications but where it is used its particular properties are extremely valuable. Since any part of one side will fasten to any part of the other it is used for adjustable fastenings such as closing cuffs and ankles on waterproof garments. Another advantage in this context is that it can be opened and closed easily, even when wearing gloves or mittens, and it is useful to provide a secondary, reasonably waterproof closure over zips on such garments. This ease of handling is also useful for disabled people who find buttons or other fastenings difficult to handle or who need additional openings in garments so that they can dress themselves without assistance.

Unforunately, the very ability of the hook side to close anywhere on a section of loop side means that it will also close on any other reasonably fibrous surface. Thus garments fastened with it can, depending on their material, fasten almost anywhere as well as in the right place, and when undone the fabric begins to be damaged by the tearing action of the hook side. Repetition of the attachment of the hook side to items other than its correct opposite number will cause the hook side gradually to acquire a build-up of fluff which limits its effectiveness. The same effect will occur if garments are washed or cleaned without the fastening being closed on itself. Because of these difficulties, it is important to select carefully which side of the fastening to use on which side of a closure and how much of each to use. In adjustable fastenings, a small section of hook side normally moves over a larger section of loop side. Another reason why the fastening has limited use as a substitute for zips or buttons is the poor appearance arising from its relative inflexibility, especially on lightweight garments. At the other extreme, however, it is substantial enough to be used a great deal as a fastening for casual shoes.

Seam binding and tape

In some types of garment, neatening of seam edges by means of overedging is inadequate or inappropriate and the fabric edges are bound with bias cut strips of woven fabric, often a satin construction, passed through a folder. A typical garment that would require this type of finish would be an unlined wool jacket or coat that was not constructed to be reversible but where a double cloth had been used, perhaps plain on the outside and check on the inside. The inside would be intended to be seen and a binding would give a suitable finish. Another use is in the finish of trouser pockets. As with binding on the outer edges of reversible garments, sharp corners such as might occur on facings would be rounded.

Tape is often used along the joining stitching in a superimposed seam if there is a risk that the seam may stretch in wear and either distort the garment or cause the stitching to crack. Typical areas for use would be shoulder seams on garments made from knitted fabrics and waist seams on dresses, especially where a flared or gathered skirt is joined onto the bodice. Machines with appropriate feeding systems can be set so that they do not stretch the materials while they are being sewn and in this case the tape can be run on flat from a roll as the seam is sewn. If stretch cannot be controlled during sewing it might be necessary to pre-cut tape pieces to length. The operator then ensures that the garment parts being sewn fit in to the length of tape. This is only possible on fairly short and straight seams; it would be impossible to handle the complete circle of a waist in this freehand manner. For economy, a narrow cotton tape in black or unbleached white is often sufficient although on more expensive garments colour matched ribbon would be used. The possible problems of bulk and show-through must be considered and guides will be needed on machines to place the tape or ribbon in the correct position under the seam-joining stitching – for example, under the 401 stitch in a (401.504) safety stitch.

For constructions such as sleeve-attachment in men's tailored jackets, where varying amounts of ease are needed at different stages in sewing the armhole seam, a programmable upper and lower feed machine can be used to set a tape or cord around the sleeve head with the correct amount of fabric eased on to it, and the sleeve can subsequently be attached to the body of the jacket as if the seam were being sewn flat.

Shoulder pads

Shoulder pads have long been a standard item in tailored garments both for women and for men but from time to time they become a fashion item and are seen in a much wider range of garments including knitwear and lightweight blouses.

The pads themselves are available in a variety of shapes and thicknesses to suit garment styles and to give the requisite amount of bulk, and in a variety of materials and constructions, depending largely on whether they are required to be washable or only dry-cleanable, and whether they are to be used in a lined or unlined garment.

The simplest are made from foam with a lightweight knitted polyamide covering and they would be used in unlined garments such as blouses, dresses and knitwear. They are tacked to appropriate seam turnings using a buttonsew machine and are both washable and dry-cleanable. If a particularly neat appearance inside the garment is required, the pads might be covered with the actual garment fabric but it is essential to preserve the three-dimensional shape of the pad. Washable and dry-cleanable pads for lined garments often consist of an outer layer of a non-woven material sandwiched over a foam or fibre inner. Large stitches through all the layers would hold the pad together. They would be attached by methods similar to those for the unlined garments.

For lined garments which will only be dry-cleaned, such as men's tailored jackets, the pads are normally built up of several layers of foam or various non-woven materials and these layers may be needle-punched together. The pad is attached to the edge of the jacket at the armhole seam and also to the interlining, forming the chest piece, and accurate positioning is vital. Many companies now make use of pads on which there are small areas of adhesive resin of the type used in fusible interlinings. These pads can be attached to the jacket using an iron or, to be really sure that the jacket is in the correct shape that it would have when worn, using the type of shaped shoulder press that is common in menswear production. A flap can be folded back on the pad so that, after tacking into position by means of the adhesive, it can then be sewn to the garment without the sewing passing through all the thicknesses.

Eyelets and laces

Garments frequently require small holes in them in the form of eyelets for a variety of purposes such as for the prongs of buckles on belts, for ventilation on waterproof garments, for the emergence of drawstrings at waist or around hoods and for use with lacing as a fastening.

Machines are available of the chainstitch buttonhole type which will stitch a small round hole and these are often used on belts, especially on more expensive raincoats. Since the prong of the buckle is normally of polished metal, the sewn eyelet does not suffer great wear. A more common and more hard-wearing alternative to a sewn eyelet is a metal eyelet and reinforcing washer in brass or steel with a plated or coloured, lacquered surface. Eyelets likely to become wet must be rustproof. These eyelets are appropriate to all the uses described above but a special machine is required to attach the two sections which make up the eyelet. The centre of the visible circle of the eyelet has a short tubular projection on the back. The attaching machine presses the two eyelet sections together through the fabric, with the projection through the centre of the reinforcing washer, and spreads out the end of the tubular section over the edge of the washer so that they become permanently held together.

Different sizes of eyelet are available as appropriate to the end use and garment type and it is essential that the material to which they are attached is sufficiently substantial. Underarm ventilation holes do not take any stress and would be strong enough applied through a single thickness of any material that is likely to be used but any application that is to have a drawstring or lacing of any kind through it would need to be reinforced with another layer of fabric or interlining.

A drawstring or the lacing of a fastening could be one of many materials, from the plaited braid shoelace type described earlier, possibly with filling yarns to make it round, to narrow strips of leather or suede, or to fabric run through a narrow folder producing a spaghetti or topstitched effect. In most cases, these would have to be finished in some way at the cut end, possibly in a sufficiently bulky manner that the end could not be drawn accidentally through the eyelets. The plastic sealed end common to shoelaces could be used, even on the sewn fabric ties, and the sewn ones might also be tied decoratively in an overhand knot. Where synthetic materials are used the ends can be cut and sealed simultaneously and, if necessary, knotted afterwards. Another functional and decorative end is provided by the shaped metal or plastic item often referred to as an acorn. Where an end finishing is not used, a drawstring may be sewn to the garment with a short lockstitch tack, for example at the centre back for a waist drawstring tied at the front.

It should be remembered that, in the interests of safety, the Children's Clothing (Hood Cords) Regulations 1976 prohibits the use of drawstrings in the hoods of all outer garments, (for example, raincoats and anoraks), which measure not more than 44 cm across the chest when laid out flat. An enclosed elastic is normally used.

Zip fasteners

These are the principal items used in clothing which are partly textile in nature and partly non-textile, hard material. They provide a neat and strong fastening in garments and can be functional or decorative or both. They provide two edges which will mesh together and resist pulling apart when stressed, on a tape support which can be sewn into the garment. They can vary in the materials of the tape, the form and materials of the meshing sections and in the overall construction and function of the zip. The latter most affects their methods of attachment to garments.

The tapes are most commonly woven and can be of cotton, polyester, polyamide or mixtures. The meshing sections can be individual teeth of metal, preferably brass although aluminium may be used on some cheap zips, or they can consist of plastic teeth. Alternatively, they can take the form of a continous spiral of plastic, usually polyamide. Whichever form they take they must be securely fastened to the tape and when closed, remain securely meshed together against all reasonable lateral forces. When fully opened, an end stop holds the zip together and this must also be strong enough to withstand considerable forces when the garment is being put on or taken off. The slider must move smoothly up and down when required but keep the zip closed against a lateral pull by means of a small stop which rests between the teeth. Ball and chain sliders or ones with large rings are usual on skiwear and other outdoor garments since they can be grasped by gloved hands. For ease of sewing to the garment, a construction that gives a flat back to the zip but a well defined ridge of teeth or coil on the face side enables the machinist to sew accurately with the presser foot as a guide.

Zips are available in a variety of forms, principally:

(i)   made to length with stop and slider;
(ii)   invisible, made to length with stop and slider;
(iii)   continuous with added stop and slider;
(iv)   made to length, open ended with slider;
(v)   made to length, open ended with two sliders.

The first, which is *made to a particular length*, is the simplest, being commonly used in ladies' and children's wear. In heavier versions it would have teeth of metal or plastic but in lighter versions a plastic spiral is normal. An opening of appropriate length is left in a seam as it is joined and the zip is inserted into the opening. When the zip is fully open, some strain should be taken on the backtack at the end of the seam as well as on the stop on the zip. The zip may be concealed by being set centrally in the seam or to one side, as shown in the seam diagram in Figure 5.2(i), and a zip guard may be included, especially on skirts and trousers.

Special narrow toed or single sided presser feet for sewing zips were described in Chapter 4. These enable the stitching to run closer to the teeth or spiral than the width of a normal presser foot. Skilled operators are required for this work in order to achieve straight stitching with even edge-to-edge or overlapped fabric and an avoidance of any stretch in the fabric as it is sewn. Even the common differential feeding effect when a soft fabric is sewn on top of a more rigid one can cause the fabric to be

(i)

(ii)

Fig. 5.2. Zip insertion. (i) Concealed skirt zip insertion. (ii) Men's trouser zip fly construction.

stretched onto the zip and the garment will then not lie flat in wear. Careless sewing can also insert a twist into the garment if differential feeding occurs as the operator sews down one side of the zip and up the other, leaving the top edges stepped.

Two types of zip which require less skill are the *invisible* and the *continuous* types. Invisible zips have the teeth turned onto the inside of the garment and they are used mainly in ladies' skirts to give a smooth line over the hip with a barely detectable gap in the seam and no visible stitching. Their attachment, using a special presser foot, was described in Chapter 4. Apart from a neat appearance in wear, they offer advantages in terms of operator skill during assembly because the zip is sewn to a single thickness of fabric rather than to a folded edge, with the seam allowance clearly visible, and accuracy is easy to obtain. When considering using invisible zips, the design of the garment is important as they cannot be used across a seam such as a yoke or basque seam on a skirt. The stitching which attaches the zip to the garment is so close to the zip teeth that the extra bulk of a cross seam would cause it to jam.

Continuous zips are of the polyamide spiral type and can be purchased either as a reel of closed zip or with the two sides separate. In the closed form, they can be inserted into a variety of seams, for example, in the back of a child's or lady's dress and a twin needle machine can be used. The end stop and the slider are added later by means of special machines. No top stops are needed, provided there is a seam across the top as part of the garment's construction. One of the most important advantages of continuous zip tape, however, is found when it is used unjoined as it often is in the construction of men's trousers. It is a common construction sequence with men's trousers that each leg is completely assembled, with a partly or even completely finished waistband, and the garment is then completed by joining the crutch seam and the zip. Attaching a length of tape and spiral to each side of the trouser, flat and in the correct position, is a simple job compared with attaching a complete zip to the fly section. The crutch seam can then be joined, the waistband completed if necessary, and the stop and slider added to the zip. An example of a typical construction of the fly area of a man's trouser is shown in Figure 5.2(ii).

Zips which can be opened at the lower end are required in garments such as cardigans and jackets which have to be completely undone rather than stepped into. They are also used when a garment section might be removed for some situations of wear. Examples of this are anoraks and ski jackets with zip-out sleeves or with an inner body-warmer which attaches by means of a zip. The two sections of the garment can only be joined or separated when the slider is fully to the bottom of the zip. This type of zip may have chunky, plastic teeth and slider and be decorative as well as functional.

Insertion of an open-ended zip into a garment can be much easier than the closed type since the two sides can be separated. This is a help in the more complicated types of constructions needed for jackets and anoraks such as where a lining must also be sewn to the zip. Away from clothing, open-ended zips are seen where the reasons for their use appear to be entirely connected with construction rather than function. An example is a tapered sleeping bag, of a type not designed to attach to another one, where the zip finishes, with an open end, immediately above the shaped foot section. There is no functional need for the zip to separate at the bottom; indeed, if accidentally separated it is difficult to rejoin because there is so little free movement of the two sides. It appears to be used solely to assist construction in that it enables each side to be sewn on separately.

Zips with two sliders are used on longer length jackets and waistcoats where there would be a strain on the bottom of the zip when the wearer is seated. Both sliders must be fully to the bottom for the zip to be joined or separated but in wear, the lower slider can be pulled up and the lower end of the zip opened, when required.

Buttons

Buttons are hardware items used in conjunction with buttonholes for the fastening of garments. They can add decoration as well as providing a closure and, in addition, buttons can be used alone as decoration.

The variety of materials from which buttons can be made is considerable, including the natural ones of wood, bone, horn and mother-of-pearl as well as the man-made ones of metal, polyester, polyamide, acrylic, urea formaldehyde and casein. In addition, plastic and metal can be combined such as when a metal ring encircles a button, and plastic can be covered with the fabric of the garment. As is normal with such materials, the natural ones provide buttons with some variability in colour and pattern and possibly in size and shape, at a higher price, while the man-made materials are more uniform as well as less expensive. Which is chosen depends largely on the garment type and its market but the prime requirement from the point of view of garment construction is that for situations of moderate to high volume production it must be possible to sew the buttons on by machine. This requires that the buttons can be held in a clamp in the machine while sewing takes place and for very high volume production such as that of shirts it requires that they can be fed to this clamp automatically from a hopper system.

Buttons are sewn to garments by means of the type of cam-controlled, automatic-cycle machine described earlier. They make use of single thread chainstitch, lockstitch or simulated hand stitching, the latter being used only on tailored outerwear. Single thread chainstitch, as was explained earlier, offers insecure button attachment but the machines are in wide use and their replacement with lockstitch machines would be costly.

Buttons which are sewn directly through the face have either two or four holes and it is important that where they are functional rather than decorative they are sewn with a sufficient thread shank that the button is not so tight against the garment that it distorts the buttonhole. On a four-hole button the direction of sewing does not matter but on a two-hole button the stitching should be parallel to the buttonhole to minimise distortion and the need for a long thread shank.

The other type of button which is available has no holes showing on the face but has its own shank on the back. This type must be clamped in the machine on its side so that the stitching passes alternately through the hole in the shank and to one side of it. Fabric-covered buttons are also of this shape. A selection of buttons was described when discussing buttonsew machines.

Tack buttons, snap fasteners and rivets

The use of metal components on garments has increased in recent years, especially with the wide acceptance of denim in jeans, skirts and jackets for casual wear. A sewn button on the waistband of a pair of jeans tends to suffer such abuse that the sewing is quickly overstressed or abraded and the button becomes detached. The fabric is capable of withstanding considerable stress and there is a need for the strength that can be provide by metal tack buttons or other metal snaps or studs as fastenings and by rivets as reinforcement. Similarly, rivets on pocket corners provide greater strength as well as providing a more interesting decoration than a sewn bar tack.

Tack buttons

Tack buttons consist of two sections. The outer button fastens with the buttonhole and has a similar appearance to the previously described shank button, except that it is not attached by sewing. The inner tack penetrates the fabric from the inside of the garment and is secured into the shank of the button by means of a special machine. There is no thread to come undone or be abraded and the broad base of the tack spreads the load which is placed on the button when it is in use. The two parts can be brass or steel and the button can be made with a decorative design or logo but it must be rustproofed. Once attached to the garment, they cannot be moved and it is thus more important that positioning is accurate than it is with sewn buttons. The garment fabric must be sufficiently strong, with the addition of an interlining if necessary, to take the stress to which such a button will be subject.

Snap fasteners

Snap or stud fasteners come in a variety of types but all consist of four elements, a cap and socket which fit together and form the outer, female part of the fastening and a stud and post which form the inner, male, part of the fastening, not normally seen when the garment is fastened. The cap and post may also consist of prong rings where the fastening is being used in lightweight, non-decorative applications. Prong fasteners are the only type suitable for use on knitted fabrics. This type is suitable for use on infants' playsuits and pyjamas and it is designed to avoid puncturing the fabric with large holes. It also lies completely flat. Failures usually arise from the method of application rather than defects in the fasteners. Fasteners should never be attached through a single thickness of material, but a backing fabric should be used, especially with knitted fabrics. The size used must be appropriate to the number of thicknesses and weight of fabric. The rim of the ring must not cross varying thicknesses of fabric and fastening through binding is preferably avoided. A common-sense test is to insert the fingernail between fabric and rim; if this can be done, failure is probable. The four sections of one type of snap fastener, in this case the type with a spring in the socket, and the assembly of them, is shown in Figure 5.3.

Snap fasteners can be made from plastic, steel or brass with a design on the cap if required. The metal can be enamelled and thus colour matching to the garment is possible. They can also have plastic caps on an otherwise metal assembly which gives further design and colour possibilities. They have wide uses, both decorative and functional, and in appropriate sizes and materials are used from heavy denim jackets to infants' stretch suits. They are quick to attach using appropriate machinery which automatically feeds the separate sections into position.

Fig. 5.3.   Spring snap fastener.

Rivets

Rivets are used for decoration and reinforcement on garments, mainly jeans, and may consist of one or two sections but in both cases a special machine is required to attach them. When the rivet is used alone, the tubular section on the back of the rivet that is passed through the material is spread out by the machine on the inside of the garment. In the two-part system the rivet is attached to a cap or a washer on the other side, and, depending on the appearance required, either side may be used on the outside of the garment. A variation known as a rivet and burr can be used in twos or fours to attach the ends of the metal logo plates used decoratively on jeans.

Performance properties of components and trims

The performance requirements of the items which are incorporated into garments in addition to the main fabric are largely the same as those of the main fabric but with the additional complication that they comprise a wide variety of materials, many of them non-textile. Garments must be capable of being constructed, worn, and washed and/or dry-cleaned in particular ways and to a particular standard which is appropriate to the end use of the garment and the market it will be sold in. Assuming that an acceptable standard has been set for the main fabric, all other items must be compatible with it.

Where items are textile in nature, the requirements are similar to those for the main fabric. *Shrinkage* during manufacture and cleaning must be controlled so that the garment retains its size and is not distorted. Other textile performance properties such as *strength, pilling, snagging, creasing* and *abrasion resistance* may also be important. *Resistance to heat* may be important if a garment made wholly or predominantly from natural fibres is trimmed with a synthetic ribbon or lace or a PVC binding as the ironing temperature required to give a good appearance to the main part of the garment may be high enough to cause damage to the trim.

For non-textile items, the main requirement is often strength. This is not difficult to achieve where metal is used but metal is not suitable for every application. Bikini fastenings, for example, must be strong but they are also exposed to the sun and if made from metal they can absorb enough heat to cause burns when they touch the skin. In this situation, a plastic, usually in the form of polyamide, would be used. Where a metallic appearance is required, it can be achieved by plating the polyamide.

Where items are made from metal, the main consideration is the problem of *rusting* if they are made from steel. For most trims, buttons, clasps etc, the base material would be steel or brass, the former being cheaper but also subject to rusting, even when electroplated. For inexpensive garments, those that will not be washed or exposed to rain or sea water, or for removable items such as dungaree clips, brass or nickel-plated steel may be satisfactory, the plating offering protection from rusting unless scratched. For more expensive garments and those requiring higher performance, brass should be used.

If there will be frequent exposure to salt water, as on some sports clothing, plastic is more suitable. If there is doubt as to the base material of an item with a plated finish, steel items can be identified by their magnetic properties.

One of the most important properties of all items which go together to make garments is their *colour*, both initially and after wear and cleaning. It applies to all the items discussed in the present chapter and also to the sewing threads described elsewhere. Thus it is normally necessary for all the components of a garment to match the main fabric or to provide a specific colour contrast, in whatever circumstances they are viewed, for the match to remain throughout the lifetime of the garment, and for contrasting colours not to run or bleed into one another.

Where items are chosen to match the main fabric, the degree of match required will vary according to the visibility of the item. Zip fasteners and lining fabrics are normally partly or wholly concealed by the garment and an adequate match can be obtained from the range of stock shades carried by the manufacturers. Buttons, depending on their raw material, may be surface dyed to match but this is not a difficult process. The highest standards of *colour matching* are required of sewing threads and despite the commonly used threads being available in several hundred shades from stock and a further thousand or so shades at short notice, special dying is occasionally required.

Where a high level of colour matching is required, the actual matching of thread or other items to material is a difficult process requiring equipment, experience and skill. There are several problems present in any matching situation, relating to the person doing the matching, the materials being matched and the surroundings. Leaving aside the problem of actual colour blindness which would bar a person from working with colour in any way, individuals vary in their ability to distinguish shades. Thus two people may see a shade match differently, one regarding it as a good match and the other a poor match. Tests are available to check people's ability to see colour accurately and these tests should be administered to anyone involved in choosing or checking a colour match.

Phenomena in the materials themselves can also affect the ease of achieving a good match. *Metamerism* is the phenomenon whereby a colour may match perfectly under one illuminant but be a mismatch under a second. Therefore certain dyes will produce a shade which matches a standard in, say, artificial daylight but not in the tungsten light used domestically. The dyer, therefore, should choose dye combinations carefully so that as well as matching under the specified illuminant, the match is reasonable under other illuminants. This is a relatively easy task these days since the advent of computer dye recipe predictions. The computer can examine all possible combinations of three dyes and inform the dyer beforehand as to the level of metamerism he can expect in the final product. Some retail stores use special tubes which use less energy but can give a different colour effect from domestic lighting or the lighting used in manufacturing. Such stores will need to ensure that the match is good in the display situation in the store as well as domestically, although the match may not be perfect while the garment is still in the factory. Garments which are made to be sold by the method of selling known as 'Party Plan' will require colour matching to be at its best under tungsten lighting.

Another difficulty with dyestuffs is that they may *fluoresce*, that is, absorb light in the ultraviolet part of the spectrum and re-emit it in the visible part. This phenomenon is actually made use of in white materials to make them look brighter but if it is present in dyestuffs of other colours it may cause shades to match in strong sunlight but differ in poor daylight or tungsten lighting.

Yet another problem is known as *dichroism* which is an apparent change of colour as the direction of viewing is changed. It tends to occur more with fabrics than with threads and other trims but it can affect the judgment of their colour. The best method of achieving satisfactory matching in these varied circumstances is by the use of a special lighting cabinet which contains one of each of the types of illuminant under which a match might need to be made. The box is painted a standard grey on the inside, the samples are viewed at a standard angle to the light, and the lighting in the room surrounding the box is also specified. If a light box is not available then matching should be done in good natural north daylight or in a room lit by BS Artificial Daylight. The fabric samples used should be at least 10 cm square, held at an angle of 45° to the light source and maintained stationary with the thread whilst a decision is made. They should be viewed against as plain a background as possible. Whether a light box is used or not, if sewing threads are being matched, the thread should be sewn into the fabric since a single strand will generally appear paler than the thread on the package. If a clothing manufacturer does not have satisfactory conditions for thread matching to the high standards that are required, the service can normally be provided by the thread suppliers on receipt of a fabric swatch.

Even when it has been established that the personnel engaged in colour matching have satisfactory colour vision, there can still be problems of agreement between visual observers, and many garment manufacturers and retailers now require fabrics and components to be matched instrumentally. These computer-controlled instruments make use of what are called colour difference equations which enable a manufacturer to specify a single colour difference tolerance, between his colour standard and delivery batches of fabric or other items, which is valid over the whole of colour space. The effect of this is to specify a maximum allowable shade variation, regardless of shade. How large a colour difference is acceptable will depend on a particular garment manufacturer's standards for his market but to many visual observers it would be undetectable. The two most common equations used in the UK are CMC (Colour Measurement Committee) Equation which is now the British and European Standard and the M&S 89 Equation which is used by all suppliers to Marks & Spencer.

In matching fabric and other items, the surface characteristics of the items being matched can have a significant effect upon the final visual shade. It is not possible to produce a coloured continuous filament thread, with its high lustre, so that it will appear exactly the same as a coloured spun or corespun thread which has a fibrous, matt surface. In addition, the surface character or twist of the thread may be changed as it goes through a sewing machine and this may affect its shade. The local density of a fabric in a seam may also cause difference in the shade of the seam compared to a single ply of fabric elsewhere in the garment and this may affect apparent thread match. Buttons, ribbons and other items may also have a glossy surface compared with the main fabric which will make matching difficult.

Having chosen a suitable shade to match the material to be sewn or to contrast with it for decoration, it is important that the selected shade remains colour fast throughout the life of the finished article. The *colour fastness* of any material is the resistance of its colour to the different agencies to which it may be exposed during manufacture and use. This usually means wash fastness and light fastness but other factors may be involved such as fastness to rubbing, pressing, cold water, sublimation, chlorination, dry cleaning, bleaching, and perspiration. Colour fastness is assessed in terms of change of shade in the item itself and staining of material adjacent to it. The tests used for colour fastness in sewing threads and other components follow the same lines and use the same Grey Scale methods of assessment as are used in investigations of other textile materials. The need for colour fastness to some of these agencies is largely self-explanatory but others may be less clear. Colour fastness to rubbing is necessary so that items used for contrast do not stain any adjacent fabric against which they may be rubbed constantly during use. Hot, wet pressing represents one of the severest tests of fastness and to test it a wet sample of thread or other trim is placed between one piece of wet cloth and one dry piece and pressed with a hot iron for 15 seconds. In practice, wet and dry parts of a garment could well be pressed together during ironing. The cold water test covers the situation where a garment containing a strongly coloured trim is left lying wet. This condition could be more severe than washing since no relative movement occurs and permanent staining could result. This particular problem can vary with the fibre content of the material being stained and bulked synthetic fabrics present a particular difficulty. They are sometimes referred to as 'scavengers' as they tend to attract any spare dyestuff to themselves.

Where thread is concerned, a wide range of colour fast shades is available in cotton threads for use on cotton fabrics and in polyester and polyamide threads for use on cotton, polyester and polyamide fabrics but these are not always sufficiently colour fast for use on bulked synthetics such as Ban-lon. Special polyamide threads are available to cope with this situation. The problem of *sublimation* arises when garments are subjected to permanent press curing processes. Temperatures as high as 175°C can be required and at this temperature some dyestuffs can sublimate, that is the dye vaporises and may be deposited on a cooler fabric surface and cause staining.

Permanent press treatment of garments to give them easy care properties generally involves chemicals and high temperatures which may adversely affect sewing threads in several ways. The main factors are shrinkage, strength loss and sublimation. Cotton threads are generally unsuitable because of loss of strength and shrinkage although they are normally free from sublimation. Spun polyester and polyester corespun are suitable with respect to strength and shrinkage and dyes are generally used on them that are fast to sublimation but it is advisable to mention the particular end use when ordering the thread. *Chlorination* is a hazard when articles are exposed to certain bleaching agents, swimming pool water and many anti-felting treatments for wool, the latter being particularly severe. Cotton threads are unsuitable as they can become bleached but polyester is normally satisfactory.

Where any items are being put together in a garment in a situation of contrast, the colour fastness requirements are higher than when they match and it is always advisable to notify the supplier of a contrast item that it will be used in that situation, as well as notifying him of any special processes to which the garment will be subject, so that special care can be taken with dyeing or different materials can be used if necessary.

A special problem of colour, though not of colour fastness, requires a mention here and that is the problem of *yellowing* of white materials and threads. Aside from any problem of white garments becoming soiled in manufacturing, problems occasionally arise when apparently perfectly clean garments are found to have yellow stains in places on them when they are unpacked prior to sale. Considerable investigation has been applied to this problem and an important factor appears to be exposure of the garment to oxides of nitrogen or hydrogen sulphide in polluted atmospheres. The pollution could arise from such things as vehicle exhausts or boiler or cooker emissions and tends to be worse during the winter months. Numerous other factors are also implicated such as fluorescent brightening agents which may be prone to yellowing and which may migrate and concentrate in certain areas of the garment such as hems and seams, chemicals present in (or contamination of) cardboard and polythene used for packaging, and the particular tendency of some white polyamide fibres to yellow if exposed to certain pollutants. Close scrutiny of packaging materials, fabric finishes, sewing threads and associated trimmings will reduce the possibility of yellowing and work continues to find satisfactory chemical inhibitors which could be applied to these items.

Outside the situations already described, other less common and rather specialised ones exist which present special hazards to components from the point of view of colour and other problems. Such situations are the extreme laundering and dry-cleaning conditions used with contract rental workwear and those such as medical and food applications where threads might be required to be non-toxic and fast to autoclaving. Component manufacturers can normally advise on the most suitable thread and sewing conditions and, if necessary, special finishes can be developed.

6
Alternative Methods of Joining Materials

It has already been stated several times that the dominant process in the assembly of garments is sewing. Many attempts have been made to develop other processes but achieving the speed and flexibility of manufacture which is required, along with the seam appearance and performance, have proved difficult. The processes which have been developed as alternatives to sewing are very important, but their use is confined to limited situations. Those to be considered are:

(1) Fusing
(2) Welding and adhesives
(3) Moulding

(A) FUSING

By far the most important area of garment construction where an alternative process has significantly taken over from sewing is in the attachment of interlinings. The purpose and nature of interlinings were described in the last chapter but the discussion was confined to interlinings which are sewn into garments. When interlinings are sewn in, it can be difficult on parts such as collars to avoid a wrinkling of the interlining inside the collar and pucker around the edge. On large parts such as jacket fronts, the attachment of interlinings by sewing is expensive and requires skill if a high standard is to be achieved. The alternative process which has been developed is that of fusing, whereby the interlining is bonded to the outer fabric by means of a thermoplastic resin.

The fusible interlining consists of a base cloth, which may be similar to that used for a sew-in interlining, and which carries on its surface a thermoplastic adhesive resin, usually in the form of small dots, which will melt when heated to a specific temperature. If it is laid flat with the resin side onto the garment part and heat and pressure are applied, the resin will flow into the fabric of the garment and it and the interlining will become permanently attached. For the remaining assembly of the garment this laminate, as it is called, will be handled as one piece of material. This simple explanation hides a great deal of technology but it serves to introduce one of the most significant developments in garment construction methods to have taken place in recent years. Not all garment fabrics can be fused, and there will always be some situations where sew-in interlinings continue to be used, but in the vast majority of garment making today, fusing is the more common process. The reasons are both economic and technical.

The advantages of using fusible interlinings

(1)   In most cases the use of fusible interlinings shortens manufacturing time with a consequent *reduction in direct labour cost*. In large area applications such as jacket fronts the fusing operation replaces complex baisting operations. In some small area applications such as reinforcing tapes it replaces sewing but in others it can actually add a stage to the manufacturing process. If the parts of a collar are to be sewn together in a jig, a sew-in interlining can be laid into the jig at the same time as the collar parts at only a small extra cost in labour. If the collar is to be fused it must be done separately from the assembly of the collar.

(2)   There is a *reduction in the skill* required in many operations involving fusing compared with the sewing in of interlinings and this leads to a reduction in training time.

(3)   It is easier to achieve *consistent quality* in the lamination process than it is with many of the operations of sewing in of interlinings, especially on modern lightweight fabrics. Traditionalists sometimes claim that, in individual cases, a craftsman using traditional canvas interlinings can produce garments with a subtlety of contour, a softness and a crease recovery that fusing cannot, but the overall cost of manufacturing by this method is high enough to be uncompetitive for all but a few people, and this softer appearance, when rarely seen, has become less fashionable.

(4)   Fusible interlinings provide opportunities for *alternative methods of garment construction*, in some of which the interlining might be said to be operating as a 'work aid' in the sense that the term was used earlier, with all the advantages of speed and quality that work aids can confer. Most notable of these methods are those involving slotted interlinings. In this case the interlining will have been purchased cut to a specific narrow width, perhaps that of the pattern piece for a waistband, with lines of long narrow slots, about 20 mm by 2 mm, cut out of it along the intended folds of the waistband. When fused to the waistband, and sewn to a skirt or trouser along one line of slots, the band will more easily fold in the

Fig. 6.1. Skirt waistband with slotted interlining.

correct positions to give the correct width. This type of application is shown in Figure 6.1. It can be used in many other applications as well such as forming the edges of pleats and hems.

The requirements of fusing

The process of fusing interlinings to garments must fulfil certain requirements and avoid certain problems if the garment is to have a satisfactory appearance and performance throughout its life.

(1) The laminate produced by fusing should show the *aesthetic qualities* required by the designer in the finished garment. This relates in particular to the stiffness or draping qualities of the garment. These increase beyond those of the two components, singly or together, in a way which is not predictable. Achieving the required stiffness, handle or draping qualities is a matter of trial and error before manufacturing begins. The factors over which the garment manufacturer can exercise choice are the drape of the fusible's base cloth and the type and quantity of the fusible resin forming the bond. In the search for a softer handle, the choice may be a compromise between the strength of the bond, as measured, and those qualities referred to as stiffness, handle and drape, based on a subjective judgment. Other fabric properties which could be adversely affected by the fusing on of interlinings are crease recovery and air permeability. A laminate will normally show crease recovery properties somewhere between the better component and the worse and it may vary with the grain direction of the fabric. Fusing normally reduces air permeability and if it is both low to begin with in the outer fabric, and an important requirement in the finished garment, consideration must be given to it when interlinings are chosen.

(2)   The *strength of bond* of the laminate must be sufficient to withstand handling during subsequent operations in the garment manufacturing process as well as the flexing which takes place in wear. The bond must resist either the temperature and degree of agitation of a washing and drying cycle, with perhaps subsequent ironing, or the solvents, temperature and agitation of a dry-cleaning process, and in some cases both. The garment should carry a care label appropriate to the requirements of the fused interlinings as well as to the rest of the garment materials. If there is not a complete and even bond over the whole surface of the laminate when first fused, or if delamination takes place at some stage in the garment's life, it will appear as a 'bubbling' in the outer fabric of the garment. Parts which appear to be satisfactorily fused initially, could have a bond which is below the required strength and which will subsequently fail. Certain fabrics are particularly difficult to fuse to and notable among these are showerproof rainwear fabrics. Both the showerproof finish on the fabric and its typically smooth, hard surface make a good bond difficult to achieve.

(3)   Fusing must take place without either *strike-through* or *strike-back* occurring. When the softened adhesive resin is pressed into the garment fabric, it is important that it does not go right through to the face side of that fabric, and that it does not go back to the outside of the interlining base cloth. These problems are known as 'strike-through' and 'strike-back' respectively. If strike-through occurs it may show on the right side of the garment as a pattern of dots of resin and if it occurs on a garment subject to high temperature ironing such as a shirt collar, it may be picked up on the iron and lead to marking of the garment. If strike-back occurs it can contaminate parts of the equipment used in the fusing process, and may also adhere to the garment lining during pressing.

(4)   The fusing process must not cause *thermal shrinkage* in the outer fabric. Fusing commonly takes place at around 150°C and at this temperature many fabrics may be subject to thermal shrinkage. If it occurs it can cause garments to fit together badly during manufacture and be incorrect in size after manufacture.

(5)   A further possible effect of the heat of the fusing process is that of *dye sublimation*. Fabrics may change colour to a level which is unacceptable and in a way which causes a mis-match between the fused and unfused parts of the garment.

(6)   Since the fusing process involves pressure, there is a risk that pile fabrics may be subject to *crushing* during fusing. Fused and unfused parts of the garment, when sewn together, may have a different appearance.

(7)   Where showerproof fabrics are fused, there is a possibility that the presence of a fused interlining in the garment may *wick water* through the fabric in the fused areas while the unfused areas remain satisfactorily showerproofed. Water resistant interlinings have been developed for these situations.

The achievement of the above requirements, and the avoidance of the problems described, require that care is taken in the selection of an interlining for a particular outer fabric at the design stage, having in mind the intended appearance, handle and end use of the garment and the equipment available for fusing. It also requires careful control of the fusing process in the factory. Fusing operations pose problems of a different order from those of cutting, sewing and pressing for the simple reason that a satisfactory outcome of the operation cannot be judged visually. While some of the problems described show immediately, in most cases they will only appear after wearing or cleaning, by which time many faulty garments may have been made. In most other clothing manufacturing operations, the eye provides the information required to make a judgment about acceptability. In fusing, it will be seen that the temperature at which it takes place, the pressure that is applied, and the time during which the heating and pressing operate, are critical for satisfactory fusing, but their effectiveness can only be measured by specific, destructive tests performed on samples of fused fabric and interlining. Setting up and maintaining fusing operations requires a closer and more continuous co-operation among materials suppliers, production managers and the manufacturers of the equipment than is required in other operations.

The fusing process

The means of fusing are temperature and pressure, applied over a period of time, usually in some kind of specialised fusing press. The rise in temperature at the 'glue line', the interface of resin and outer fabric where the resin is active, is caused by the electric heating elements of the press. This changes the state of the resin from a dry solid to a viscous fluid. Only with appropriate pressure will this flow among the fibres of both the outer fabric and the fusible base cloth. On cooling, the resin re-solidifies and forms a bond between the two components of the laminate. The heat has to pass through fabric to activate the resin, and this requires a time measured in seconds, which varies according to the nature of the fabric and the type of resin.

Every fusible resin has an optimum temperature at which it flows satisfactorily. If this temperature is not reached then a longer time or higher pressure will not compensate, and the bond will be weak. If the temperature rises too high the resin becomes too fluid, giving rise to strike-back and strike-through. Most specifications of optimum temperatures for fusing include a tolerance to cope with small variations in operating conditions.

In addition to the outer fabric of the garment, three factors determine the properties of the fused laminate:

(1)   the base fabric of the interlining;
(2)   the type of fusible resin;
(3)   the pattern of application of the resin to the base cloth.

(1) The base fabric of the interlining

Base fabrics are available in the woven and non-woven constructions described for sew-in interlinings and also as warp knits. The warp knits are either a locknit or weft insert construction.

Locknit, using more yarns and with more interlinking of loops, gives a satisfactory stability where simple warpknit would not be stable enough. The most usual fibre is nylon, which gives very soft handle and draping. In some applications, the smooth surface may fulfil part of the role of a body lining. Weft insert fabrics consist of vertical chains of loops with yarns laid in horizontally and interlaced with the vertical chains. This construction should, in theory, give the vertical suppleness and horizontal resilience of a woven interlining, but in practice the properties are rather unpredictable. Finishing involves heat setting and, depending on the nature of the inserted yarn, may include chemical treatment.

(2) The type of fusible resin

Just as there is a range of stitch and seam types to achieve a range of assembly objectives and finishes, so there is a range of types of resin to cover a range of laminating requirements. The choice of resin is restricted by limits imposed by the outer fabric, the fusing equipment to be used, the end use requirements, and the precise behaviour of the resins in response to heat. The particular requirements of resins are as follows:

(a) The fusing temperature needed must not be so high that it will damage the outer fabric or its colour. The usual maximum is 175°C, with 150°C most common.

(b) The fusing temperature needed must not be so low that the bond is inadequate to withstand garment making. The lower limit is generally 110°C though leather may require even lower temperatures.

(c) The resin must provide a bond which is suitably resistant to washing and/or dry-cleaning.

(d) The thermoplastic nature of the resin must be such that adjustment of temperature is sufficient to permit it to penetrate the outer fabric to give a bond, without flowing excessively to give strike-through or strike-back.

(e) The resin must contribute to the achievement of the desired handle of the laminate.

(f) In the majority of end uses the resin must be white or transparent. It must also have low dye retention properties.

(g) The resin must be harmless in processing and in end use.

An ideal resin would have a high degree of cross-linking ability, that is, it would be a thermosetting resin with no danger of being affected by subsequent higher temperatures. Such resins are still under development.

The resins used are mostly chemicals whose names will be familiar from other uses. All are capable of modification during manufacture to give a wide range of properties, both as fusible resins and for these other uses. In the present context, a detailed understanding of the properties of the resins is not necessary, but it is important to appreciate the range that is available.

(a) Polyethylene

Polyethylene coatings are available in different densities and with different values of a property known as the melt flow index. The value of this index determines the extent to which the resin flows during the fusing operation and the higher its value, i.e. the more easily it flows, the lower will be the subsequent resistance of the laminate to dry-cleaning solvents. The effect of varying the density of the resin is to give a greater resistance to dry-cleaning solvents, and a higher softening point, with increasing density. All the polyethylene resins used in fusible coatings are washable and, in the higher densities, they are both washable and dry-cleanable. They require high bonding pressures on the fusing press and their main use is in interlinings for shirt collars.

(b) Polypropylene

This resin is similar in properties to high density polyethylene but reaches its softening point at a higher temperature. This makes it especially suitable for fusing applications where rapid, high-temperature drying is part of the garment laundering process. The resin will withstand temperatures at the glue line of 150°C before delaminating.

(c) Polyamides

Polyamides can have a wide range of fusing properties, according to the proportions of the basic ingredients of different nylons employed as well as the amount of plasticiser added. The objectives are to vary the melting range and lower the softening temperature. Polyamides are very widely used in dry-cleanable garments. Polyamides in the higher temperature melting range are generally washable up to 60°C but in the lower melting ranges they are dry-cleanable only.

(d) Polyesters

Polyesters have a similarly wide range of fusing properties as a result of varying the constituents. These resins are used in garments which are dry-cleanable and washable, because polyesters are less water-absorbent than polyamides and therefore resist washing better.

(e) Polyvinyl chloride (PVC)

This resin is generally printed onto base fabrics as a plasticised paste and the fusing temperature is determined by the amount and type of plasticiser used in its formation. It is both dry-cleanable and washable. It is commonly used in large area applications on coat fronts.

(f) Plasticised polyvinyl acetate (PVA)

This resin is normally in the form of a continuous coating for fusing to leather and fur at low pressures and temperatures. It is not dry-cleanable and has limited washability.

A small number of other chemicals have been tried but they are not in widespread use.

(3) Methods of applying resins to base cloths

There is further scope for varying the properties of an interlining and its effect on the outer fabric of a garment by varying the application of the resin to the base cloth. The most popular methods used are:

(a) scatter coating;
(b) dry dot printing;
(c) paste coating.

All the methods involve the use of carefully selected particle sizes of the various resins. Scatter coating uses the largest particles, from 150 to 400 microns, dry dot printing uses particles from 80 to 200 microns, and paste coating uses the smallest at 0 to 80 microns (1,000 microns equals 1 mm).

(a) Scatter coating

Specifically designed scattering heads are used to provide an even scatter under automatic control. The resin is then softened in an oven, pressed onto the base cloth and cooled. This is the cheapest method of making a fusible but the product is not as uniform nor as flexible as printed coatings.

(b) Dry dot printed coating

The powdered resin fills engraved holes on a roller. The base cloth passes over a heated roller and then against the engraved roller. The powdered resin adheres to the cloth in the form of dots. Oven heating follows the printing operation to ensure permanent adhesion. The temperature and pressure on the two rollers is varied for different resin types. Patterns of dots can vary from 3 to 12 dots per cm according to the garment manufacturer's requirements. Generally, lighter weight garment fabrics require interlinings with smaller dots in higher concentration, while heavier weight fabrics require larger dots in lower concentration to allow good penetration into the fabric surface and give a satisfactory bond.

(c) Paste coating

Fine resin powders are blended with water and other agents to form a smooth paste and are printed onto the base cloth. Heat removes the water and the dots coalesce into solid resin. This type of coating gives precisely shaped dots and is used to produce the finer dots used in shirt collar fusibles.

The above are the most frequently used methods. Others used are: preformed systems, where a preformed net is laminated to a base cloth to form precise dot patterns such as are used on top collar fusibles; extrusion laminating, producing a continuous film of polyethylene, also used in shirt collar applications but resulting in a very stiff product; and emulsion coating, for instance by dipping the base cloth into a bath of emulsion, squeezing out excess resin by rolling and drying in an oven to produce double-sided coatings.

Choice of resin type and method of coating relates to cost, fusing characteristics, suitability for use with particular fusing equipment, durability when washing and dry-cleaning and particular garment end use. It will be clear from the variety of base fabrics, resin types and resin applications that are available that the total range of possibilities when these are used in combination is very wide. Within one company, which makes a limited range of garment types and has only one method of fusing, a small selection only will be needed. Making the correct choice requires careful investigation at the design stage, often with the help of the interlining companies and their laboratory facilities. Cost will often be a consideration but it should be remembered that the cost of the interlining is often small in relation to the total cost of the materials in the garment, whereas the cost of failure of unsatisfactory garments, returned after wearing and cleaning, could be extremely high.

The means of fusing

Fusing equipment must provide control of three factors:

(1) temperature;
(2) pressure;
(3) time.

(1) Temperature

This must be high enough to achieve the necessary temperature at the glue line which will change the dry thermoplastic resin into a partially molten state in order that it will flow. For each resin there is a limited range within which the correct level of flow is achieved. Too low a temperature gives poor flow and poor subsequent adhesion. Too high a temperature gives too much flow, resulting in strike-back and strike-through and a reduction of performance in most respects.

(2) Pressure

The equipment must provide enough consistent pressure to ensure intimate contact between interlining and outer cloth over the whole surface of the interlining. This ensures correct transfer of heat to the glue line and correct penetration of resin among the fibres of the outer fabric. Too low a pressure reduces penetration with consequent low adhesion. Too high a pressure provides excessive penetration of resin resulting in strike-back and strike-through.

(3) Time

The equipment must give enough time to allow the temperature and pressure to induce melting of the resin and penetration of the outer fabric in order to produce a satisfactory bond, but not too much or strike-back and strike-through result. It will be appreciated that if a thick fabric and an interlining are put into a heated press in a cool state, it may be several seconds before the resin reaches the required temperature.

These three factors are interrelated. A change in one may necessitate a change in the others, though there is a limit to the extent to which one factor will compensate for another. If the temperature in the press is not high enough, no amount of extra time will enable the resin to soften and flow.

Fusing equipment

The equipment used for fusing can be divided into:

(1)   specialised fusing presses;
(2)   hand irons;
(3)   steam presses.

(1) Specialised fusing presses

A number of different types of fusing press have been developed over the years, providing control of the heat and pressure applied to the garment part and providing for fusing to take place on flat sections of garments that have not yet been sewn. In many companies, such fusing presses are sited in the cutting room and the fusing operation takes place before transferring the garments to the sewing room. On some garments, notably men's jackets, it is necessary to add further sections of fusible interlining to the already three-dimensional garment during construction and for this, different equipment must be used.

(i)   (ii)

Fig. 6.2. Flat bed fusing presses. (i) Vertical action. (ii) Scissor action.

Fusing presses vary in the way they operate and these differences affect both the quality of the fusing and the productivity of the operation.

(a) Flat bed fusing press

A diagram of the principle of operation of this type of fusing press is shown in Figure 6.2. It consists of two horizontal metal platens between which the fabric and interlining laminate are sandwiched. The top platen is unpadded but the bottom platen has a resilient cover, typically silicone rubber, though it may be a felt pad. Both platens have an outer cover of PTFE which can be easily cleaned to prevent staining and build-up of resin, which would cause garment parts to adhere to the platen. Heat is provided by electric elements, usually in the top platen only, but sometimes in the bottom also. The elements are so disposed as to provide a uniform temperature over the whole surface.

The press manufacturer aims for a standard of control allowing a variation of 5°C either way from the required temperature over the whole surface area. Pressure is applied by closing the platens together mechanically, hydraulically or pneumatically. The pressure system must be robust, provide accurate closing over a large area and be free from distortion through heat, wear or mechanical faults. The resilient bottom cover should be changed regularly to avoid pressure problems. Vertical action closure, as shown in Figure 6.2(i), gives more accurate pressure than the scissors action shown in (ii). Fusing time is normally controlled by an automatic timer, whose cycle can be varied to suit different requirements. It is typically of the order of 8–12 seconds.

In the simplest mode of operation, the operator places the garment part face down on the lower platen, places the interlining resin side down on top of it in the correct position, and closes the press. This is slow and time-consuming as the operator can do little that is productive for the duration of the fusing cycle. These presses do not cover a very large area, often not more than one metre by half a metre, and the number of garment parts which can be fused at one time will depend on their size. If a small end section of a larger garment part requires to be fused it may be possible to insert only the end of the part into the press. A change in the type or style of garment to one needing large areas of fusing could present difficulties for a company having only a small area fusing press. Where small parts are being fused, output may be increased by laying them on a sheet of card which is then placed in the press. By this method, the placing of garment and interlining parts can take place while the previous parts are being fused. Accuracy of positioning of the interlining on the garment part is important, not just for the garment, but for the cleanliness of the press. Where the whole area of a garment part is being fused, the interlining pattern is normally slightly smaller than the garment pattern so that there is no possibility of the interlining extending over the edge of the garment part. If this happens, resin is transferred to the cover on the lower platen and subsequently to the face side of another garment part. This is a potential problem whatever the method of fusing used.

Variations in the design of these presses can improve productivity, in particular by having a twin tray system which slides in and out from under the top platen, or a three-station carousel which has two operators at separate loading and unloading stations. In both of these, loading and unloading takes place during the fusing cycle, but the principle of operation of the press remains the same as the simple version described above, in that the garment parts are held firmly between the platens for the duration of the fusing cycle.

Among the advantages of this type of fusing press is that, in the simplest version, their small size and relatively low cost allow their use by the smaller clothing manufacturer. They also tend to reduce fabric shrinkage since the fabric is held under pressure throughout the fusing cycle. A disadvantage, though, is the tendency to crush pile fabrics such as velvet because of the length of time that they are held under pressure.

(b) Continuous fusing systems

These systems operate by passing the garment part, with its interlining placed on it, past a heat source and, either simultaneously or subsequently, applying pressure. Heat is provided in one of three ways:

(i)   With direct heating, the conveyor belt carries the components to be fused into direct contact with a heated surface, either a drum or curved plates.
(ii)   With indirect heating, the components to be fused are carried through a heated chamber.
(iii) With low temperature, gradient heating, the components are carried through a pre-heating zone. Heating is either direct or indirect. With this approach the temperature reached at the glue line is only just above that required to make the resin a viscous fluid and in some cases fusing takes place satisfactorily with a glue line

Fig. 6.3. Continuous fusing press.

temperature of only 120°C. This reduces the possibility of heat shrinkage in the outer fabric and is a feature of some of the most recent fusing presses. An example of (ii) is shown in Figure 6.3.

The maintenance of the required temperature is less of a problem inside a fully enclosed, continuously operating press, than with a flat bed press, especially with modern electronic temperature controls. On drum presses, the tension of the conveyor belt presses the components continuously against the heated drum, during the complete fusing process. Where conveyor belts carry the components past heating plates (direct) or through a heating chamber (indirect), nip rollers apply pressure to the assembly after heating. The pressure time is very small compared to that in flat bed presses and has to be more precisely controlled. The loading on the rollers is applied by springs or pneumatically at their ends. Rollers must be maintained parallel, unbowed and free of wear to give even pressure. The rubber covering of the rollers is available in a range of hardnesses. Usually shirt top collar fusing requires the hardest rollers and outerwear fabrics require softer rollers. Fusing times depend on the speed of the conveyor belt which can be adjusted to give various dwell times in the heated zone.

Companies engaged in high volume garment production generally use continuous fusing systems, both for the quality of the fusing they give and for the productivity gains. Presses are now available of such a size that as many as six operators can be loading simultaneously from specially designed workplaces. Unloading may be by operator at the far end, or by automatic catcher, or the press may divert the fused parts back to the loading station. It should be mentioned here that care is needed in handling newly fused parts while they are still hot as distortion or marking can occur.

These fusing presses can require a total floor area as high as 30 square metres. By contrast, special narrow continuous fusing presses are available for use where companies require large quantities of narrow parts fused. They are particularly used for waistbands and belts and in a

Fig. 6.4. Continuous fusing press. (Reproduced by permission of Bandwise Reliant Ltd.)

company making only trousers, this might be the only fusing press they would need. High productivity is obtained by cutting the interlining in continuous strips directly from the roll (by cutting through the roll at the required width), and setting this to run continuously through the press. Waistbands are cut slightly longer than will be needed and are fed into the press, onto the interlining, one after the other by the operator. A small overlap should be made in the waistbands so that there are no gaps where adhesive from the interlining would be transferred to the press. The operator can stop the press when necessary. The fused waistbands can be rolled up automatically at the far end of the press and in many cases can be presented in this form to the sewing operator. If waistbands are being attached to trousers or skirts through a folder, time is saved if they are in a continuous strip. The joins in the waistbands will become waste between garments. A continuous fusing press is shown in Figure 6.4.

Continuous fusing presses generally reduce any problems associated with fusing pile fabrics such as velvet because the duration of pressure on the fabric is short. For the same reason, though, fabrics prone to heat shrinkage are likely to shrink more when fused in a continuous press than when firmly held in a flat bed press.

(c) High frequency fusing

In the fusing presses described so far, heat has been provided by electric heating elements. This limits the number of thicknesses of fabric which can be fused at once because of the time taken for the heat to transfer through the fabric to the resin. If multiple layers of fabric and interlining could be stacked up and fused simultaneously, productivity might be increased. Over a number of years, attempts have been made to do this by generating the heat by means of high frequency energy, in the same way as in a microwave cooker.

The alternating waves from a high frequency generator are absorbed by the material, generating friction and heat between the molecules. The platens of the press are the plates generating the high frequency field and the heating effect is uniformly distributed in length and width and is the full height between the platens. The effect is known as dielectric heating. The heating effect is different between natural and man-made materials and the fusible adhesive material generally heats up faster than either the interlining base fabric or the garment farbric. This should result in bonding at the glue line without excessive heat being generated in the fabric. Multiple plies of garment and interlining can be stacked up to 70 mm high, and since the heating effect is not dependent on its distance from a heat source, the adhesive at each joint should be raised to the same temperature. Less pressure is needed than with conventional fusing presses. The time required to generate the heat depends on the capacity of the high frequency unit and the weight of the load to be fused. For a typical 30 kW unit, operating times of 1–3 minutes may be achieved for loads of 5–20 kg.

The difficulty which arises with this method of fusing is that the press must be set to allow for the particular natural or man-made materials being used, the weight and thickness of those materials, and their moisture content. This is not easy, especially in the case of the moisture content. If incorrect estimates are made, it is possible for the press to overfuse and bond the whole stack together, or underfuse and produce a poor bond on each garment part.

Only a small number of these presses are in operation so far in the UK.

(2) Hand iron

Only those interlinings which can be fused at relatively low temperatures, low pressures and in relatively short times are at all suitable for fusing by hand iron. There are a number of difficulties. The operator cannot know the temperature at the glue line and cannot apply pressure uniformly. The operator estimates the time subjectively. Only small parts can be fused with any degree of success, and then only by pressing the iron for a fixed time onto the fusible, covering the area step by step and using steam to help the heat transfer. It is particularly in this situation that garment parts may appear to be satisfactorily fused initially but deficiencies will show up as delamination during wearing or cleaning of the garment.

When the iron is used merely to position an interlining part or tape temporarily, to be followed by pressing on a steam press, then fusing conditions are more satisfactory. This is common in menswear where additional, reinforcing, fusible tapes are often added during the construction of a jacket, in positions such as pockets, vents and hems. The garment is placed on a shaped press of the type to be described in the next chapter, the interlining sections are positioned using the hand iron, and the press is closed to effect complete fusing. On jacket hems, a slotted interlining tape is often used and once this is fused on, the iron can be further used to press up the hem along the line of slots before further sewing.

(3) Steam press

In this case fusing takes place on presses of the type used for intermediate and final pressing of made up garments. Temperature at the glue line is achieved by steam from the head of the press. The temperature reached depends on the steam pressure at the press head, the efficiency of the press and its cladding. Pressure is provided mechanically or pneumatically by closing the press head on the buck. Vacuum in the lower part of the press, or buck, assists rapid cooling. The head is less likely to meet the buck with even pressure if it works with a scissors action. Best results are obtained if the pressing cycle is controlled automatically. The resins which fuse most successfully on a steam press are polyvinyl acetate and the lower melting range of polyamides, but fusing is not as effective as when using a dedicated press.

A specialised use of a steam press for fusing is in the positioning, and initial attaching, of fusible shoulder pads in men's jackets, as described in Chapter 5. A shoulder press would be used.

Methods of fusing

All the descriptions of the fusing process that have been included so far, have represented it as a single piece of interlining, laid resin side down, on a single piece of garment fabric, laid right side down. This is referred to as single fusing and it is the safest in the sense that it is easiest to set the press conditions to achieve the correct temperature at the glue line. Several other configurations are possible, both in terms of the presentation of the parts to the fusing press, and in the parts that are included in the garment. Some of the variations will now be described and illustrating them will demonstrate some of the methods of garment construction that involve fusible interlinings. The main variations are:

(1) reverse fusing;
(2) sandwich fusing;
(3) double fusing.

(1) Reverse fusing

In this method the outer fabric lies on top of the fusible. It is sometimes used in fusing shirt and blouse collars. On flat bed presses with elements only in the top platen, it is necessary to adjust temperature settings. Since the interlining part is normally slightly smaller than the garment part, accurate positioning may be difficult.

(2) Sandwich fusing

This is effectively carried out only on a horizontal continuous press where heat is applied both from above and below. Two pairs of components, forming two laminates, are fused together, with the two outer fabrics on the outside of the sandwich (of four layers) and the two interlinings on the inside. With correct temperature settings, the glue line temperature may be achieved in both laminates but the potential for strike-back occurring and causing all the layers to adhere together is considerable. A small amount of fusing time will be saved but preparation will take longer and the quality of the results may be unsatisfactory.

(3) Double fusing

This is the fusing of two sorts of interlining to the outer fabric in one operation. It is most commonly used in shirt collars and men's jacket fronts.

(a) Shirt collar fusing

The majority of shirts manufactured today are made with one-piece collars rather than the more expensive, traditional two-piece collar. In the creation of a satisfactory one-piece collar with a definite break line, fusible interlinings play a very important part. Two different constructions are in common use, both requiring two thicknesses of interlining to be fused to the top collar section in what is referred to as a skin and patch construction.

(i) *One-piece collar with turning*. This construction is shown in Figure 6.5. One layer of fusible interlining skin is fused to the edge of the fabric, except on the neck edge, and a second layer of fusible interlining patch, cut to fit within the sewing line and with a 3 mm slot along the break line, is fused on top of it. This double fusing process requires the achievement of two correct glue line temperatures in the two layers of resin. The collars are normally fused with the patch lining towards the hot press surface, if only one platen is heated, and it is necessary to ensure that the glue line temperature furthest away, i.e. the one between the face fabric and the interlining skin, reaches the required level. This may require the glue line temperature nearest to the press surface, i.e between skin and patch, to be slightly above that required. However, because of the generally thin face fabrics and interlinings and the tolerance built into the interlinings, the two glue line temperatures can be balanced to give good performance without excessive flow of resin.

In this construction, precision is all important in the cutting and

Top collar
fabric

Fig. 6.5.   One-piece collar construction with interlining in the seam.

Top collar
fabric

Fig. 6.6.   One-piece collar construction without interlining in the seam.

locating of the interlinings. They are usually die cut and the two sections are spot welded together before being placed on the collar piece. A locating notch ensures correct positioning on the collar. This type of collar can be sewn in an automatic jig or profile stitcher and the interlining skin gives support to the fabric during stitching. It does, however, produce a thicker collar edge than the alternative method. All the component parts are cut and fused warp to warp to ensure minimum shrinkage during fusing and after-care.

(ii)   One-piece collar with nett interlining construction. This construction looks similar at first glance to the one described above but both the skin and the patch interlinings are cut to the same size and fit within the stitch line on the collar piece. This is shown in Figure 6.6.

The interlining edges are used as a profile for stitching directly onto the fabric collar plies, usually with a small wheel beside the presser foot acting as an edge guide. Automatic profile stitching machinery cannot be used. There is no excess interlining in the seam and this gives a thin edge that does not require topstitching.

Fig. 6.7. Jacket front with floating chest piece.

Fig. 6.8. Jacket front with fully fused forepart.

(b) Fusing of tailored jacket fronts

A wide variety of different constructions are used for the foreparts of men's jackets and a small selection only will be described here. The main requirement is a different level of support in different sections of the jacket between the shoulder and the hem and an additional support in the chest area which does not go into the lapel. To retain a good appearance in the jacket, despite the movement of the body, the interlining should provide a recovery from bending in the horizontal direction, coupled with a softness and flexibility in the vertical direction.

(i) Floating chest piece. In this construction, shown in Figure 6.7, the body interlining is fused over the whole of the front and a chest piece is made by fusing two interlinings together and attaching them to the front by means of a fusible bridle tape.

(ii) Fully fused forepart. This construction of jacket front has a body interlining fused right across and a chest piece and shoulder piece fused on top of it. This is shown in Figure 6.8.

(iii) Multizonal with extra fusible felt shoulder. Interlinings are available which are graduated in weight, usually in three stages, across the width of the cloth. If the interlining parts for the garment are cut across the piece it is possible to create a garment with heavier interlining at the top and lighter at the hem. With some garment end uses, such as washable school

Fig. 6.9. Jacket front with multizonal fusible interlining.

blazers, this might be adequate on its own. For a higher quality garment, additional lapel and shoulder pieces are fused onto it. If the lapel becomes too bulky by this method, a separate piece of interlining may be used in that area. This method is shown in Figure 6.9.

Not all types of fusing press are suitable for the methods of fusing described here and, in every case, very careful setting of the press conditions is necessary.

Quality control in fusing

It is clear from a number of statements made so far that careful control of the fusing process, after careful selection of interlinings, is essential. Assuming that a company has purchased a press which is appropriate to its needs, and sited it where extraneous factors such as draughts will not affect it, checks must still be made on a routine basis that the press and the garments being produced on it are satisfactory. Separate checks can be made on the factors of temperature, pressure and time and on the quality of the bond being achieved in the laminate.

(1) Checks on temperature

It is necessary to calibrate fusing presses before beginning to operate them, in order to relate actual glue line temperatures to thermostat settings in all the conditions and over all the time cycles likely to be met during normal manufacturing conditions. The glue line temperatures required for fusing will always be lower than the thermostat temperatures displayed owing to the insulating effect of press cladding, interlining and outer fabric. A further factor is the heat required to boil off the regain, the natural moisture contained within materials, which is a variable factor. Two methods of checking temperature are available.

(i) A portable *pyrometer* is a device which consists of a long wire probe which can be inserted into a press, between plies of interlining and fabric, and which shows on a dial the temperature achieved after a certain time of closing of the press. It can only be used on a flat bed press and should itself be calibrated using heat sources with known temperatures such as boiling water. The probe, or a set of probes, should be placed in the press so that readings are obtained over the whole area of the platen. Fusing presses are heated by means of a number of heating elements and it is essential to monitor that all are working. When making these checks, the time of closure of the press should also be noted.

(ii) *Thermopapers* consist of a narrow strip with a series of heat-sensitive areas. Each section along the thermopaper is marked with a temperature and it changes from white to black if that temperature is reached while it is in the press. This is the only method of heat measurement which can be used with a continuous press and the time of throughput should also be noted when checks are made. This method can, of course, also be used on a flat bed press. Thermopapers should be passed through the continuous press at intervals across its width, sandwiched between interlining and fabric.

Whether the press is being calibrated initially, or is in use for fusing, it must be allowed sufficient time to reach its working temperature after switching on. This time could be half an hour or more and arrangements must be made for it to be ready by the start of production each day. If a flat bed press is left idle over a break, or a continuous press is not left running, they may not be ready for use immediately afterwards as various unheated parts will have cooled down. Both types of press must be run through several cycles before being used again.

(2) Checks on pressure

Adequate and even pressure over the whole area of a fusing press is essential and, although there will probably be a dial showing the pressure in the compressed air line supplying the press, this does not provide a very good indication of the actual pressure on the platens. In practice, only the evenness of the pressure can be measured, whether it is adequate being determined by whether the results are satisfactory in terms of fused garments. The method uses strips of paper, in different ways according to the type of press:

(a) Pressure in continuous presses Provided access can be gained to the rollers in the press, strips of paper can be passed through the press which is stopped when they are partially through the rollers. Pulling out the strips by hand will show if there is any bowing in the rollers. In practice, the achievement of even pressure is far less of a problem with this type of press than with a flat bed press.

(b) Pressure in flat bed presses In this case, strips of paper are placed round the perimeter of the lower platen, projecting by a small amount.

The press is closed and the evenness of pressure, at least towards the edges, is shown by the ease or difficulty of withdrawing the strips.

(3) Checks on time

In the calibration of a press, the representation of time on the press controls must be related to the actual time of fusing, that is the time of press closure for a flat bed press or the time of heating in a continuous press. It should not be assumed that the time in seconds given on a dial is what is actually happening. Both types of press can be checked with a stop watch.

In the course of checking the temperature on each type of press, the time cycle required for the desired temperature to be reached will be discovered. This will change for different fabrics and interlinings, as, with thicker fabrics, more time will be needed for the heat to penetrate to the glue line. When a garment is designed, and the interlining is selected, checks should be made to establish the fusing conditions which must be specified for production.

(4) Checks on garment quality

To ensure that the quality of the fusing of the garments is satisfactory, the *strength of the bond* between the outer fabric and the interlining must be tested by measuring the force required to peel them apart. Of interest is the initial bond strength after fusing and cooling, as well as the bond strength after the washing or cleaning procedures which will be specified for the garment. Tests for bond strength should take place at the design stage when interlinings are being selected and as a routine quality control procedure during production.

Tests for bond strength are made by fusing a large enough section of fabric and interlining so that it covers the full width of the press. Strips 5 cm by 15 cm are cut from this laminate in the lengthwise direction. A small amount is peeled apart by hand so that clips can be attached separately to the interlining and the face fabric and the force required to continue peeling apart the two sections is then measured. The most accurate method of measurement uses a laboratory tensile testing machine which records on a chart the variations in the peel bond strength along the length of the strip. If this facility is available it may be used at the design stage but it is unlikely to be available for routine testing during production. More appropriate is a spring balance which, with practice, will give reasonably good and reproducible results. The sample is suspended from a fixed point by the clip attached to it, the spring balance is attached to the clip on the interlining, and the force required to peel them apart is noted. Alternatively, a series of different weights can be used, and the strength of the bond accepted as adequate if the lightest weight which will peel the bond apart is above a certain level.

It is not easy to specify the figures which should be obtained for peel bond strength for a particular combination of interlining and outer fabric. Figures must be obtained which can be related to actual satisfactory performance of garments in wearing and washing or dry cleaning and with time a company can build up a library of useful information. For each new style of garment, a figure must be established as the required standard. Tests for peel bond strength should be carried out at least twice each day during the production run of the style, the figures recorded, and action taken to investigate the cause if inadequate strengths are discovered. By measuring the bond strength at intervals across the press, a check is made on the uniformity of temperature and pressure across the press since they determine the quality of the bond.

In establishing the correct level of peel bond strength at the design stage, sample pieces should be subjected to the appropriate washing and/or dry-cleaning tests and the peel bond strength checked after drying. This will show whether there is an unacceptable loss in strength during these processes. The samples can also be examined visually for delamination. During the production run, weekly wash or dry-clean tests should be made on garment parts or, preferably, on complete garments. This should be part of an overall programme of checks on the performance of the materials and construction of the garments being manufactured and should include wearer trials.

As part of the investigations made at the design stage to decide on a satisfactory interlining and fusing conditions, the outer fabric should be checked for *heat shrinkage* and *colour change* during fusing. Shrinkage must also be checked for during washing and dry-cleaning since this is a common cause of delamination.

A final point to make concerning the control of quality standards in production relates to *cleanliness* of the press and surrounding area. Fusing presses tend to acquire a build-up of resin on their various parts which is made worse by the addition of frayed threads and lint from fabrics. This can be severe enough to affect the evenness of pressure in a press and it can also lead to the transfer of adhesive resin onto the face side of garment parts and to threads and lint being trapped between the garment fabric and the interlining during fusing.

Alternatives to the fusing of interlinings

In recent years some attempts have been made to bypass the operations of making an interlining with a resin on it and fusing that interlining on to the garment part. If an appropriate adhesive paste, perhaps with some type of filler added, could be 'printed' directly onto garment parts to a suitable density, it might be possible to achieve the support and control that interlinings provide and to do it more economically. As yet, such methods are only used to a very limited extent and they take the clothing manufacturer into fields which are more those of the specialist adhesive chemist than the garment maker and the technical problems are considerable.

(B) WELDING AND ADHESIVES

The process of fusing just described applies to the attachment of interlinings to garment parts over an area which may be large in the case of a jacket front or it may be small in the case of a reinforcing tape. Whatever the situation, the fused part is not subjected, in the course of normal wear and tear, to any forces which would tend to pull it apart. Over the years, many attempts have been made to join normal garment seams by methods other than sewing, usually using some means of sealing or sticking the seam. It will be remembered that a large proportion of the seams used in garment construction are superimposed seams, and when sewn with the correct selection of stitch type and sewing thread these can be made adequately strong for a particular fabric and garment end use. Unfortunately, when this type of seam is joined with any kind of adhesive or some method of melting a thermoplastic fibre fabric and bonding the material together, the seam may easily pull apart, unless it is substantial and possibly ugly. The effect is similar to the undoing of the hook and loop fastening described earlier or to the peeling of adhesive tape from a roll.

The situation in which an adhesive or sealed seam works well is in the lapped seam but in the majority of materials this presents problems of raw edges. Experience of a hook and loop fastening on a garment or on footwear shows how strong it is against a shearing force and the same applies to a long seam which is bonded together. Unfortunately the more complicated lapped seams which lend themselves well to sewing by means of folders cannot easily be constructed for any other method of joining.

Further properties of sealed or adhesive seams also cause problems. The seams tend to be less flexible and have less stretch and recovery than sewn seams and both these problems can cause the seam to break down. If a seam is incorrectly joined, it may be impossible to alter it. While stitching is, in most cases, simple to undo and re-sew, seams joined by other methods are likely to become damaged if separation is attempted.

All these difficulties, however, do not mean that there is no scope for using such methods of construction. Their use is limited, but very important where it is used. The main areas of use of the type of methods outlined here are as follows:

(1) the welding of decorative motifs to garments;
(2) the sealing of the edges of sewn garment parts and other garment components to prevent fraying and avoid the need for additional sewing;
(3) the waterproofing of previously sewn seams in garments made from waterproof materials;

(4) the attachment of garment parts by means of adhesives where subsequent stitching, such as topstitching, will prevent the parts peeling apart.

Welding

The first three of the processes listed above require a welding process to take place. Welding as a process in garment manufacture involves the sealing together of thermoplastic materials but the heat is not applied externally as is normally the case with the fusing of interlinings. The heat must be generated within the thermoplastic materials; for example, in special threads which have been woven into the back of a decorative motif during its construction. The process used can be similar to that described under high frequency fusing, or, more commonly, it is done by means of ultrasonics.

If two hard materials are vibrated against each other, they become hot at the point of contact. If plies of thermoplastic materials are placed between the points of vibration, heat will be generated internally in the materials where they touch and, if this heat is sufficient, they will melt and can be pressed together so that a bond is formed. A device which changes an input of electric current into mechanical vibrations is known as a transducer and it is this which is used to generate the heat. If the speed of vibration is below about 18,000 cycles per second, audible sound will be produced which could be painful and even dangerous to work with. For this reason, and for technical reasons to do with the welding of clothing materials rather than other types of materials, frequencies in the ultrasonic region of around 20,000 cycles per second are used. In *ultrasonic welding* of clothing materials, the vibrations developed in the transducer are transferred to a 'horn' and the heat is generated between this vibrating horn and a stationary anvil. Fabric plies are placed between the horn and the anvil, and the horn, in addition to vibrating, maintains the pressure necessary to form a weld once the surfaces to be joined have been melted. Horns can vary in size up to a maximum of about 25 cms by 4 cms if rectangular or about 9 cms in diameter if round. The actual shape of the horn relates to the particular welding operation to be achieved.

The amount of heat generated depends on the amplitude of the vibrations, the frequency, the pressure between the two surfaces, and the length of time they are allowed to continue vibrating in contact. The amplitude is pre-set for a particular application, depending on the materials to be welded and the type of operation, that is, joining, edge finishing, etc. Pressure is adjusted by experiment and the time is usually around 2 seconds. The horn and anvil remain cold to the touch at all times.

The materials to be welded must be at least 65 per cent thermoplastic, though there is scope for welding materials with a high natural fibre content if a plastic film is inserted between the plies being sealed together.

The methods described so far make use of a welding machine working on a 'plunge' principle, that is, it welds a limited area or length of material at a time. Typical uses are the application of motifs to garments, the cutting and sealing to length of ribbons and straps, and the shaping of small garment parts which would otherwise be costly and time-consuming to sew. Motifs must be designed to be attached by the welding process and have suitable threads woven into the back of them. Ribbons and sewn straps made of suitable materials can be simultaneously cut to length and heat sealed at the ends to prevent fraying. It is particularly useful where narrow straps or ties for a garment have been made by sewing through a folder since the ends are, in this case, very awkward to neaten. A neat, non-bulky end is achieved very rapidly by means of welding.

Another item which can usefully be cut to exactly the right dimensions and sealed at the same time is the hook and eye tape used as a fastening on bras. This is supplied as a continuous strip and cutting it into sections with scissors is inaccurate and leads to a costly neatening operation afterwards. In instances such as this where the garment part to be welded will be worn against the skin, care must be taken that the edge remains sufficiently soft that it will not cause discomfort.

More substantial operations which have been welded are waistband ends on sports shorts. The waistband can be bound on to the garment in the manner described previously and a specially shaped horn made to cut and seal the waistband end into a pointed shape and, at the same time, weld in the buttonhole. Another use on the same type of garment could be to create a small vent at the lower end of the side seam. Both these operations are costly to do in the conventional way. Welding saves time and guarantees accuracy of shape in the finished part. This type of construction is acceptable on a garment for the less expensive market but would not be appropriate on expensive styles.

Welding is also important as a method of waterproofing the seams on garments made from materials rendered waterproof by means of a coating of PVC on the outside of a textile material. A sewn seam in materials of this type would allow ingress of water between the layers of the material or through the needle holes, depending on the configuration of the seam. If the PVC surface layer can be welded after sewing it will seal the PVC across the gaps. A superimposed seam is normally sewn at a seam allowance of 5 mm, turned to one side, and welded on the outside in a plunge process that seals 10–15 cm of seam at a time, the actual length depending on the size of the horn and anvil being used. The process of sewing followed by sealing is time-consuming and costly but the garments are designed for high performance protective wear for outdoor situations and can generally command a high price. On some materials, a sufficiently strong seam can be achieved by welding alone, in a configuration similar to that achieved after sewing and welding. In either situation, whether sewn first or not, the seams become bulky and inflexible compared with the rest of the material of the garment. Garment design is important, both because of this bulk and because of the cost of assembling the seams, and garments of this type normally have a minimum of seams of carefully planned shape. Since they are usually loose-fitting outer garments the loss of shaping possibilities is not important though material costs can be high when, for instance, jackets are cut in one main body piece with no shoulder, armhole, yoke or centre back seams.

In addition to the stamping and plunge type operations described above, the welding principle can be used in rotary machines. In this case a rotating wheel replaces the anvil and, if the wheel has a dot pattern on it, an effect similar in appearance to stitching can be created. The garment parts must be conveyed accurately through the machine to obtain the correct seam line. The appearance of the machine is similar to that of a flat bed sewing machine but without the thread control systems. In deciding whether to weld or sew garments, the constraints previously described must be remembered.

Adhesives

Welding and adhesives are being described together because there are some similarities in the problems which arise in the construction of seams using them, but there are also a number of differences. The term adhesive is here used to mean a substance which is 'sticky' in the conventional sense of the word, whether it be a film of adhesive transferred from silicone paper which sticks immediately, or a similar material which must be heated so that it melts and sticks. It is different in principle from welding which uses the garment material to form the bond and a means other than direct heat to achieve it.

A limited number only of garment construction methods make use of adhesives for seams but three applications are worth describing. One is the use of an adhesive thread which can be sewn into the edge neatening of a hem as one of the looper threads. When the hem is pressed up to the correct position, the thread melts and holds it in place without sewing. The obvious restriction here is the problem of alteration of the garment length. Another use of adhesives is in seams which will take no strain or which will subsequently be topstitched. Patch pockets can be attached to garments by means of a strip of adhesive around the edge, the top corners being reinforced subsequently with a sewn bar tack. Yoke seams can be similarly attached using an adhesive and topstitched afterwards. Adhesive seams such as these are not in common use at present and it is not proposed to describe in detail the methods of achieving them.

The third use of adhesives does not relate to the construction of seams but is again a means of waterproofing them, in this case when the materials are waterproof by virtue of a coating on the inside rather than the outside. Many waterproof materials nowadays are made from a strong woven nylon with an inside coating of neoprene, PTFE or other synthetic material, often of a type that gives breathability as well as waterproofing. Aesthetically these materials are often superior to the PVC-coated materials described earlier and with good flexibility and handling properties they can easily be sewn with strong seams, either superimposed or lap felled. These are then rendered waterproof by the application of a sealing tape along the seam on the inside. A special machine heats the tape to make it stick and then rolls it under pressure firmly into place along the seam. Although these materials can be sewn more easily than the PVC-coated materials, the process of seam sealing adds greatly to the manufacturing cost of the garment and, as with the previously described garments, careful garment design is required to reduce the number of seams and control their shape.

(C) MOULDING

The inclusion of moulding under a heading of alternative methods of joining garments is not entirely accurate since the process of moulding actually eliminates seams as opposed to creating them by a different method. However, it has some importance as an alternative method of manufacture and is best included here.

The development of moulded garments brings together a number of technologies, without which moulded garments would be impossible. These include automatic knitting machinery, thermoplastic yarns, texturising processes to give fabrics made from these yarns an acceptable handle, stretch fabrics, and heat setting. Moulding causes the fabric of the garment to be permanently stretched or shrunk or both, by heating it until it just begins to soften, deforming it into the required shape, and then cooling it so that the new shape becomes permanent. Knitted fabric is essential since it must be capable of being both stretched and compressed and the synthetic content must be at least 65 per cent.

A particular development some years ago applied the technique to ladies' trousers which it proved possible to make with no sewing other than a seat seam. The appropriate size of knitting machine was used to knit tubes for the legs and a hem was knitted in at each end. Each tube was heated and moulded over a suitably shaped form to provide a hip, knee and ankle shape, and a section of each was cut out so that they could be joined together at the seat seam to make a pair of trousers. Other garment types, or parts of them, have been moulded by similar methods but for this type of garment the process has not been widely used. Moulding forgoes an important element in the creation of aesthetic appeal in garments which is the placement of seams, and styles made by this process are inevitably rather simple.

The one exception to this lack of success is the moulding of bra cups, where the combination of a garment which changes little in shape and a fashion for a softer, lighter, less supporting construction has enabled the technology to be widely applied. A high stretch material of polyamide and elastane is normally used and the sections to form the cups must be cut larger than the actual cup size. This is a disadvantage since it wastes fabric but it is necessary so that the edge of the cup can be clamped in the moulding machine. Moulding takes place over a hemispherical metal surface and the central area of the cut cup becomes moulded to that shape. No attempt is made to make the moulded cup exactly the shape of the section of the body it will cover since some stretch remains in the material and the garment is designed to be worn in a slightly stretched state. Following the moulding stage, the spare fabric is trimmed from the edges of each cup, and construction of the bra continues in the same way as for a bra with cup sections that are sewn together to create the shape. The saving in seaming costs for the cup is, to some extent, offset by the additional fabric which must be used. Moulded bras represent a significant proportion of the total number of bras now manufactured but this could change if fashion reverts to a firmer, more structured look.

7

Pressing

Pressing makes a large contribution to the finished appearance of garments and thus their attractiveness at the point of sale. To appreciate the revolution wrought by modern pressing methods and equipment, it is necessary to examine nineteenth century photographs. These exhibit rumpling and fullness in the clothing which men and women about to be photographed today would not tolerate. The problem is clearly demonstrated in the photograph of Brunel, taken in the nineteenth century, and shown in Figure 7.1.

The purpose of pressing

(1) To smooth away unwanted creases and crush marks

In garment manufacture, creases and crushing occur in garments as a result of operator handling and these are particularly bad where garments are handled between operations in bundles, whether tied up tightly or piled on trolleys or in boxes. However, the increasing use of materials with a high standard of crease recovery, along with the reduction in work in progress that results from the installation of hanging transport systems or the working of team systems, has reduced the problem for many types of garment.

(2) To make creases where the design of the garment requires them

Creases are obvious design features in trousers, skirts (where a series of creases is often referred to as pleating) and some collar styles. Creases are less obvious but still require pressing when they are hems and cuff edges, front edges, top edges of waistbands, pocket flaps and patch pocket edges as well as pressed open seams, which from a pressing point of view are two creases sewn together.

Fig. 7.1. I. K. Brunel: Pressing in the middle of the nineteenth century. (Reproduced by permission of the Victoria and Albert Museum.)

(3) To mould the garment to the contour of the body

This does not refer to the specialised technique of garment moulding described in Chapter 6, but to the enhancement of shape already largely determined by seams and darts. It is mainly effected in wool or wool-rich fabrics in the types of garment referred to as tailored. This sort of moulding involves two kinds of deformation (together or separate): shrinking and stretching. After moulding it is not possible to unpick the seams and return garment parts to their former flat state. The chief areas where this moulding takes place are around the ends of darts, collars, shoulders, armholes and sleeveheads, and sometimes trouser legs. Thus the chest and waist of a tailored jacket created by the pattern's seams and darts can be accentuated by pressing on shaped presses. A general principle can be stated which is that where the body has a prominence, extra length is created, and where the body has a hollow the fabric is shrunk.

(4) To prepare garments for further sewing

The term 'underpressing' is reserved for pressing operations on partly constructed garments, while top-, off- or final pressing is used for completed garments, the actual term varying according to the sector of the industry. The stages at which a garment is underpressed will depend on many factors. It normally takes place when several sewing stages have been completed but are still accessible by the press equipment. An obvious example would be a jacket and its lining before assembly, after which pressing of the separate sections would no longer be possible. Underpressing also makes further sewing easier to do, or easier to do to a high quality standard. It may be possible to topstitch a collar which has not been pressed, but it is likely to be more quickly and accurately sewn if it has.

(5) To refinish the fabric after manufacturing the garment

Especially during underpressing, the surface of the fabric may be temporarily changed. A common symptom is gloss or glazing, induced by extreme pressure of press or iron in order to achieve a firm edge or seam. The surface fibres are heavily flattened in such a way as to form a partial mirror. A related but lesser symptom is a generalised flattening of the nap of the fabric, which no longer shows the richness intended by its designer. With the longer-fibred naps, as in corduroy or velvet, this becomes much more important.

In summary, pressing makes the final presentation of the garment, ready for sale.

Categories of pressing

The process of pressing serves to highlight the variety and extremes which exist within the clothing industry across the different garment types, the levels of style change and the volumes of a style that are produced. Specialised pressing equipment is costly and often relates to a specific garment type, and even a particular shape. Style change may render it redundant. As with sewing machinery, the more flexible the equipment, the more skill is required of the operator. It is useful to divide garments into categories according to the amount and type of pressing they require.

(1) Garments which require no pressing

This category includes bras and other foundation garments, stretch swimwear and dancewear, and briefs and other items of underwear. Manufacture achieves a satisfactory finished appearance through topstitching of seams and the use of fabrics, sometimes synthetic and usually knitted, which do not require shaping, refinishing or creasing. In factories making garments solely from within these types, there may be no pressing equipment whatsoever.

(2) Garments requiring minimal pressing or finishing

The term 'finishing' is used here since this category includes garments which require no more than a light steaming since pressing in the sense of applying pressure is not necessary. Typical are simple, single ply garments such as slips and nightgowns, often in knitted synthetics, tee shirts and other knitted leisurewear, quilted or wadded items such as anoraks, and some laundered and garment-dyed products.

(3) Garments requiring the use of an iron in underpressing and final pressing

For the opening of seams and the creasing of edges and for pressing garments with gathers and fullness, and in situations where style change is frequent, pressing with an iron is common because it is simple and flexible.

(4) Garments requiring extensive underpressing and final pressing

This category includes garments which require the pressing open of seams and the setting of edges during manufacture, which are often of more mouldable fabrics, which use large areas of interlining and which are usually wholly or partly lined. It includes men's jackets, trousers and waistcoats, many skirts, women's tailored jackets and trousers, topcoats, trench coats and other lined rainwear. Style change in many of these garments is infrequent and a range of specialised, shaped, press equipment has been developed.

(5) Garments requiring pleating or 'permanent press' finishing

These special effects will be described separately later.

The means of pressing

The means of pressing are heat, moisture (usually as steam) and pressure, singly or in combination. These means deform or reform fibres, yarns and fabrics in order to achieve the effect intended by the designer.

Equally important, after the application of heat and moisture, is the application of vacuum, which sucks ambient air through the garment as it lies on the buck (the lower part of a press) or pressing table. This rapidly dries out residual moisture from the garment (and the buck cladding) and ensures that the set imparted by pressing is retained. The suction is created by an exhauster operated by an electric motor. In the simpler finishing processes, it will be seen that hot air or infra-red heating may serve the same purpose.

Research in the past into the pressing of wool and polyester/wool mixture fabrics has shown the importance of temperature in obtaining a satisfactory standard of pressing but also the difficulty of achieving the required temperatures. Although the pressure of the steam in the supply line to the press will be above atmospheric pressure, and the steam temperature consequently above 100°C, the steam released from the supply line and through a press and its cladding will cool as it expands. Steaming of garments on a press without the head of the press locked closed produces garment temperatures just short of 100°C and it is only by locking the press head closed for at least 10 seconds and adding further steam that the required temperatures of around 130°C can be achieved. For polyester/wool trousers, where a durable crease can be set into the material, a period of head lock of 30 seconds should be used to achieve the necessary temperature and at the same time allow the molecules of polyester in the fabric to rearrange themselves in the position of the crease. An application of vacuum for 5 seconds or more is needed to cool the fabric and prevent the development of unwanted creases during handling by the operator immediately after removal from the press. Precise positioning of the trouser on the press is essential since these creases, once set, are virtually impossible to remove.

It is important to realise that pressing during garment manufacture is often only one set of applications of heat, moisture and pressure during the life of the fabric. The fabric is set during finishing, by a variety of processes depending on the type of fabric and its fibre content, and will be re-pressed for the consumer after dry-cleaning or by the consumer after domestic washing.

A concern of the garment manufacturer, especially one using woollen fabrics, is the possibility of excessive shrinkage during pressing, resulting from relaxation of tensions from inadequate setting during fabric finishing. The problem with tailored garments is that a certain amount of consistent shrinkage is required in order to mould the garments during pressing, but not so much dimensional instability as to result in sporadically undersized garments. Some manufacturers carry out their own shrinkage operation before spreading and cutting, usually by a form of steam blowing or decatising, but occasionally by immersion in cold water with a wetting agent followed by air drying at room temperature (the so-called London shrinking). Knitwear is normally finished flat to the correct dimensions by inserting a wire frame into the garment before the application of steam and vacuum. This is crucial for acrylics, and the stabilisation process may additionally be carried out before cutting.

Pressing equipment and methods

In categorising garments into the various types that require pressing, reference was made to some of the equipment that is used and it might seem that different companies adhere rigidly to different types of equipment. In practice, many companies combine the use of several types of pressing equipment to achieve satisfactory and economical pressing.

(1) Iron

The traditional form of iron, heated by a gas flame inside the metal casting, had its last stronghold in the touching up of men's jackets. Temperature was estimated only by the rate of saliva evaporation from its bottom surface. A damp rag provided moisture and a piece of linen was the drying agent.

The most common type of iron in general use nowadays is steam electric. The iron is heated by an electric element, controlled by a thermostat, and supplied with steam, either from the factory's main steam supply, or from a small boiler adjacent to the pressing unit. The steam function of the iron is activated by the touch of a button, when a powerful jet of dry steam is produced. At extremes, the weights of irons vary from about 2 to 15 kilos. Several shapes are available including a roughly triangular one similar to a domestic iron, the 'tailor's shape' which has a pointed nose and parallel sides, and a narrow one used for operations such as seam opening on sleeves and trouser legs.

There is a range of workplaces available for ironing. In a situation where a variety of parts and shapes of garments has to be pressed, a simple pressing table, similar in shape to a domestic ironing board, is used. Modern tables have a supply of vacuum to hold the garment in position and dry and set it after ironing. This vacuum facility can also be used as a work aid in the sense that the term was used earlier. A section of a flat garment part can be held in place while the operator moves the remainder of the part to create a fold or pleat which she then presses. The position of the fold can be marked on the press cover for accuracy. The flat table can be fitted with swivel arms, which present bucks of varied shapes to allow the laying of sleeves, shoulders and collars without distortion or the danger of creasing. Each of these has the vacuum facility. Alternatively, the basic table may consist of a very large flat area, or a smaller curved surface, each with additional sections to be swung into

Fig. 7.2. Ironing units showing a variety of surface shapes. (Reproduced by permission of Continental Pressing Technic Ltd.)

position if required. The principle is one of flexibility, with some units able to accept a change of pressing surface so that the most suitable shape is always available for the production of a particular batch of garments. A blowing function is also available on some of these pressing surfaces which gives a billowing surface on which to press. This enables some difficult materials, such as thin, hard rainwear fabrics, to be pressed with less risk of seam impressions showing.

Self-contained units, incorporating a steam boiler and electrically driven vacuum and air blowing facilities, are increasingly used both in the underpressing of tailored garments and the pressing of unstructured garments, because they can be moved from place to place at much less cost than conventional steam presses or the older irons, both of which are linked to the factory steam supply. This means that they can be sited within a production line of sewing operations to enable underpressing to be undertaken at minimum cost. Examples of some of the types of ironing unit that are available are shown in Figure 7.2. The iron would be rested at the right hand end of the flat surface or alternatively the weight of the iron could be taken on the spring fitment on the upper gantry. This reduces operator fatigue in continually picking up and putting down the iron.

The use of an iron and pressing table may require considerable skill on the part of the operator, especially when finally pressing complex dresses or blouses, because of the handling involved around a surface shape which is never exactly that of the garment. Additionally, the amount of steam and vacuum used is left to the operator, and the quality of the pressing may suffer if the operator is tempted to hurry in the interests of high output.

(2) Steam presses

A steam press consists of a static buck and a head of complementary shape which closes onto it, thus sandwiching the garment to be pressed. A general-purpose, manually operated press is shown in Figure 7.3. It consists of a frame carrying the buck, which is generally rounded in shape for pressing a variety of garments, linkages to close the head by a scissors action, a pipe system distributing steam to head and buck, a vacuum system to provide suction through the buck, a table around the buck to aid handling of the garment, and foot controls for head closure and vacuum, with hand and/or foot controls for steam. There is also a means of varying head pressure.

When pressing a garment such as a skirt, a typical pressing cycle might be: steam from the buck is applied, the head is locked to press the garment, further steam from the head or the buck may be applied, and the head is then released and vacuum applied to cool and dry the garment before it is moved around the buck for the next part of it to be pressed. When pressing is completed, the garment is hung on a hanger. Adequate time of application of vacuum is essential if the garment is not to remain damp and to distort at this stage. In the case of a manually operated press, the duration of steam, pressure and vacuum are left to the skill and judgment of the operator, as is the manipulation of the garment around the buck, often rather different in shape from the actual garment.

Where large quantities of a garment shape are being manufactured, there is scope for using bucks, and, of course, matching heads, which are close to the shape of the garment. In particular, in men's jacket production, the total pressing of all the parts of the garment is broken down into many stages, both of underpressing and final pressing, and at each stage a specially shaped press is used. An example is shown in Figure 7.4.

In many cases, an iron is available beside the press for the operator to touch up local areas of the garment before pressing with the head of the press. This facility can also be used to add sections of fusible interlining to partly constructed garments, especially tailored jackets. The example quoted previously was of a slotted tape interlining being added to the hem of a jacket. It would be attached in position by means of the iron, fused properly by closing the press, the hem could be folded up along the slots, again by means of the iron, before pressing the hem up finally with the press.

Manually operated scissor-action presses have been improved considerably by the use of electronically controlled pneumatic power. The compressed air takes the heavy, fatiguing work of closing the press from the operator, and allows the introduction of automatic timing of the

Fig. 7.3. General purpose steam press. (Reproduced by permission of Continental Pressing Technic Ltd.)

pressing cycle. A decision can be made at the beginning of a production run as to the correct cycle for the fabric and garment style, and the press can be set to reproduce it. The original devices which achieved this were known as programme card controls, in which sections of a plastic card were removed which represented periods of time for the different

Fig. 7.4. Jacket shoulder press. (Reproduced by permission of Continental Pressing Technic Ltd.)

functions of the press. A small electric motor drove the card through the control box, tripping micro-switches, and thus engaging and disengaging the functions of the pressing cycle: head approach, steam, head lock and vacuum. Different cards were prepared to suit different fabrics. Latterly, this type of control has been replaced by microprocessor controls.

Another improvement is in the mechanical principle in the operation of steam presses. This employs a vertical head movement instead of a scissors action, giving the benefits of much finer control and a more even distribution of pressure over the whole surface of the buck, especially where contoured shapes have to be aligned. At the same time additional functions can be incorporated such as head vacuum and air blowing from the buck. The combination of these three factors enables easier pressing of fabrics such as gabardines, where impressions of seams and pockets can cause a problem. The air blower is used in conjunction with head vacuum at the end of the pressing cycle to reduce impressions. The correct pressing cycle can be designed and maintained through the use of microprocessor controls.

A development in press operation is the carousel press. Here a pair of bucks rotates between the operator and either a single or a double head, depending on whether the bucks are identical or an opposite pair for pressing the left and right of a garment part. The operator loads the garment onto one buck which is then moved away to be aligned under the head, often behind a screen that keeps steam away from the operator. Both scissor action and vertically acting heads can be used but the latter is increasingly common. While the machine carries out the controlled pressing cycle, the operator loads the other buck. This enables the operator to achieve a much higher output because the handling time of the operation takes place during the pressing cycle, leading to higher machine utilisation. An example of a carousel press is shown in Figure 7.5.

Trouser pressing is conventionally carried out in two operations, in addition to the underpressing of the seam: legging on a flat press which sets and creases the legs, and topping in a series of lays around the top of the trouser on a contoured press. If the trouser features a pleat at the waistband, the leg crease must be run into it accurately. The problem is to provide firmly set creases at the same time as an even finish to the fabric overall, without impressions of pockets, fly and seams showing. Traditionally, these impressions were removed in a subsequent 'touching up' operation with an iron, on those fabrics such as gabardines where the steam press leaves an unacceptable finish, but on most fabrics this should not be necessary. Trouser legging also moulds the legs by pressing away fullness in the underside below the seat area, and by shaping the calves in closer fitting trousers. In addition, the presser must set the crease in the correct position in order that the crease might hang centrally over the shoe of the wearer. Usually the pattern cutter designs the pattern in such a way that the presser achieves the desired effect by aligning inside leg seam on outside leg seam up to the knee and the inside leg seam then runs back a few centimetres at the crutch.

A number of machines combine the topping and legging in one operation by suspending the trousers, from the waistband, vertically over an upright 'buck' and pressing from each side. Certain difficulties arise with this method, in particular, achieving consistency throughout the size range and flexibility of mechanical pressure on critical areas such as waistbands, pockets and fly. The term trouser covers a wide range of garments, including jeans, women's trousers of perhaps simpler

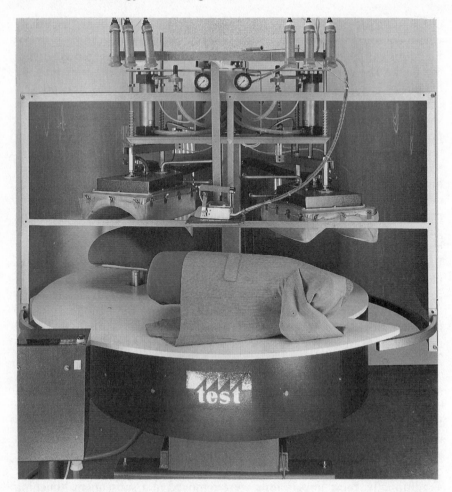

Fig. 7.5. Carousel press. (Reproduced by permission of Continental Pressing Technic Ltd.)

construction and requiring a less sharp crease, men's trousers including four pockets, and suit trousers. Whether combined topping and legging is acceptable at the moment will depend on the construction of the trousers, the sharpness of the crease and the required quality standards at the point of sale. Thus separate topping is still frequently used.

The machinery available for pressing legs also includes double leggers, which press two legs simultaneously, with the top hanging down between two separate bucks, onto which one complete head closes. This is shown in Figure 7.6. Vertically acting heads, carousels and microprocessor controls are also available. In an attempt to avoid impressions and gloss at the side seam, a split head action (with a vertically acting head) applies steam to the whole leg but no pressure to the seam area. Automatic unloading after pressing, which keeps the legs flat, is also available, the

Fig. 7.6. Trouser press: double legger. (Reproduced by permission of Continental Pressing Technic Ltd.)

first serious approach to mechanising the handling elements in a pressing operation. Other than this example, handling between press and hanger is still a significant part of pressing operations.

Press cladding

Bucks of steam presses and the tables used with irons (vacuum boards) are commonly covered with a heat-resistant silicone foam. This is protected on the outside by a top cover of woven polyester (or stretch nylon with the more highly contoured bucks). Although it is generally heat-resistant it is normal to protect the underside of the silicone foam from the continuous heat of the buck by a layer of synthetic felt. The silicone foam has a life of several months without compacting. It remains resilient enough over a long period to absorb the thicknesses of seams and inhibit impressions in the finished garments. Both the stretch nylon and the woven polyester top covers should be smooth enough to allow easy manipulation of the garment from one pressing lay to the next.

The heads of steam presses may be covered with a sandwich of materials which contains, from the metal head outwards, a layer of metal gauze, (sometimes copper or more often aluminium) which makes for even distribution of steam, a layer of synthetic felt to protect the next layer, the main layer of knitted cotton padding, and a final layer of outer cover as on the buck. An alternative for certain fabrics and applications is an aluminium grid plate, with perforations for the emission of steam, and contoured to fit the head of the press. While these general approaches to covering head and buck are typical, there are many variations according to the needs of the operation. For instance, a need for firmer pressing will reduce the thickness of padding in a few underpressing operations to merely an outer covering.

Control of the pressing process

Despite considerable developments in steam presses in recent years, especially in programmable controls designed to ensure that all of the garments in a batch receive the same, satisfactory, cycle of steam, pressure and vacuum, there is considerable variation in the success of the pressing of individual garments. The easiest aspect of the pressing process to measure is the time cycle but with many presses connected to the same steam supply and to the same vacuum line, an individual press may not always receive the supply that it should. Thus the required temperatures may not always be achieved, nor may satisfactory cooling. In addition, there may be unevenness between a head and a buck which affects the pressure achieved on a garment.

Until recently it has not been possible to measure the effect of any of these parameters but equipment has now been developed by the Clothing Technology Centre to monitor press equipment. Sensors are able to quantify the conditions inside the press by measuring the temperature profile during the pressing cycle, the pressure on the garment and the strength of the cooling vacuum. Evenness of each parameter across the area of the press can also be measured, as can thickness and compressibility of cladding. This equipment has greatly increased the possibility of setting presses correctly to achieve an acceptable standard of pressing. Test methods for factors such as sharpness of crease have also been developed.

Creasing machines

A special type of small press performs an extremely useful function in what is, in effect, an underpressing situation. Creasing machines fold over and press the edges of clothing components such as pockets or cuffs to prepare them for easier sewing. In particular, a patch pocket which has already had the top hem sewn, is pressed ready for the operator to sew it to the garment with no handling of the seam turnings. The operator positions the component over an appropriately shaped die and blades manipulate the fabric to form the creases around it and exert pressure during the pressing cycle. The means of pressing may be heat alone, coming from elements in the machine, or heat and steam for some fabrics.

(3) Steam air finisher

This equipment is often referred to as a 'puffer', a form press or a 'dolly' press. It consists of a frame carrying a steam distribution system, compressed air distribution system and a pressing form which is a canvas bag in the approximate shape of the garment to be pressed – that is, a body shape but with no sleeves. There are controls for steam and air release, and timers controlling the steam and air cycles. The equipment aims to reduce the positioning and re-positioning in pressing operations by pressing the whole garment at the same time, though finishing is a better term in this situation since very little pressure is applied to the garment. The operator pulls the garment on to the form from above, and the form is then expanded to its full size and shape as steam is blown through it from the inside. A cycle of, perhaps, 8 seconds steaming is followed by a further period of hot air drying, also by blowing from the inside.

This equipment can remove accidental creases and refinish the fabric, but will not form creases or mould the garment. It is extremely useful for garments such as nightdresses, tee shirts and blouses, and is sometimes worth using for simple dresses, even though the hem might have to be pressed flat separately with an iron or a steam press. Distortion along buttoned openings is prevented by a sprung, padded, clamp which holds the section of garment in place and an additional attachment is a spring-loaded sleeve former. Care must be taken when finishing garments in knitted fabrics which may stretch, as the size and shape may be distorted to that of the bag covering the unit. If this is a problem, a slipover may be made from a rigid, woven, press-covering fabric, to the pattern shape of each size of garment, and put on the covering bag as a restrainer before pressing each size of the garment style.

A variation on the shape described here can be used for jeans and other casual trousers which do not require a crease. The trouser is clamped in a ring at the waist and clamped again at the ankles. Steam followed by hot air is blown through it, while maintaining slight downward tension on the legs. An example of a steam-air finisher for trousers is shown in Figure 7.7.

(4) Steam tunnel

Another garment finishing process where pressure is not applied to the garments but where handling during the process is reduced is in steam tunnel finishing. It can be used for a variety of simple garments in man-made fibres and blends. Some garments would be on hangers, fed under automatic control through a cabinet on a motorised rail, and passing through sections with superheated steam and drying by air blowing. Alternatively, tee shirts and similar knitwear are loaded onto frames and passed through the tunnel on a conveyor. The tunnel reduces the need for any other pressing process before or after its operation and

Fig. 7.7. Steam-air finisher for trousers. (Reproduced by permission of Continental Pressing Technic Ltd.)

sometimes eliminates it. The aim of the steam is to relax natural fibres, that of the heat to relax man-made fibres. With the garments on hangers or frames, gravity or tension pulls out the wrinkles, and the turbulence of air blowing provides additional energy to relax wrinkles in woven fabrics. Such turbulence should be restricted with fabrics such as acrylics, since excessive agitation makes the fabric pliable and subject to deformation. This fabric responds well to infra-red drying, a feature of some tunnels. The setting of steaming and drying conditions in the tunnel can be varied for different fabrics. The operators have only to load and unload the hangers or frames. An example is shown in Figure 7.8.

Pleating

Pleating is a special type of pressing, the aim of which is to produce an array of creases in a garment, of some durability and according to a geometrical pattern. This may be an overall pattern of small pleats, formed as a result of machine pleating a complete roll of cloth, or larger pleats formed by hand pleating of garment sections which have been previously cut to shape and, in the case of skirt sections, hemmed. Examples of machine pleating are fluting and crystal pleating and of hand

Fig. 7.8. Tunnel finisher. (Reproduced by permission of Continental Pressing Technic Ltd.)

pleating, box pleats and the fan-shaped pleats which taper to nothing at the waist and are known as sunray pleats. Like other forms of pressing, the means of pleating are heat, moisture and pressure.

Machine pleating is of two types. The first is a rotary machine in which the rollers are fitted with complementary dies similar to gears. Extensive areas of tiny pleats such as crystal pleating or accordion pleating can be produced on this machine. Different geometrical patterns can be achieved only by changing the complementary dies. Second is a blade machine in which pleats are formed by the thrust action of a blade or blades. The pleats are set by heat and pressure as they pass between a pair of mangle-type rollers. Some machines have steaming boxes which steam the fabric before pleating. The pleating takes place between two layers of paper and the pleated fabric is re-rolled for delivery along with the paper. This process is normally carried out by specialist firms, rather than by clothing manufacturers. The subsequent cutting of garment sections from the pleated fabric is not easy and sizing can be very variable.

In hand pleating, the fabric is folded between two complementary card patterns, which are scored in such a way as to fold at the lines where pleats are required. The fabric is placed on the first card, the second card is laid over the top, and the cards with their enclosed fabric are then folded tightly into the pleat pattern that is scored on the card. With flimsy fabrics it is possible to insert two plies.

In traditional hand pleating, the folded cards with their enclosed fabric are rolled up inside a further layer of unpleated card, tied round to hold them in place, and put into a steam box or autoclave. This enables pressure to be built up and steam temperatures of around 130°C to be achieved. This sets the pleats, whose durability is related to the temperature and duration of the steaming, as well as the nature of the fabric being pleated. The time in the autoclave could be as long as half an hour and the autoclave is large enough to take several dozen garment parts at once. Only a small number of clothing manufacturers have their own autoclaves, mainly those who expect always to include pleating in their garment styles and/or those who are geographically remote from the main centres of clothing manufacture. In these centres, specialist firms provide a pleating service. Cut garment parts are hemmed if necessary, then sent out for pleating, and making up continues when they are returned. This delay in between sewing operations is disruptive of production flow and is one of the problems of including pleating as a feature in garment styles. Another problem is the cost, much of which is the result of the large numbers of pleating cards which are needed.

A way of reducing both these problems, for certain types of pleat, is provided by a specialist pleating press which enables a garment manufacturer to do pleating within the factory more simply than can be done with an autoclave. The press consists of large, upper and lower flat platens, both of which are heated, and a supply of steam to the lower platen. The garment part is sandwiched between card formers which are steam permeable and the pleats folded into place. Only pleats which will lie flat can be done by this method; it will not do sunray pleats. Several garment panels can be put in the press side by side and a typical pressing time is one to two minutes. Heat, humidity, pressure and time can all be varied to obtain sharp pleats. A separate cardboard-folding machine enables the clothing manufacturer to make his own pleating cards. If necessary, in box pleat and similar designs, the two cards of a pair are folded to slightly different dimensions to allow for fabric thickness.

Before any pleating process is planned for a fabric, checks should be made to ensure that it will not suffer from shrinkage or a change in colour during the process. If there is a likelihood of colour change, other sections of the garment should be put in the autoclave along with the parts to be pleated.

Permanent press

The process known as 'permanent press' was developed some years ago as a way of giving good crease recovery after washing to cellulosic fabrics. It declined with the rise in popularity of polyester/cotton and polyester/viscose blends, where the polyester content assists crease recovery and improves fabric strength. The permanent press treatment reduces fabric strength. More recently, in an attempt to compete with man-made fibres, the process has been marketed again with 100 per cent cotton fabrics of high enough initial strength to allow for some degradation.

The process involves treating fabric, during its manufacture, with a post-curing resin. An ordinary resinated, crease resistant fabric would be cured at a high temperature at this stage, prior to delivery to the garment maker. A permanent press fabric is only dried after the resin treatment and is then made into garments. The process is often used for trousers and in this case they would be pressed to form the creases at the seams and hems and down the front and back. The garments are then passed through an oven and the resin in the fabric cured at a high temperature. When the garment is washed and dried, the fabric returns to the shape it was cured into, that is, smooth across the panels and creased where required. Care must be taken at the design stage of the garment to ensure that all the components will withstand the high temperature curing – in particular, that there will be no dye migration or shrinkage.

The state of pressing

Not nearly as much attention has been paid to the technology of pressing as to the technology of sewing and cutting. What has been achieved is the means to press all fabrics and garments, refinishing the fabric and producing a temporary or durable set in the three-dimensional shapes required.

A number of interesting points may be noted.

(1) The percentage of total manufacturing work content involved in pressing is generally not known across the industry.
(2) The actual pressing time as a percentage of the total time in pressing operations has not been analysed as it has for typical sewing operations.
(3) The possibilities of automation have been explored for some steam presses, but most pressing operations require the continual intervention of the human hand.
(4) The great advances in the general area of permanent press and easy care are by no means complete, although this concept involves also textile structures and finishing as well as sewing and fusing technology.

8
Clothing Manufacture

Towards the end of a study of the technology of clothing manufacture, it is appropriate to consider the way forward for the clothing industry, in terms of likely technological developments. Reference has been made many times to the labour-intensive nature of the sewing process and to the small proportion of a sewing machinist's time which is actually spent sewing, and it is the sewing area of garment manufacture which has long been expected to offer the widest scope for imaginative research and development.

The term 'operation' has been used loosely throughout to denote some stage in the manufacturing process. Operations are the divisions of the total work content of garments. Each operation consists of a work cycle which is the sequence of elements of cutting or sewing, fusing or pressing, required to perform a job or yield a unit of production. Operations define the work done by people in a factory.

In the sewing room, the breakdown of the total work content of a garment into operations has traditionally included long, medium and short operations, the actual length being influenced by the amount of work content in the garment, the predicted quantity of output of an individual style, and the number employed in the company manufacturing it, with the consequent potential for specialisation among its operators and managers. In this case an operation was the amount of the work content of a garment that was undertaken by one operator.

On this principle, a garment manufactured in small lots or as individual garments in a small company would tend to have long operations, if not a form of make-through organisation, where an operator constructs virtually the whole of the garment. The throughput time for a garment in this case would be the actual making time for the garment.

By contrast, the operation length would be short for garments manufactured in volume in a large company with a large workforce, and with specialist managers as industrial engineers who would plan the best utilisation of people and machinery. The organisation of production in this case would be that of a Progressive Bundle Unit or PBU, with the successive operations in the garment performed by different operators, and with, normally, considerable quantities of partly made garments working their way through the production line. The throughput time for a garment in this case could be days or even weeks.

Thus this operation or unit of work undertaken repetitively by an operator could vary in size from, perhaps, hours for a handmade bespoke jacket to fractions of a minute for the bulk production of briefs. Between the two extremes lies every possible variation.

Traditionally, two themes in the design of operations vie with one another. These are the technical requirements of the process and the managerial requirements of planning a production line. The production line itself could take several forms, varying gradually between the make-through and the Progressive Bundle Unit described above. Make-through methods were, and still are, used for the very small volume couture or bespoke garments and also for runs of perhaps a few hundreds of a style for the high fashion retail sector. Technologically, they require that garments are assembled by very simple methods, predominantly lockstitch with overlocking if available. Typically much of this work is undertaken by homeworkers who have access only to a lockstitch machine with no work aids of any kind. If overlocking is essential, it may be done before despatch to the homeworker or when the garments are returned to the organising company. Garments made by the latter route tend to be very untidy. Whilst virtually any fabric, unless it has high stretch, can be assembled entirely on a lockstitch machine with an overedger used for neatening, it is almost certainly the case that it could be assembled to higher standards of appearance and performance, and at a more competitive price, if it could be assembled using the wide range of machines and attachments that have previously been described. This is only possible if construction is as a sequence of operations, with the most appropriate machinery used for each one, and this was one reason for the widespread development and use of the PBU as a production system.

The other apparent advantage of assembling a garment as a sequence of operations, each undertaken by a different operator, was the opportunity to motivate operators to high rates of work by individual financial incentive schemes. These determined a further technical requirement of the design of operations, in addition to the use of a particular machine and attachments, which was that an operation should encompass only one basic skill, and preferably only one level of that skill. Thus, pressers would not normally sew, and sewing operators would not be making the best use of their sewing skills if they were pressing, trimming or doing any other job requiring less training time than sewing. In addition, operators trained on lockstitch machines would not be using their skills to the full if employed on a buttonhole machine which requires minimal handling skills, and an operator skilled enough to attach collars to shirts would not be best employed sewing darts.

A final technical requirement in the design of operations is that there is often a necessary sequence of construction. One seam may have to be sewn before another. A seam must be sewn before it is pressed open, though it may not have to be pressed open immediately after sewing. A number of seams may be sewn before all are pressed together.

The managerial requirements of operation design in the PBU relate to the need for operators to be highly trained on the specific tasks that form the sequence of operations in the assembly of a particular garment style, and for the flow of work through these operators to be tightly controlled and well balanced. Longer operations need longer training times since rates of repetition are lower. Short operations are quicker to learn but can result in a disproportionate amount of time being spent organising the bundle of garments that is presented to the operator. The pressure is on operators to develop limited skills to a high level. This maximises production for the company and earning levels for the operator who is working on a payment-by-results system. In terms of the flow of work through the sequence of operators, there is a need to balance the work content of operations so that there is the right flow of work for every member of the production sequence, as well as the right total amount of work to fill each operator's working day. This has to be achieved despite variations in operators' rates of working and a tendency to a high level of absenteeism. Inevitable unevenness is smoothed out by high levels of buffer stocks between operators. The achievement of this high level of training and smooth line balance is dependent on long runs of the same style of garment, on sophisticated management skills in industrial engineering, and on the availability of capital to invest in the variety of machinery that is required.

Through the 1970s it appeared that production runs of most styles were set to become longer and longer and the answer to economical production was to mechanise the processes of assembly that were being used and refine the methods used in operator incentive schemes. These schemes are heavily dependent on sufficiently long runs, preferably many weeks, of the same style of garment so that operators can reach a steady rate of working and a suitable rate can be set for the job. In the 1980s the trend towards longer production runs began to reverse and in many sectors of the industry the demand changed to more and more varied styles in ever smaller quantities. These variations result from the increasingly market-driven nature of clothing retailing and now affect much of the 'middle market' that forms a large part of the UK clothing industry and that hitherto could rely on continuity of demand for its products.

This sector of the industry has spent the last few years considering how it can organise its production so that garments are made efficiently and to a satisfactory quality standard but with as short a throughput time as possible. This has generated an increasing requirement for flexible machinery, multi-skilled operators and lateral thinking about the actual methods of assembly that are used for garments. While the organisation of production may still be as a Progressive Bundle Unit, it is increasingly likely that one of the newer methods of production organisation, described briefly at the end of the section on Basic Sewing Machines and Associated Work Aids in Chapter 4, will be used. The first of these systems was the one known generally as a Unit Production System, or UPS, where garments are transported singly on a hanging transport system, there is a small quantity of garments between each operator, and operators are generally specialised to one operation for the duration of the production of the style. The second was the team system, also known as modular manufacturing, described in its commonest form where the operators work standing up and each operator can do several of the stages in the construction of the garment. They take a single garment through these stages before passing it on to the next operator in the sequence and moving back to start another garment.

Whichever method or organisation is used, the garments are assembled as a sequence of operations but, in the team system particularly, these operations can no longer be identified as the work undertaken by an individual operator. They become simply the identifiable separate stages in a garment which are as they are for reasons of machinery (i.e. machine plus attachments) and/or sequence. If the number of these stages can be reduced by innovative thinking about methods of garment assembly, the level of investment in machinery can be reduced. An example would be that although edges are traditionally neatened using the 503 or 504 stitch, if a 512 or 514 stitch is already in use for seam joining it is not detrimental to the garment if it is also used for neatening. Different garment types will offer different opportunities for this technique.

A useful analysis of the need for production flexibility in the clothing industry is provided by Tyler (1).

Having considered the nature of sewing operations within the organisation of garment assembly, it is now possible to return to the theme of the way forward for the clothing industry in terms of likely technological developments.

As was stated at the end of Chapter 4, there has been considerable automatic machinery developed for the earlier, two-dimensional stages of the assembly of such items as shirts and men's suits, and for two- and three-dimensional operations on underwear, where high volume production continues to be the case and where the limited style and fabric changes that do occur have little effect on the machinery used. However, this machinery is only automatic in the sense of handling materials whilst they are being sewn and in most cases still requires loading by a human operator. It is also only available for a few of the assembly operations for each type of garment, the rest of the garment being assembled by operators working at machines of less specialised types, in the same way that is used for all other, less high-volume types of garments. Figures of up to 80 per cent machine utilisation have been achieved for the fully automatic or mechanised workplaces described here, but for the rest of garment assembly the amount of the operator's time actually spent sewing is, as has already been stated, typically around 20 per cent. It is worth considering this breakdown of time further.

Activity	Single needle lockstitch without thread trimmer and needle positioner	Single needle lockstitch with thread trimmer and needle positioner	Overlock machine without chain cutter	Overlock machine with chain cutter	All machines average
Bundle handling	5.6	4.2	6.0	14.9	5.7
Work docket	2.4	2.1	2.3	2.6	2.4
Present work to machine	18.4	17.4	24.8	15.6	20.1
Sew	19.5	22.2	22.1	33.0	20.2
Realign	14.8	17.9	12.4	5.0	14.2
Remove and aside	3.6	4.7	5.3	7.2	4.4
Trim threads	6.7	2.7	6.7	–	6.0
Needle position	3.5	0.8	–	–	2.4
Relaxation	7.9	7.9	8.0	10.1	7.8
Talk to supervisor	2.0	3.4	2.1	1.1	2.3
Change thread	0.9	0.8	1.3	1.9	1.0
Rethread needle	4.5	3.8	3.0	5.2	4.3
Machine repairs	1.2	1.5	1.3	0.2	1.3
Miscellaneous fabric handle	6.8	7.0	3.5	1.8	5.7
Other	2.2	3.6	1.2	1.4	2.2
	100.0	100.0	100.0	100.0	100.0
Work stations observed	366	50	97	9	605

Fig. 8.1. Table of sewing machinists' activities. (Excerpted and reproduced by permission of the Shirley Institute.)

The analysis of typical sewing machinists' activities from which this figure of 20 per cent is taken was carried out by Grills and Brown (2) for the Shirley Institute in 1975 and it is likely that in many companies the picture they found has not changed radically since then. An abstract from their table of results in Figure 8.1 shows the percentage of time spent on each category of activities for three machine types (eight were studied).

The authors point out that 'differences in percentages among different machine categories for similar activities are due to sampling error and real differences in the operations carried out, the latter being the more important cause'. An explanation of the non-sewing activities may be helpful and will also show the areas where the recent trends in the organisation of production described above may alter the figures.

Bundle handling signifies untying and laying out the bundled parts before the operation as well as reassembling and retying after the operation. This relates specifically to the progressive bundle type of production system and is substantially reduced in either a unit production system or a team system.

Work dockets signifies the cutting of a 'coupon payment ticket', as a record of work done, for payment purposes. Even in PBU systems this is increasingly being replaced by simpler or automatic methods of recording the work done by individual operators, where there is computer processing of pay and other information. In a UPS, the computer control of the system is such that individual work flow is recorded. In a team system it is commonly the case that the team is paid as a group and the record of workflow is simply a record of the number of garments completed compared with the target number.

Present work to machine involves separating and picking up the parts, matching plies and orienting the needle for further sewing.

Sew, Realign, Remove and aside are self-explanatory.

Trim threads and *Needle position* mean cutting the thread chain from the needle to the workpiece after sewing and adjusting the needle position before that. Here, the quantity of lockstitch machines with thread trimmers and needle positioners, and those without, is today likely to be reversed.

Relaxation, Talk to supervisor, Change thread, Rethread needle and *Machine repairs* are self-explanatory.

Miscellaneous fabric handle includes turning out, especially points and corners, cutting, notching and trimming.

Other means rewinding bobbin spools and similar activities.

The average proportion of all time spent on sewing was 20.2 per cent. This will have increased slightly in many companies with the popularisation of automatic thread trimming, and in the companies operating UPS and team systems, it will have increased some more by the removal of much of the bundle handling elements, but since a great deal of the industry still works on bundle systems, the average will not have changed much.

In the study, the proportion of time spent on sewing actually varied from as little as 3 per cent to as much as 45 per cent. Those showing less than 10 per cent were sewing short seams requiring great accuracy and change of direction. Work handling amounted to 44 per cent of the total time and, if 'Miscellaneous fabric handle' is included, 50 per cent. Twenty per cent of the total was presenting work to the machine.

The industry has considered three basic approaches to improving the non-sewing parts of sewing operations:

(1) an analysis of the psycho-motor skills used by operators, leading to improved methods of training operators;
(2) a study of the methods the operator uses at the workplace, to develop both equipment and new methods step by step which will bring about a gradual but continuous reduction in the work content of operations;
(3) the development of robotics to transfer the manual elements to a dedicated but flexible computer-controlled machine.

Analysis of psycho-motor skills

This analysis conveniently breaks down into three sections:

(a) the effector processes (the motor system), which are the visible part of skill, the organised movement of hands, feet, and other parts of the body;

(b) the receptor processes, that is, how the senses take in and transmit information from the environment;

(c) the central activities, taking place in the cerebral cortex, which link and organise the other two processes.

Regarding *effector processes*, it is predominantly the skills of hands and fingers which govern clothing production, resulting in the rapid, highly dextrous manual movements of the sewing machinist. Skilled performance is most evident where movements of different limbs are co-ordinated as in the movements of the foot, the knee and the two hands of the machinist, who on completing a line of sewing, stops the machine and operates the underbed thread trimmer with the foot, raises the presser foot by means of the knee lift, and removes the sewn fabric parts in a smooth and continuous process.

Regarding *receptor processes*, the sewing machinist uses principally three or four to transmit information.

Vision is used to recognise shapes and profiles, sometimes in unusual attitudes, to discriminate between the right and wrong side of the fabric, to assess when two edges of a seam will not fit, to gauge distances and to provide a continuous series of cues about the matching of parts being sewn, the orientation of edges to the needle and the appearance of work completed.

Among the most important and often unrecognised sense a machinist depends on is the kinaesthetic sense which provides information about the position of limbs and the pressures they exert. It provides the means for control of movement, both gross and delicate, from deep-seated nerve endings in muscles, tendons and joints. To enable the operator's eyes to concentrate on the area in front of the needle point, the position of the foot pedal, and hence the speed of stitching, is sensed kinaesthetically. Similarly, the tensioning of the two plies of fabric being joined is sensed kinaesthetically in the fingers. Such sensations are seldom at the level of consciousness in an experienced machinist, but have been 'internalised' during the training process.

The sense of touch is used to gain information about fabric surfaces and the force of grip required to manipulate them.

From time to time, the sense of hearing will come into play to signal a defect in the running of the sewing machine.

Regarding the *central activities*, a skilled performance is partly based in the conditioning of reflexes, but appears to be more complex than that. Each response to a stimulus grows out of those which have preceded it in a continuous stream. The complex co-ordination of senses and movements, the precise timing and rapid rate of decison-making below the surface of consciousness indicate that the level of skill achieved by sewing machinists can be very high.

The procedures of training require an analysis of the range of activities in the operations to be learnt, not only in terms of the result desired but also in terms of the movements required and the perceptual cues necessary for its accomplishment. The basic skill components can then be isolated and taught separately before the complex co-ordinations of actual operations are attempted. Clearly, control of machine speed with accurate stopping, and fabric control before, during and after sewing, are components of the total skill requirement which is built up through practice on appropriately designed exercises and, finally, on operations themselves.

A study of the methods used

A study of the methods the operator uses can be analysed by looking in more detail at the Grills and Brown research in conjunction with the different stages of sewing operations which have been identified. These can be grouped into five phases as shown in Figure 8.2.

Phases 1 and 5 are concerned with transport of materials into and out of the workplace, changing thread and dealing with the work docket. The first principle is that the operator should not be diverted from a task by having to go to fetch work from a remote location. The second is that the work should be presented to the operator between hip and shoulder height. The third is that the work should require the minimum manipulation before and after sewing. In a progressive bundle unit this might be achieved by presenting operators with larger bundles though there is not always scope for this since bundle size is determined largely by a combination of the piece length of the cloth and the length of the marker. In a unit production system all three principles are adhered to simply because it is the designed purpose of the system to present each operator with single garments in the correct position for working on them. In a team system, interoperation handling is also greatly reduced as the garments are either taken through a succession of operations by the same operator or handed directly to the next operator in the team.

Phases 2 and 4 are concerned with presenting work to the needle, involving separating and picking up parts, matching plies and orienting the parts to the needle ready for sewing, realignment and trimming threads and disposal within the workplace after sewing (50 per cent of time). This involves a number of principles, to be applied where appropriate:

(a) Separating and picking up the two plies to be sewn simultaneously using opposite symmetrical motions.
(b) Positioning parts to be picked up as near to the operator as possible,

Phase

(1) Material into workplace

(2) Present to the needle

(3) Sew

(4) Dispose

(5) Materials out of workplace

Fig. 8.2. Five phases of a sewing operation.

and planning storage of parts within the workplace in three dimensions.

(c) Providing a defined and fixed place for all tools and materials.

(d) Designing the sequence of activity to provide for continuous, smooth and rhythmic motions which are easier to control and more accurate than intermittent motions, for example, in the sequence from sewing to disposal.

(e) Designing a larger table surface which normally avoids parts of the garment hanging over the edge to the left of the needle, thus encouraging free movement of the garment during presentation to the needle and realignment.

(f) Assessing the most effective distance from needle point to the front edge of the table (this is commonly fixed at 15 cm or so, but might be varied to accommodate longer runs of sewing).

(g) Distributing work among different limbs to relieve the hands. This is increasingly easy to achieve by using programmable machines so that the activities of backtack, thread trim and foot lift become foot controlled instead of, as previously, hand controlled.

(h) Ergonomic factors such as seating, lighting and temperature.

Phase 3 is concerned with sewing (20 per cent of time) and the needle point engineering which makes it easier and more accurate, as well as rethreading the machine (4.3 per cent of time). Sewing machine manufacturers have in the past invested a great deal in the development of higher speeds for sewing machines. Beyond a certain point, the objectives of this investment were largely irrelevant to reducing the work content of operations. The first reason is that higher machine speeds affect only 20 per cent of the average operation time. The second reason is the time taken by the foot to depress the pedal, and the effects of acceleration at the beginning of the sewing run and deceleration at the end. The result of these two factors is that increasing the machine speed from 5,000 to 6,000 stitches per minute on a typical fairly short sewing operation would reduce overall time for the operation by less than 2 per cent. It is also the case that at a given level of accuracy of stitching, the limits of speed in sewing together two pieces of fabric is about 10 metres per minute, that is, 4,000 stitches per minute with a stitch length of 2.5 mm. This limit depends on the human operator, not on the machine. Speed of sewing might be increased if the tolerances on the seam could be increased but this may not produce acceptable quality. It is relevant to note here that typical speeds of machines used in team systems, where operators are required to be multi-skilled and often work standing up, are no higher than this.

Another reason for limiting machine speed was demonstrated by Munden (3) in an investigation into the effects of machine speed on the regularity of stitch density. He concluded that when sewing a seam at low speeds, minimum presser foot pressure is required if an exact stitch density is to be obtained, since at low speeds maximum presser foot pressure causes compression and stretch of the fabric, so that stitches fall too close together. However, as the machine speeds increase to 5,000 stitches per minute, maximum foot pressure is required, since under these circumstances, with minimum foot pressure, no contact between fabric and presser foot occurs due to the effect of the feed dog inducing bounce in the presser foot. At speeds in excess of 5,000 stitches per minute, even under maximum presser foot pressure conditions, the presser foot will not be serving its purpose and irregular, inconsistent and low density results will be obtained. This result is laid at the door of basic sewing machine design. The designs of the 1850s, running at approximately 200 stitches per minute, had not basically changed by the 1970s but were expected to run at 7,000 stitches per minute. A fundamental redesign of the hinged, spring-loaded presser foot is required if it is to be efficient above a point somewhere between 3,000 and 5,000 stitches per minute.

Much more fruitful sources of reduction in work content are other aspects of needle point engineering such as the specialised presser feet, special purpose feeds, folders, tape feeds, edge trimming knives and multi-needle machines that were described in previous chapters. These all contribute, not only to more consistent quality, but also to shorter working time.

One area which has not until recently attracted much attention is the figure found by Grills and Brown for rethreading the needle following thread breaks (4.3 per cent of total time on average). This is an aspect of the unreliability of the sewing machine which is important in operator-controlled operations but is crucial in automatic, machine-controlled operations. Some of the cause can be found with the sewing thread and thread manufacturers are increasingly aiming towards knot-free thread as an aid to solving the problem.

The development of robotics

This is a much more recent approach to improving the non-sewing parts of sewing operations.

In 1965, Arthur D. Little Inc. published a report to the Apparel Research Foundation in the USA, a study entitled 'State of the Art Investigation of Automated Handling of Limp Fabrics'. This study was at least as significant as the subsequent second volume describing an experimental programme leading to the building of demonstration 'Rink' equipment. The study divided automation into five consecutive elements:

(i) *Separation and pick up*. The researchers state, 'In order to quantify by ranking the difficulty of accomplishing any of these steps, we applied, from judgment, a difficulty factor. The higher this difficulty factor, the more difficult the task is to automate from a technical as well as a possibly economic standpoint. These difficulty factors are assigned in the values of 1 to 5. One is the easiest; 5 is the most difficult. For other elements of automation, difficulty factors go as high as 25.' They considered three conditions:

(a) An aligned stack straight from cutting and undisturbed, with each ply within plus or minus 1/32″ of any other ply. This condition could apply only to the first operation following cutting. (Difficulty Factor 1.)

(b)   A non-aligned stack in a flat stack with each ply aligned within ¼″ of another ply. (Difficulty Factor 2.)

(c)   A non-aligned stack of three-dimensional pieces, with tolerance limits as for (b) and in which two or more individual pieces have been sewn together. (Difficulty Factor 5.)

(ii)   Orientation of piece in direction and plane. Again three conditions were considered:

(a)   A piece of irregular shape but with one straight edge which can be detected and oriented by a simple three point sensing system such as three photocells. (Difficulty Factor 2.)

(b)   A flat, irregularly shaped piece without a straight edge is far more difficult to orientate, requiring recognition of the total shape. (Difficulty Factor 4.)

(c)   A piece of irregular shape in three dimensions requires a matrix of sensors, detecting pitch and yaw on at least two axes out of three. (Difficulty Factor 10.)

(iii)   Mating. 'Mating is defined as bringing two or more plies or pieces under proper orientation with each other in plane and rotation.' Again three conditions were considered:

(a)   Aligning two flat pieces, one on top of the other by the straight edges common to both, which would then be joined by sewing, is the simplest. (Difficulty Factor 2.)

(b)   A more difficult case involves aligning two pieces of irregular shape with no straight edge. (Difficulty Factor 4.)

(c)   The most difficult case involves aligning two pieces both of which have an irregular three-dimensional shape, such as mating a shirt sleeve to the body of the shirt. (Difficulty Factor 10.)

These cases are by no means exhaustive and, for instance, do not include aligning more than two pieces, matching checks or the insertion of fullness.

(iv)   Control through the work point.

(a)   The simplest is where two mated pieces require the application of a fastener, such as a stud, through the two plies. (Difficulty Factor 1.)

(b)   The next order of difficulty involves sewing along the straight edge of two mated plies. (Difficulty Factor 2.)

(c)   More difficult again is the sewing of an irregularly shaped edge on two flat plies mated together. (Difficulty Factor 4.)

(d)   Most difficult is the sewing of mated, irregular, three-dimensional shapes. (Difficulty Factor 25.)

One difficulty mentioned is the likelihood that complete mating cannot be achieved before sewing and therefore the need for breaking a sewing operation into sections with a sew-mate-sew sequence.

(v) Accurate stacking so that subsequent operations can be performed on the combined piece. Again the same type of analysis emerges:

(a) A flat piece with a straight edge. (Difficulty Factor 1.)
(b) A flat piece with an irregular shape. (Difficulty Factor 2.)
(c) A three-dimensional irregular piece. (Difficulty Factor 5.)

Even though the orders of difficulty quoted are achieved by judgment and are therefore to some extent subjective, this is a remarkable analysis, taking the understanding of what takes place in sewing operations a lot further than hitherto. It is clear that as sewing operations move away from an aligned stack, straight edges and two dimensions, the difficulties are compounded (in other words as sewing operations move away from cutting and progress along the line). The 'Rink' demonstration device actually constructed involved no order of difficulty higher than 2. The researchers then ranked a proposed automated series of operations for the manufacture of shirts and of work trousers. Operations such as set collar, close collar, set sleeve and hem bottom on the shirt were ranked as high as 285, and some operations on the flies of trousers as high as 212.

Another major research project, funded by the Pfaff Company, was the transfer street, designed to carry out all operations on a left shirt front, including front edge folding, buttonholing, pocket attaching and hemming. A similar transfer street performed the shorter series of operations on the right front. The cut stack of shirt fronts was clamped in a tray and delivered to the machine. Pick up from the tray was by pressure-sensitive adhesive tape; it was then placed on a plate which moved the single front to the folder. After this, belts fed the fronts to subsequent operations. Pre-folded and pressed pockets were fed from magazines and transferred in a clamp device to the machine for attaching pockets. In all the automatic handling devices the work piece was oriented in direction and plane by controlling it from an aligned cut stack. Control over mating similarly derived from exact location in a cut stack. Control during sewing was through clamps. The machine as a whole never became commercially successful; it provided, in contrast to the Little report, a great deal of the technology which led for instance to automatic pocket setters, sequential buttonholers and buttonsewers and to pick up and disposal devices. Again none of these operations attempted anything with a higher order of difficulty than 1 or 2 in the Little hierarchy.

Neither of these developments attempted more than relatively simple handling of standardised parts. Later developments have turned their attention to robotics and the concepts of 'flexible manufacturing', which are more in line with the needs of a fashion industry.

A robot is a reprogrammable, mechanical manipulator. A robot has to have a memory and be capable of being programmed to repeat an operation precisely and continuously until reprogrammed. It must be capable of moving in three dimensions or two planes plus a rotary movement.

A paper published by Sinclair (4) in 1986, reporting on work undertaken by the 'Manchester Group', that is, the Shirley Institute, Salford University Industrial Centre and the Hollings Faculty at Manchester Metropolitan University, lists five problems which must be solved before robots can undertake a significant proportion of the operations in clothing manufacture:

(a)   The recognition of arbitrarily shaped objects.
(b)   Ply separation and pick up in a controlled manner of both large and small two-dimensional flexible garment parts.
(c)   Alignment of flexible parts to each other and to the assembly machine in the same operation.
(d)   Realignment of parts during the operation without loss of control.
(e)   Sensing the need for and taking appropriate corrective action during the operation.

258 operations on eight garment types were analysed in terms of robot capabilities and it was concluded that if there was a major investment in research and development to solve these five problems, it would be possible to automate 37 per cent of the operations on these garments. However, these represented only two-dimensional operations. The remaining, three-dimensional, operations would remain beyond the capabilities of robot technologies in the foreseeable future.

Despite this widely held view, research is proceeding on a number of fronts.

In the area of vision systems for the recognition of arbitrarily shaped objects, Taylor and Taylor (5) describe several methods of using cameras to scan garment parts to identify their type and orientation, either at the beginning of an assembly sequence or at a later stage. Depending on the subsequent operation to be performed, the part may be moved to correct an erroneous orientation, perhaps by a robot, or sewing may take place correctly regardless of orientation.

A paper by Taylor and Koudis (6) analyses the handling activities of typical sewing operations in a similar manner to that given in Figure 8.2 and suggests that the difficulty of automating this handling may be assessed by imagining the results of trying to perform such operations manually but with eyes closed and perfectly numb fingers. An operator separating and picking up fabrics with the fingers generally uses three techniques: pinch, peel and rub, singly or in combination, and it is these techniques that are reflected in the 'pick and place' devices that have been developed.

The paper by Taylor and Koudis describes five different methods which have been developed to separate fabric plies, namely vacuum, adhesives, pinching, pins and air jets. A very high degree of reliability is required in any devices that are developed since, if the separation process was required once for each time a 3-second operation took place, a reliability of only 95 per cent would give on average one failure per minute. An operator would need to be continually available to rectify these intermittent failures. Factors which affect the separation process are the cohesive forces between layers, such as could occur in a stack of knitted cotton which has been compressed at the cutting stage, and the degree to which the edges are bound together, either by the edges fusing during cutting or because of interlocking fibres.

A further review, of the devices available to the industry in the USA in 1987, is provided by a report to the Apparel Research Committee published in that year (7). This gives a classification of limp fabric handling devices which can be used to define standard and specialised equipment. The classification indicates how they achieve the activities of ply separation, ply removal, transport and orientation and registration.

The pinching concept of ply separation is exemplified by the Clupicker, one of the most successful pick and place devices yet developed, which is manufactured by Cluett Peabody & Co. Ltd and is designed to be adjustable to cope with a wide range of fabrics. It has a picking wheel with a rough surface which rotates and causes the top ply to slide against the second ply. This creates a fold of cloth which enters a shoe adjacent to the wheel and is gripped. Retaining fingers drop to hold the remainder of the stack and prevent the picker from taking two plies at a time. When the picker lifts, it takes the top ply with it. Placing is basically the reverse process. Picking speeds of 12 pieces per minute are feasible with this machine. Multiple pickers would be used on larger garment parts – for example, four would be used on a shirt front.

Brotherton and Tyler (8) describe an investigation into Clupicker performance in which they found it to be generally very reliable, provided it was supplied with cut stacks with accurately aligned edges. One fabric only gave significant problems with different picking performance between different colours. Subsequent investigation of this fabric with the Kawabata KES-f surface tester showed a surprisingly large difference in surface roughness between the two colours of the same fabric. The general conclusion formed from this investigation was that much basic work on the fabric/machine interface still needed to be done.

Further work in the area of fabric handling is reported by Iype and Porat (9), Govindaraj *et al.* (10), Ono *et al.* (11) and Leung *et al.* (12).

Other developments in recent years have returned to the earlier idea of the transfer line but with new options for piece identification by means of vision systems and for movement by means of robotics. The Textile/ Clothing Technology Corporation, known as TC Squared, was set up in the USA in 1980 to investigate the automation of apparel manufacturing in an attempt to achieve substantial reductions in costs. By 1985 a laboratory prototype machine had been built at the Draper Laboratories, the contract research organisation to whom the initial work had been given. The Singer company then took over to translate the technical success into a commercially viable system. The sections of the line consisted of:

(a) an automatic loader to insert parts to be loaded into the transfer line;

(b)   a viewing table that allows the automatic vision system to recognise the parts;
(c)   a robot that can fold and align the edges;
(d)   a transfer door that slides the parts to the sewing station;
(e)   a sewing unit with feed belts and a sewing machine under computer control.

Lines were planned which would assemble a complete jacket sleeve or trouser leg, and which would need three vision systems, two or three folding robots, and three sewing stations. This work is described in papers by Abernathy and Pippins (13), Bray and Vento (14), and Tyler (15). Tyler suggests that the most difficult area of the system may be the folding robot as the placing part of the pick and place operation has generally received less study and evaluation than the picking part.

The Japanese TRAASS (Technology Research Association for Automatic Sewing Systems) project, some of which is described in the work by Ono *et al.* above, has been running for 10 years and has produced some robotic systems for the sewing operations in making ladies' blazers, but a total system appears still to be many years away. Marlowe (16), in commenting on this, suggests that although technical solutions may, in many cases, be in sight, the equipment has so far been of such extreme complexity as to cast grave doubt on the economic viability of the systems envisioned. In his paper, which is mainly on the future of programmable sewing, he describes systems for monitoring thread tension and sewing faults such as mis-stitching while it is happening, for automatic switching of presser foot type when garment type changes, and for pre-programming such parameters as stitch length, presser foot pressure and top-feed ratio. He suggests that these more modest developments could significantly reduce sewing room changeover time between different batches of work and improve a factory's ability to respond quickly to changes in demand. Such incremental improvements appear to him to offer more realistic prospects of commercial benefit to the industry than the tantalising mirage of robotic systems, commercial exploitation of which seems likely to remain beyond our grasp, even well into the next millenium.

The last ten years have seen research into automated, robotised systems in several countries proceeding with limited but important success, driven largely by an increasing need to react better to the economic pressures of cheap imports into those countries. Those same ten years have seen extensive changes in large areas of the clothing industry caused by changes in the retailing scene, changes which require greater flexibility and improved speed of response. Present predictions suggest that these two themes will continue alongside each other, with automation developing further where volume remains high enough and with flexibility and speed of response fulfilling the requirements of fashion. It is not possible to predict just how long it will be before the two themes merge to give truly automated, flexible manufacturing.

Further Reading

The following books and articles will assist the reader in following the subject further.

The bibliography of clothing manufacture has never been large but it has been usefully expanded in recent years. Some earlier publications are still useful, even some from as much as thirty years ago, but unfortunately they are becoming increasingly difficult for the reader to locate.

Two general books which contain a wide range of detailed material, much of which is still useful despite its age, are *Apparel Manufacturing Handbook*, by Jacob Solinger (Van Nostrand Reinhold, 1980) and *Sewn Products Engineering and Reference Manual*, edited by Manuel Gaetan (Bobbin Publications, 1977). Further books will be mentioned in relation to individual chapters.

A number of journals make an important contribution to the subject. *Bobbin*, published in the USA, covers a range of topics but particularly technology. The following four journals include useful articles from time to time and also reviews of machinery exhibitions around the world: *Manufacturing Clothier*; *Clothing World* (published by CAPITB); *Textile Asia*; and *Apparel International*.

Hollings Apparel Industry Review, (HAIR), published by Hollings Faculty, Manchester Metropolitan University, includes useful industry statistical analyses as well as technical and research articles.

Textile Outlook International publishes mainly economics-related articles and company profiles which are useful as industry background but has occasional useful technical articles.

International Journal of Clothing Science and Technology publishes some of the scientific research currently being undertaken in the clothing field.

Specific articles will be mentioned in the following sections but the reader is best advised to monitor the journals on a regular basis in order to have the latest information and analysis.

Chapter 1:   Background to the Clothing Industry

Up-to-date information on employment, output and other aspects of the clothing industry can be obtained from *Employment Gazette*, *Hollings Apparel Industry Review* and *Textile Outlook International*.

Chapter 2:   Cutting

A useful earlier work is:

Trautman, J.E. (1979) *Material Utilisation in the Apparel Industry*. Apparel Research Foundation Inc., Arlington.

An important recent book which also contains substantial additional references is:

Tyler, D.J. (1991) *Materials Management in Clothing Production*. Blackwell Scientific Publications, Oxford.

Articles about various aspects of cutting room work include:

Tyler, D.J. (1989) Excess Costs in Garment Manufacture due to Fabric Faults. *HAIR*, 6(1).
How much do Fabric Flaws Cost Your Business? *Apparel International*, October 1991.
Gratsch, J. The Myth of Tension-Free Spreading. *Bobbin*, February 1991.
Sinclair, D. (1987) Single Ply Cutting in the Clothing Industry. *HAIR*, 4(3).
Disher, M. The Cutting Edge. *Manufacturing Clothier*, September 1991.
The Cutting Room. *Manufacturing Clothier*, April 1992.
Paterson, A. Cutting Room Innovation. *Manufacturing Clothier*, March 1993.

Chapters 3 and 4:   Sewing and Sewing Machinery

It is impossible to discuss sewing without the language and system of diagrams developed by the organisations who publish national and international standards.

The British Standards Institution, Linford Wood, Milton Keynes, MK14 6LE, UK, publishes:

BS 3870: 1991: Stitches and Seams. Part 1: *Classification and terminology of stitch types* and Part 2: *Classification and terminology of seam types*.

British Standard 3870 is identical with ISO 4915: 1991: *Textiles – Stitch types: Classification and terminology* and ISO 4916: 1991 *Textiles – Seam types: Classification and terminology*, published by the International Organisation for Standardisation (ISO).

Useful examples of adaptations and additions to sewing machines are given in:

Low Cost Work Aids for the Clothing and Garment Industries, NEDO 1974.

Many of the Technological Reports published by the Clothing Institute contain useful research findings and are still relevant. A name which frequently appears among the authors of these reports is C.M.C. Dorkin who, in addition to carrying out a great deal of basic research herself, stimulated and managed a considerable body of work by others. Her influence on clothing research is immeasurable. Particularly useful Technological Reports are listed below:

Burtonwood, B. & Chamberlain, N.H. (1966, 1967) The Strength of Seams in Woven Fabrics. Part 1, *Technological Report* No. 17, CI, and Part 2, No. 18, CI.
Blackwood, W.J. & Chamberlain, N.H. (1970) The Strength of Seams in Knitted Fabrics. *Technological Report* No. 22, CI.
Dorkin, C.M.C. & Chamberlain, N.H. (1961) Seam Pucker, its Cause and Prevention. *Technological Report* No. 10, CI.
Dorkin, C.M.C. & Chamberlain, N.H. (1962) Lockstitch Seams in Knitted Fabrics. *Technological Report* No. 11, CI.
Dorkin, C.M.C. & Chamberlain, N.H. (1963) The Facts about Needle Heating. *Technological Report* No. 13, CI.
Townsend, T. & Chamberlain, N.H. (1974) More Light on Structural Seam Pucker in Lightweight Fabrics. *Technological Report* No. 16, CI.
Deery, F.C. & Chamberlain, N.H. (1964) A Study of Thread Tension Variation during the Working Cycle in a Lockstitch Sewing Machine. *Technological Report* No. 15, CI.
Crow, R.M. & Chamberlain, N.H. (1969) The Performance of Sewing Threads in Industrial Sewing Machines. *Technological Report* No. 21, CI.

In addition:

Hurt, F.N. & Tyler, D.J. (1973) The Influence of Fabric Finishing Conditions on Sewing Needle Temperatures. *Clothing Research Journal*, 1, 1.
Lewis, J. (1973) Cloth Finishing Procedures for Preventing Sewing Damage in Wool and Wool/Synthetic Fibre Double Jersey Fabrics. *Clothing Research Journal*, 1, 3.
Leeming, C. & Munden, D.L. (1973) Sewability of Knitted Fabrics. *Clothing Research Journal*, 1, 2.

Recent research into seam pucker, using such modern techniques as KES-f and laser measurement of seam appearance are reported in various articles in the *International Journal of Clothing Science and Technology*. Further relevant articles are as follows:

The Sewing Room. *Manufacturing Clothier*, September, 1992.
Marlowe, P. Programmable Sewing Progresses: But Where To?. *Bobbin*, January 1992.
Programmable Sewing Machines. *Manufacturing Clothier*, July/August, 1991.
Disher, M. Profile Stitching. *Manufacturing Clothier*, December/January 1991.
Cannon Jones, A. Methods Improvement in Men's Tailored Manufacturing. *Bobbin*, October 1990.
Disher, M. Button Sewing and Buttonholes. *Manufacturing Clothier*, February 1992.

Chapter 5:   The Use of Components and Trims

Labels and Labelling. *Manufacturing Clothier*, May, 1992.
Start, B. Embroidery and Garment Decoration. *Manufacturing Clothier*, December/January 1993.
Fairley, M. Creative Embroidery. *Apparel International*, April & November 1992.
Trim Details. *Manufacturing Clothier*, June 1992.
Holme, I. A Novel Printing System with Great Potential. *Manufacturing Clothier*, April 1992.

Chapter 6:   Alternative Methods of Joining Materials

The main part of this chapter is about fusing for which there is some useful literature. There are a number of the Clothing Institute's *Technological Reports* which are relevant:

Dorkin, C.M.C. *et al.* (1968) The Practical Performance of Fusing Presses. *Technological Report* No. 19, CI.
Dorkin, C.M.C. *et al.* (1968) The Testing and Utilisation of Fusible Interlinings. *Technological Report* No. 20, CI.
Morris, P.A. (1971) The Physical Properties of Textile Laminates made from Fusible Interlinings. *Technological Report* No. 23, CI.

A recent and useful book is:

Cooklin, G. (1990) *Fusing Technology*. The Textile Institute, Manchester.

The British Interlining Manufacturers' Association (BIMA) has produced a useful series of Bulletins which collectively cover most of the issues in fusing technology, including base cloths, the chemistry and application of fusible resins, methods of fusing, fusing equipment, testing procedures, trouble-shooting and some typical garment construction applications.

Recent articles are:

Cussons, P. Interlinings. *Manufacturing Clothier*, June 1992.
Robey, D. Tailored to the trends. *Bobbin*, June 1992.
Levin, S. Frame Fusing for the 90s Look. *Apparel International*, May 1990.

Chapter 7: Pressing

A useful publication on practical aspects of presses which is available to CTC members (some colleges are members), is *Technology Review* No. 5: Evaluating Steam Pressing, Clothing Technology Centre, Kettering, Northants, July 1990.

Recent articles are:

Friese, R. State-of-the-art Pressing and Finishing. *Manufacturing Clothier*, March 1992.
Stewart, A. *et al*. CIM Solutions for Pressing Problems. *Bobbin*, March 1991.

Chapter 8: Clothing Manufacture

In this chapter, specific references are marked in the text.

(1)   Tyler, D.J. Managing for Production Flexibility in the Clothing Industry. *Textile Outlook International*, September 1989.
(2)   Grills, R. & Brown, S. (1975) *Productivity in Sewing Operations*. Shirley Institute.
(3)   Taylor, G. (based on research studies by D. Munden) The Results of Speed. *Bobbin*, September 1978.
(4)   Sinclair, D. (1986) Towards Flexible Manufacturing in the Clothing Industry. *Hollings Apparel Industry Review*, 3(3).
(5)   Taylor, P.M. & Taylor, G.E. (1991) *Sensory Robotic Assembly of Apparel at Hull University*. Department of Electronic Engineering, The University of Hull.
(6)   Taylor, P.M. & Koudis, S.G. (1987) Automated Handling of Fabrics. *Scientific Progress*.
(7)   *Automated Limp Fabric Handling Devices: Report of the Limp Fabric-Handling Task Group* (1987). Apparel Research Committee.
(8)   Brotherton, A.A. & Tyler, D.J. (1986) Clupicker Performance and Flexible Apparel Automation. *Hollings Apparel Industry Review*, 3(2).
(9)   Iype, C. & Porat, I. (1989) Fabric Alignment using a Robotic Vision System. *International Journal of Clothing Science and Technology*, 1, 1.

(10) Govindaraj, M., Chen, B. & Koechling, J. (1992) Fabric Properties as Control Factors for Flexible Apparel Production Systems. *International Journal of Clothing Science and Technology*, 4, 2/3.

(11) Ono, E., Ichijo, H. & Aisaka, N. (1992) Flexible Robotic Hand for Handling Fabric Pieces in Garment Manufacture. *International Journal of Clothing Science and Technology*, 4, 5.

(12) Laung, M., Black, D.H. & Lam, A. (1992) Evaluation of Two Pick and Place Devices used on Clothing Materials. *Hollings Apparel Industry Review*, 9(1).

(13) Abernathy, F.H. & Pippins, D. TC Squared: Apparel, Textile and Education at its Best. *Bobbin*, September 1986.

(14) Bray, F. & Vento, V. Chapter Two Begins with Singer. *Bobbin*, September 1986.

(15) Tyler, D.J. (1989) The Development Phase of the Textile/Clothing Technology Corporation Automation Project. *International Journal of Clothing Science and Technology*, 1, 2.

(16) Marlowe, P. Programmable Sewing Progresses: But Where To? *Bobbin*, January 1992.

Index

Pattern cutting

Metric Pattern Cutting
Third Edition
Winifred Aldrich
The number one, best-selling book on pattern cutting for women's wear, including a new section on computerised pattern cutting and numerous blocks.
192 pages, illustrated hardback.
0 632 03612 5

Metric Pattern Cutting for Menswear Including Computer Aided Design
Second Edition
Winifred Aldrich
In the second edition of this standard work on the subject, blocks based on easy-fitting shapes have been added to extend the range of styles that can be used. A new chapter provides an ideal introduction to computer aided design.
144 pages, illustrated hardback.
0 632 02635 9

Metric Pattern Cutting for Children's Wear From 2–14 years
Second Edition
Winifred Aldrich
Another bestseller by Winifred Aldrich, providing a simple but comprehensive system of pattern cutting for children's wear. Highly illustrated with hundreds of stylish diagrams and clear, concise

instructions, it features basic blocks which can be adapted for creative design and includes illustrated grading instructions.
165 pages, illustrated hardback.
0 632 03057 7

Pattern Cutting for Lingerie, Beachwear and Leisurewear
Ann Haggar
This comprehensive text takes the reader through the whole process from the initial planning stages to finished pattern pieces. It is illustrated by numerous examples, working diagrams and drawings and contains patterns for stretch fabrics.
250 pages, illustrated paperback.
0 632 02033 4

Pattern Cutting for Women's Outerwear
Gerry Cooklin
Highly illustrated with clear stage-by-stage instructions, this innovative book emphasises the technological aspects of pattern development for women's mass-produced clothing. A simple, integrated system of drafting block patterns is described, followed by a wide-ranging toolbox of professional pattern cutting techniques with many examples of their applications. Patterns for linings and fusibles and computerised pattern design systems are also described.
192 pages, illustrated paperback.
0 632 03797 0

Dress Pattern Designing The Basic
Principles of Cut and Fit
Fifth Edition
Natalie Bray
With Fashion Supplement by Ann
Haggar
This classic and well-known textbook
now includes instructions on recent
fashion shapes. The book contains
over 100 basic diagrams and 40
plates, combined with clear and
detailed instructions.
192 pages, illustrated paperback.
0 632 01881 X

More Dress Pattern Designing
Fourth Edition
Natalie Bray
With Fashion Supplement by Ann
Haggar
This text expands the basic course,
showing the applications of the basic
principles and methods to more
advanced styles and specialist cutting
techniques. Lingerie, tailoring and
children's patterns are included.
208 pages, illustrated paperback.
0 632 01883 6

Dress Fitting
Second Edition
Natalie Bray
Fitting can cause problems for
dressmakers and students. Natalie
Bray discusses these problems,
outlining techniques for better fit;
problems of figure, posture and
pattern adjustment; and how to
identify a defect and choose the best
method of dealing with it.
120 pages, illustrated paperback.
0 632 01879 8

**Pattern Grading for Women's
Clothes**
Gerry Cooklin
A comprehensive text on pattern
grading setting out a simple and
effective grading system, which can be
applied to most size charts used for

women's clothing. Over 50
demonstrations of master and basic
garment grades are provided,
accompanied by simple and clear
instructions. Includes 200 illustrations
and 30 detailed size charts of
international sizing systems.
400 pages, illustrated paperback.
0 632 02295 7

**Pattern Grading for Children's
Clothes**
Gerry Cooklin
This thoroughly practical guide
includes demonstration grades broken
down into easy-to-follow illustrated
stages with simple and clear
instructions, and children's size charts
from 22 countries and leading retailers
in Europe and the USA.
320 pages, illustrated paperback.
0 632 02612 X

Pattern Grading for Men's Clothes
Gerry Cooklin
An up-to-date, profusely illustrated
and comprehensive manual setting out
the practical principles and
applications of pattern grading for the
whole range of men's clothing,
including computerised grading, the
latest developments in fully automatic
grading and grades for linings, fusibles
and pockets.
304 pages, illustrated paperback.
0 632 03305 3

**Master Patterns and Grading for
Women's Outsizes**
Gerry Cooklin
Although nearly 15% of the women's
market is for outsizes, current sizing
systems are out of date and an entirely
new approach to construction and
sizing is required. This specialised and
up-to-date treatment of the subject
provides pattern cutters with a wealth
of practical information.
Approximately 192 pages, illustrated
paperback.
0 632 03915 9

Modelling on the Dress Stand
Janice Mee and Michael Purdy
The technique of modelling or 'toile' as an effective alternative to flat pattern cutting is explained, setting out the basic principles and progressing from simple to more complicated applications.
192 pages, illustrated paperback.
0 632 01884 4

Master Patterns and Grading for Women's Outsizes
Gerry Cooklin
Improved foundation garments and greater fashion awareness make it imperative for an entirely new approach to the construction and sizing of garment patterns for outsizes. This new textbook is a specialized and up-to-date treatment of the subject, and provides pattern cutters and graders with a wealth of practical information.
128 pages, illustrated paperback.
0 632 03915 9

Clothing production

Introduction to Clothing Production Management
A J Chuter
This practical text sets out the fundamentals of quality control, fault prevention, work study, effective supervision, training, balancing, layouts and other information essential for a profitable operation.
192 pages, illustrated paperback.
0 632 01827 5

The Technology of Clothing Manufacture
Second Edition
Harold Carr and Barbara Latham
The full range of clothing manufacturing technology is surveyed and discussed, including the processes of modern clothing manufacture;

cutting, sewing, alternative methods of joining materials and pressing; manual, mechanical and computer-controlled methods of production; and current applications of computerised techniques and robotics.
288 pages, illustrated paperback.
0 632 03748 2

Materials Management in Clothing Production
D J Tyler
The efficient control of materials in clothing production is discussed with emphasis on key areas for production control: principles for purchasing fabrics; material requirements planning; and the use of information technology for communications between suppliers and customers.
176 pages, illustrated paperback.
0 632 02896 3

Fashion Design and Product Development
Harold Carr and John Pomeroy
A new book which sets out the modern, commercial approach to product design in the clothing and fashion market and discusses the practical factors including materials, manufacture, costs, quality and organisation of the process.
192 pages, illustrated paperback.
0 632 02893 9

Introduction to Clothing Manufacture
Gerry Cooklin
This introductory textbook for students and newcomers to the clothing business provides a comprehensive view of the clothing industry. It explains practical aspects of clothing manufacture, from the original design to deliveries to retail customers; describes each of the basic planning and manufacturing technologies; and contains many realistic and practical examples of the

day-to-day operation of a clothing factory.
190 pages, illustrated paperback.
0 632 02661 8

Knitted Clothing Technology
Terry Brackenbury
This unique book covers the specific techniques used to convert weft knitted fabric into garments. It examines techniques of shaping and construction, specialist assembly machinery, and future trends in the production of knitted garments.
208 pages, illustrated paperback.
0 632 02807 6

CAD and Design

CAD in Clothing and Textiles
Second Edition
Edited by Winifred Aldrich
A unique insight into the practice of computer aided design. With contributions from experts in the industry, many aspects of CAD in clothing and textiles are discussed including writing of the software, sale of systems, applications, training and education.
192 pages, illustrated paperback.
0 632 03893 4

Fashion

Understanding Fashion
Elizabeth Rouse
'A wealth of information and comment of interest to anyone in the apparel business'
Apparel International

Highly illustrated, this book investigates the social and cultural significance of clothing and fashion, the influence that social changes have on styles of dress and on the development of the fashion industry and why and how fashion as we know it today has developed.
320 pages, illustrated paperback.
0 632 01891 7

Fashion Marketing
Edited by Mike Easey
Marketing is now an indispensable component of fashion and clothing courses. This book satisfies students' requirements, and has a number of special qualities that make it essential reading for anyone in the business. Theory and practice are balanced, with examples to illustrate key concepts. Where numerical concepts are included, clear worked examples ensure that the ideas are easily understood and retained.
240 pages, illustrated paperback.
0 632 03459 9

Dressmaking

Dressmaking Simplified
Third Edition
Valerie Cock
Highly illustrated, this practical textbook sets out all the basic techniques, with additional information on choosing the correct fabric for garments; sewing machines, including the four main groups of machines; and collars, with instructions on attaching a shirt collar with a band.
240 pages, illustrated paperback.
0 632 02216 7